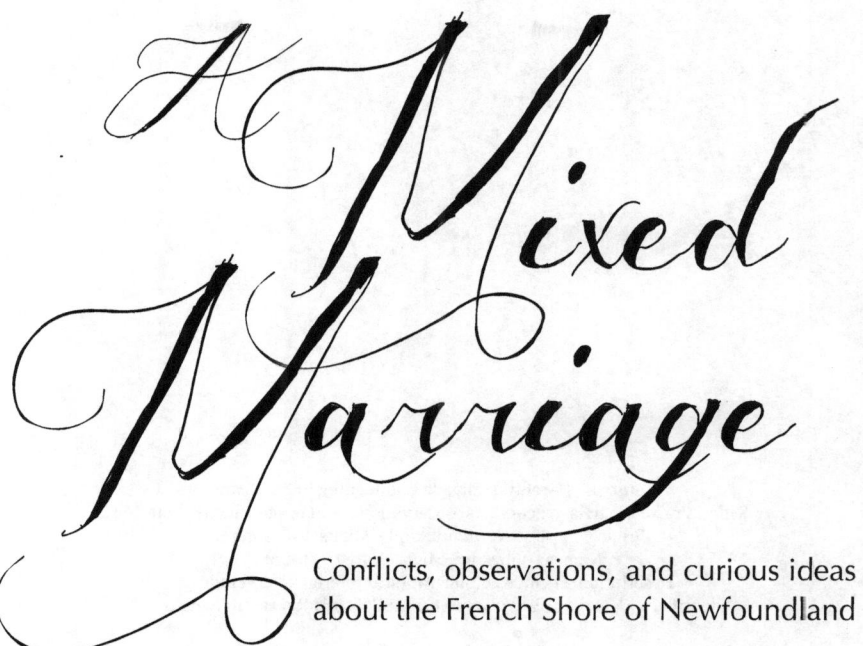

A Mixed Marriage

Conflicts, observations, and curious ideas about the French Shore of Newfoundland

Library and Archives Canada Cataloguing in Publication
Title: A mixed marriage : conflicts, observations, and curious ideas about the French shore of Newfoundland / Michael Wilkshire.
Names: Wilkshire, Michael, 1939- author.
Description: Includes bibliographical references and index.
Identifiers: Canadiana 20200206680 | ISBN 9781989417119 (softcover)

Subjects: LCSH: French—Newfoundland and Labrador—History—19th century. | LCSH: French—Newfoundland and Labrador—Social conditions—19th century. | LCSH: Fisheries—Newfoundland and Labrador—History—19th century. | LCSH: Canada—Foreign relations—France—History. | LCSH: France—Foreign relations—Canada—History. | CSH: French Shore Problem (Newfoundland and Labrador)
Classification: LCC FC2200.F8 W55 2020 | DDC 971.8/00441—dc23

© 2020 Michael Wilkshire

Published by Boulder Books
Portugal Cove-St. Philip's, Newfoundland and Labrador
www.boulderbooks.ca

Design and layout: Tanya Montini
Editor: Stephanie Porter
Copy editor: Iona Bulgin

Printed in Canada

Excerpts from this publication may be reproduced under licence from Access Copyright, or with the express written permission of Boulder Books Ltd., or as permitted by law. All rights are otherwise reserved and no part of this publications may be reproduced, stored in a retrieval system, or transmitted in any form or by any means, electronic, mechanical, photocopying, scanning, recording, or otherwise, except as specifically authorized.

We acknowledge the financial support of the Government of Newfoundland and Labrador through the Department of Tourism, Culture, Industry and Innovation.

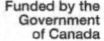 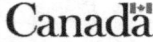

A Mixed Marriage

Conflicts, observations, and curious ideas about the French Shore of Newfoundland

BOULDER BOOKS

MICHAEL WILKSHIRE

"Cod preparation in the bay near Cape Rouge.– Drawing by Le Breton from a photograph." *Le Tour du Monde* (1863), 413.

TABLE OF CONTENTS

Preface by Michael Wilkshire 9

C.-J.-A. Carpon, *Voyage to Newfoundland* (1852)
    Prospectus 27
    Introduction 31
    Chapter 1 34
    Chapter 2 43
    Chapter 3 63
    Chapter 4 71
    Chapter 5 84
    Chapter 6 117
    Chapter 7 142
    Chapter 8 171
    Chapter 9 182
    Chapter 10 190

Account by Baron D.J. Larrey of his voyage
to Newfoundland in 1788. 205

A report on the season's activities by Captain Venancourt, commodore of the French naval station in Newfoundland in 1821, to the minister for the navy.......................... 235

A report on the season's activities by Captain Gautier, captain of the naval schooner La Gentille, based in St-Pierre, to the commandant of the islands of St-Pierre and Miquelon in 1846 249

A report on the season's activities by Captain Mer, commodore of the French naval station in Newfoundland in 1868, to the minister for the navy 261

Acknowledgments 295
About the Author 296

PREFACE

The French presence in Newfoundland from the early 18th century to the early 20th is a story of a mixed marriage, or cohabitation. Sovereignty over the island belonged to the British, but France enjoyed the right to fish along an extensive part of the shoreline. As with many long-term relationships, this one was marked by a number of sharp differences from time to time, but also peaceful co-operation. These fishing rights were enshrined in the Treaty of Utrecht of 1713, allowing France to catch and dry fish between Cape Bonavista and Point Riche on the west coast; in 1783 the limits were amended to go from Cape St. John to Cape Ray.

This volume contains a collection of French texts relating to the French Shore, also known as the French Treaty Shore, of the island of Newfoundland. Apart from the extract from Baron Larrey's memoirs, all are here translated into English for the first time, and the Larrey translation is a new one.

Between 1713 and 1783, the situation was complicated by English settlers moving into some parts of the coast allocated to the French, especially in Bonavista Bay. Wars between France and England meant that the French fishery was suspended for a while, and in the meantime

English settlers took over what had been French settlements. When peace returned, conflicts were inevitable. The change to the limits introduced in 1783 were an attempt to avoid such difficulties by moving the French to more remote parts of the island's shoreline.

The French fishery was strictly seasonal, since the terms of the treaty did not allow them to overwinter in Newfoundland. Every spring tens of thousands of French fishermen came to Newfoundland to set up, fish for cod, and salt and dry it before taking it back to France or directly to export markets at the end of the season. The premises that they occupied were flimsy, and, once abandoned, quickly fell into disrepair, so that often little or no trace remains of this two-centuries-old tradition. The memory of it, however, remains in texts such as those presented here.

C.-J.-A. Carpon was a ship's surgeon with the French fishing fleet for many years and intimately acquainted with the French Newfoundland fishery and its traditions as well as being a doctor for the crew. The regulations varied over the course of the 19th century, but generally a fishing ship with a crew of 40 or more required a surgeon, though often this regulation was skirted by giving the position to a man who was essentially a fisherman with little or no medical training (hence the necessity for the "Paper Doctor" that Carpon mentions on page 73, a do-it-yourself guide to how various medical problems should be treated). But Carpon was an exception. As an *officier de santé* (medical officer), he was licenced to practice medicine on land and would have been the best-educated member of the crew. He was ideally suited to recording his recollections of life on the French Shore of Newfoundland, and we are fortunate that he did so.

Ships' surgeons with the fishing fleet would not have been the only medical practitioners in rural Newfoundland. Every year both the British and the French navies sent a small fleet of fisheries protection vessels to oversee the fishery and ensure that the treaties were being respected. These ships would have a properly qualified medical staff, as opposed to a fish splitter who might have a smattering of medical skill, as happened with the fishing fleet.

The presence of these ships' surgeons is significant, since they treated not only the crews of the naval ships and the fishing fleet but also the local English population, and represent the very earliest form of health care in some of the most remote parts of the island of Newfoundland. In the case of the naval ships, those services were available only for a brief period, as the ships passed through different harbours on patrol, but the surgeons with the fishing fleet were there for the season, even if the skill of the practitioner often left much to be desired.

This collection of texts includes all of Carpon's book, with his recollections of his stays in Newfoundland, as well as a chapter from Larrey's memoirs in which he describes his one and only season spent in Newfoundland before he went on to an illustrious career elsewhere. Larrey's text provides a bridge between Carpon's recollections of a surgeon with the fishing fleet and the reports of naval captains charged with overseeing that fishery. Larrey was a ship's surgeon on board the *Vigilante* in 1878, and, although a naval officer, had no responsibilities relating to the overseeing of the fishery.

We have also included three reports about Newfoundland written by naval captains as part of their duties in fisheries protection: one by Venancourt in 1821, another by Gautier in 1847, and the third, the most comprehensive, written by Mer, the commodore of the French naval station in Newfoundland, in 1868. The juxtaposition of these texts allows the reader an insight into the daily life of the French fishing fleet at ground level and an official overview of the situation from naval officers judging how the situation was operating, what problems there were, and how they might be mitigated.

Little is known of C.-J.-A. Carpon apart from what he tells the reader in *Voyage to Newfoundland (Voyage à Terre-Neuve)*. It is here that we learn how, in 1847, he set sail from Granville as a surgeon on board the French fishing vessel *Deux Sophie*, destined for the northeast coast of Newfoundland. The title page of Carpon's account also states that he had spent "several" summer seasons on the coast of Newfoundland in the same capacity. He tells us in Chapter 1 that he spent the 1826 season on board the *Euphrosina*, captained by Mr. Adelue. We learn that he was qualified as an *officier de santé*, acceptance for which was a little less stringent than for the rank of doctor. One is reminded of Charles Bovary in Flaubert's *Madame Bovary*, a fictional contemporary of Carpon's who is similarly qualified. Carpon had studied in Paris under Baron Larrey and was an avid hunter and sports fisherman in addition to being curious about all that he saw around him in Newfoundland.

Standard bibliographies show no other work by Carpon apart from *Voyage to Newfoundland*, which was published by Poisson in Caen in 1852. On the title page, Carpon is listed as being a corresponding member of the Caen Agricultural Society, but he does not appear to have contributed to that organization's journal, the *Mémoires de la Société d'Agriculture et de Commerce de Caen*. The status of corresponding member was given to those who were not resident in the community of Caen; Caen residents were simply described as members. The publication of that periodical was somewhat irregular, but every few years it included a list of paid-up members, a list that includes Carpon as a corresponding member in the issues of 1852, 1855, 1858–59, 1860, and 1866. He is shown in each case as being a surgeon in the merchant navy and resident of Le Pont d'Hyenville. The first membership list to be published after 1866 was in 1871, where Carpon's name is missing. Whether this means that he had died or that his membership had lapsed is open to speculation. Subsequent membership lists also fail to include him.

The edition of *Voyage à Terre-Neuve* in the Caen municipal library contains three surprises. First, on the inside front cover there is a brief, unsigned, handwritten note stating that the author was born in Cormolain, a district of Bayeux, on 17 March 1803. Second, appended to the text is a short list of errata that was added after a number of copies had been distributed, which helps to explain some of the oddities in the text. And finally, a letter from Carpon dated 7 May 1852 to an unnamed man regarding the production of his book:

Hyenville, 7 May 1852.

Dear Sir and Friend,
I received from Mr. Poisson two boxes containing books: one package of about 20 volumes plus a basket which contained about 30. This basket, which opens by means of two flaps attached to the handle, was closed on one side only; in one of the corners was my little fish with a note from Mr. DesLongchamps and a letter which states that there is another but which I did not find. It begins with these words: "I add a few lines etc."
Promising the purchasers that their names will be published as subscribers cannot do any harm, so this list can usefully be appended to the second edition.
What means can be used to have my work promoted in the Caen Agricultural Society?
I readily agree to this, and point out to you for your information that I was born in Cormolain (Calvados) on 17 March 1803.
There are in the first edition many typographical errors, in punctuation, accents, words that have been changed, many of which you have been made aware of.

Somewhere, I cannot recall where, there are two nouns, one masculine, the other feminine, with the adjective in the feminine plural.[1]

The work is very well printed on fine paper that is mechanically produced, and I cannot see any difference between this paper and the one that must be vellum; is that the one that is contained in the small package in wrapping paper?

You see, my dear sir, that your letter has been lost. Of the two boxes, the one that forms a perfectly regular rectangle has not been opened, I am sending it to Messrs. Perrot and Hulin, who will acknowledge receipt to Mr. Poisson, when I have forwarded it to them. I beg you, please send me the errata immediately. Yesterday I delivered 36 copies for cash that I corrected by hand, but this work tires me tremendously. Would you also please tell me approximately how many volumes that box might contain?

Your devoted friend,
C. Carpon[2]

To this rather meagre biographical information should be added a number of details provided by a study of the crew lists of fishing ships sailing from Granville. These list Carpon's date of birth repeatedly as 8 March 1803, despite his assurance in his letter quoted above to the contrary, but, more importantly, show that he was one of the most experienced of the surgeons sent to Newfoundland. He made a total of 17 voyages, as follows:

---

1   In French an adjective that qualifies both a masculine and a feminine noun should be in the masculine plural. (Translator's note.)
2   Our translation. (Translator's note.)

Table 1: Record of Carpon's Experience in Newfoundland
(currency figures are in francs)

Year	Ship	Place of Residence Listed	Avances*	Au retour**	Parts***	Value of the part	Pratiques ****	Microfilm no. (Library and Archives Canada)
1826	Euphrosina	Cormolain	400.00		1.00			F-1801
1827	Indien	Coutances	510.00		2.00		1.00	F-1802
1828	Clarisse	Coutances	610.00		2.00		1.00	F-1803
1834	Pauline	Coutances	500.00		2.00		1.00	F-1838
1847	Deux Sophie	Montmartin	400.00		2.00	69.17	1.00	F-1883
1848	Deux Sophie	Montmartin	150.00	150.00	2.00	104.36	1.00	F-1879
1849	Abeille	Montmartin	400.00	200.00				F-1881
1853	Jacques François	Hyenville	600.00		2.00	46.15	1.00	F-1894
1854	Héloïse	Granville	600.00	400.00				F-1905
1855	Joséphine	Hyenville	600.00	400.00				F-1910
1857	Héloïse		500.00	300.00				F-1920
1858	Anna	Hyenville	600.00	400.00				F-1927
1859	Anna	Hyenville	600.00	400.00				F-1933
1862	Anna	Hyenville	600.00	400.00				F-1952
1863	Anna	Hyenville	600.00	400.00				F-1955
1864	Anna	Hyenville	600.00	400.00				F-1959
1865	Anna	Hyenville	600.00	400.00				F-1962

Carpon's remuneration follows a fairly typical pattern. For his first voyage his advances are 400 francs, and he has no *part* or *pratique*, but this changes as soon as he has gained some experience. After this, with the exception of 1849, he is paid one *part* up to 1853, when the practice

---

* A fixed sum paid prior to departure (also known as pot de vin in the 18th century).
** A fixed sum paid on return to France.
*** The parts (sometimes known as lots) were the number of shares of the one fifth of the net proceeds of the sale of the catch reserved for the crew according to the Granville tradition. Where no parts are listed, none were paid. By the early 1850s it became standard practice to pay surgeons a flat rate, with no parts or pratiques. In most cases, the value of the part is not shown.
**** The pratique was a bonus in the form of the value of a barrel of cod-liver oil and a quantity of salt cod.

Microfilms at Library and Archives Canada. The original records are at the Service historique de la marine, Cherbourg, France.

dies. After that, his income is quite stable, apart from a drop in 1857. To give an idea of how the surgeon was paid in relation to other crew members, the figures of 1847 may be quoted as being fairly typical. If one looks at the *avances,* only the captain was paid more (500 francs), while the other officers received 250 and the men 150; novices were paid 50. What happened after 1865 is not known; our search found no further records for Carpon, and in any case in the late 1860s the number of surgeons hired fell to only a handful, reaching 0 in 1870. Even if he was still alive by then, his opportunities for employment in Newfoundland had disappeared.

The significance of the changes in his place of residence is not known. It is plausible that in 1826, where he is listed as a resident of Cormolain, his birthplace, he was still living in the parental home. In the 1847 crew list for the *Deux Sophie,* his father is noted as Antoine and his mother as Marie-Françoise, née Le Gris. Whether his settling in Hyenville was due to marriage is also unknown, but equally plausible. One item of information that is also revealed in the crew list of the *Euphrosina* for 1826 is the inclusion of Clair Adolphe Carpon, aged 18 years, listed as a "volontaire" and also resident of Cormolain. This may well have been the author's brother (the space for recording the parents of Clair Adolphe is left blank).

The form used for the Granville crew lists includes space and headings for a physical description. It is thanks to this in the 1826 list that we know that Carpon was "petit" and "brun" (short, with dark hair), as was Clair Adolphe Carpon. The 1853 list, though, is much more detailed: under the heading for height, we find "1m60." For hair we have the sign that often confuses English readers: it appears to be a ditto mark, but in fact means "none." His eyebrows were greying, his eyes grey, his forehead broad, his nose ord^{re} ("*ordinaire*"), his mouth medium, his chin round, and his face oval. However, the hair said to be lost in 1853 was assessed as being dark in 1859; the eyebrows, greying in 1853, were also noted as dark in 1859;

the eyes, grey in 1853, are noted as brown in 1859. Unfortunately, these descriptions seem to have been very subjective and not very reliable, having little more than curiosity value.

The 1826 season was tragic for the port of Granville. As Carpon points out in Chapter 1, two ships from that port, the *Belle Julie* and the *Nathalie,* sank when pierced by ice off the northeast coast of Newfoundland. One hundred and eight men from the *Belle Julie* died, and the *Nathalie* lost its entire crew with the exception of three men who survived for 19 days on the ice before finally reaching land. Carpon notes that his ship, the *Euphrosina,* had been within sight of the *Belle Julie* just a few hours before it sank, and that he himself went to the aid of the survivors of the wreck of the *Nathalie* after they reached shore. We are fortunate to have two accounts of these disasters, one by the captain of the *Belle Julie,* Clair-Désiré Letourneur, and the other by the leader of the three men from the *Nathalie* who survived their 19-day ordeal on the ice, Gaud Houiste. Both texts can be found in the *Annales Maritimes et Coloniales (partie non officielle)*[3] and have been translated into English by Scott Jamieson.[4]

Carpon was at the time a man of 23 years of age making his first trip to Newfoundland, and these tragedies must have had a profound impression on him. For his return journey to France, he sailed on the *Comte d'Estourmel,* since his own ship, the *Euphrosina,* did not go back until April 1827. (It was not unusual for a ship to go directly from Newfoundland to the market where the fish was to be sold and to send the crew members not needed for the remainder of the voyage back home on another ship.) This return trip must have involved much retelling of the loss of the *Belle Julie* by the officers and men of the *Comte d'Estourmel,* since it was one of the ships involved in attempting to save the men.

---

3   1826, t. 2, 451–54 and 481–87.
4   *Newfoundland Quarterly* 87, no. 4 (Summer 1994): 5–7 and 7–9. Available at http://collections.mun.ca/cdm/compoundobject/collection/quarterly/id/39831/rec/2.

The places visited by Carpon in his various stays in Newfoundland were all around the tip of the Northern Peninsula in the area commonly referred to by the French as "Le Petit Nord." Prior to his season of 1834, the location of the vessels for which he was hired is not listed. In 1834 he was at Great Brehat, in 1847 and 1848 at Griquet, in 1849 at Quirpon, in 1853 and 1854 at "Havre de Haha" (probably in what is now Raleigh, Ha Ha Bay), in 1855 and 1857 at Little Islets Harbour ("Havre des Petites Îlettes"), in 1858 at Griquet again; his 1859 destination is not listed, but in 1862–65 inclusive he was at Cook's Harbour. These destinations are all in the area commonly frequented by Granville fishing ships.

The Granville crew lists also offer fleeting glimpses of his activities. One occurrence that his book does not mention is the death of one of the crew, Jean Julien Labigne, cook on board the *Deux Sophie*, who died during the return crossing on 11 October 1847 of unspecified causes at the age of 33.[5] A death certificate signed by Carpon is attached to the crew list; normally these certificates simply certified that death had taken place, and did not include the cause. The following year, on the same ship, he signed the death certificate of a sailor, Auguste Félix Clérot, who died on board on 14 September at the age of 35, probably also during the return crossing.[6] In 1849 his signature appears on two death certificates: one for Mathurin Louis François Guego, aged 48, a passenger who died in Newfoundland on 6 September 1849, the other for François Joseph Pierre Legnone, age 26, *matelot 2^e classe*, who was lost at sea after falling overboard on 30 September 1849.[7] In 1863 Carpon was again in contact with survivors of a shipwreck, this time of the *Aimable Martin*; seven survivors were taken on board the *Anna* on 22 June. Six were passed on to the naval station on 22 July, and the seventh was put on board the *Amis de Granville* on 7 July; the crew list contains a note from the captain claiming reimbursement of expenses

---

5   Library and Archives Canada, microfilm F-1883.
6   Library and Archives Canada, microfilm F-1879.
7   Library and Archives Canada, microfilm F-1881.

for their provisions.[8] In 1864 Carpon signed another document certifying that Joseph Encoignard, age 40, was lost at sea after falling overboard in an accident.[9] The above probably represent a fairly typical pattern.

Carpon makes a plea for the authorities to adopt stricter regulations to ensure that those participating in the Newfoundland fishery are given a satisfactory standard of health care. These are by no means empty words, and they need to be set in the context of continued pressure from the outfitters to relax requirements. The cost of providing surgeons and the necessary supplies was one that officials were anxious to prune as far as possible. A letter from the Ministry for the Navy and the Colonies dated 20 December 1837 outlines proposals intended to lessen the burden on outfitters, principally by allowing them to have surgeons serve not just a vessel or even a particular harbour, but harbours where communication between each of them was easy.[10] In 1868, Mer makes clear that in his opinion these amendments were potentially harmful to the health of the men. In addition to that, the ship that he was to have sailed on, the *Arthur*, lost three of its crew to tuberculosis (Jean-Guillaume Gaillard and Nicolas Gaillard while they were in Newfoundland, and Charles Fouché on the return journey to France). Their deaths are noted in the record of the *Arthur* referred to above.

It is quite likely that Carpon played a role in the introduction of closer regulation of the health care given to Newfoundland fishermen. He quotes Baron Larrey's reference to Carpon's own proposals to Pierre François Kéraudren for reform. Kéraudren was the man responsible for the introduction of the "Paper Doctor" in 1844 (*Instructions médicales pour MM. les capitaines de navires qui n'embarquent pas de chirurgien,* or *Medical Instructions for captains of ships with no surgeon on board*), with Huet, Deverre, and Du Pray—all members of

---

8   Library and Archives Canada, microfilm F-1881.
9   Library and Archives Canada, microfilm F-1959.
10   Library and Archives Canada, microfilm F-862.

a special *commission médicale*.[11] This was a layman's guide on how to treat various ailments that might be encountered in the fishing industry.

This is the extent of our knowledge of C.-J.-A. Carpon. There is, however, one word that should perhaps be added in this preface. The author conveys the impression that he is a great extrovert, participating in sessions of storytelling among his colleagues, and reproducing not just the content but also the colour of those tales. He relates what he hears. He refers to one type of whale, for example, as a "fine bague," apparently blissfully unaware that in so doing he is simply giving a French form to the English *finback*. The reader will notice that some of his information, such as the stories of struggles between whales and swordfish and his explanation of the origins of seasickness, is in fact lifted directly from Larrey's commentary on his stay in Newfoundland. One wonders too whether some of his tales are factual observations or the perpetuation of urban myths. For example, his account of an English hunter who cut up his infant children who had died over the winter and used them as bait for his traps seems so far-fetched that it stretches credulity. At other times, when, for example, he talks of bloodletting as a useful procedure, he was merely echoing received opinion at the time.

Carpon's *Voyage to Newfoundland* will be remembered chiefly as the most comprehensive recollection of the life of French fishermen on the shores of Newfoundland in the 19th century, for his detailed descriptions of the structures they used, the practices they followed, and their few festive moments, such as the feast held when the supply of salt has all been used and the return home is drawing near. Whereas Gobineau's *Voyage à Terre-Neuve* shows us a broad canvas of Atlantic Canada from the point of view of a visiting diplomat, Carpon gives us the view from ground level of the first-hand experiences of an old

---

11 *Bulletin Officel de la Marine et des Colonies (édition refondue et éditée des Annales maritimes et coloniales)* tome quatrième, 1844–87. Document dated 2 May 1844. Paris: Impr. Nationale, 1880, 14–46.

hand in different small communities. The way of life that he describes disappeared with the flimsy, temporary buildings that the French used as their base for the duration of the fishing season, but fortunately his book remains.

Larrey's chapter from his memoirs offers a different viewpoint altogether. Larrey is writing as a young man in the final stages of his medical studies who has just been appointed to a season on a naval frigate, the *Vigilante*, overseeing the French fishery in Newfoundland in 1788. His account shows a man who is committed to his calling and who, when faced with potentially dangerous situations, proves to be both decisive and effective. This was his only trip to Newfoundland: he resigned from the navy after his return because of chronic seasickness. The comments of his superiors on his conduct are highly complimentary and indicate the promise of a bright future. But who would have suspected that he was destined to become one of the most illustrious figures in the history of French military medicine? He was famous for his invention of the so-called flying ambulances that brought medical personnel to the wounded on the battlefield, allowing them to be treated on the spot and evacuated to field hospitals (a novel concept) for further care far more efficiently than previously. His system of triage, selecting patients to be treated according to the seriousness of their injury and without regard to their rank or even the side they were fighting on, was far ahead of its time. This was the period when Napoleon was a rising star, and Larrey rose with him to the position of Surgeon-in-Chief to the French army. Napoleon also elevated him to the rank of baron and remembered him in his will, where he left him 100,000 francs, referring to him as "l'homme le plus vertueux que j'ai connu"—"the bravest man I ever knew." "Vertueux" here has the old sense of brave or valiant, rather than today's meaning of virtuous or morally upright.

One of Larrey's "flying ambulances," 1797.

The authors of the naval reports—Venancourt, Gautier, and Mer—were all naval captains with the French naval division patrolling the French fishery in Newfoundland. Venancourt's report is dated 1 August 1821 at Croque, when he was commodore of the naval station for that year; it was addressed to his minister in Paris, the minister for the navy. Gautier's is different. He too was part of the naval division, but his vessel, the *Gentille*, was normally stationed in St-Pierre, and his report, dated 1 October 1846, is addressed to Brou, the commandant of St. Pierre and Miquelon. Mer, like Venancourt, was commodore of the French naval station in 1868, and his report, dated 20 September of that year, was also addressed to his minister in Paris.

These three reports provide useful information over a spread of close to 50 years and show the evolution of the advice that French authorities were receiving with regard to the Newfoundland fishery.

Venanourt's 1821 report notes with regret that a number of the fishing stations assigned to St-Pierre on the west coast were not in use. This was regrettable, in his view, not only because it represented a loss to France but also because it left the door open to English settlements being established on the French Shore. He regrets too that further advantage was not being taken of the possibilities for trading cod fished in Newfoundland with French colonies in the West Indies. In addition, he presciently points out the potential dangers for the French fishery of employing local English guardians to look after their premises in winter. He notes the danger that these families might form English settlements of their own. He suggests instead that in that area they employ local Indigenous people who were fellow Catholics and as such seen as allies. He also sees the potential of the settlement of St. George's, already a significant trading centre that was operating to the advantage of the British, not the French, with the likelihood of significant expansion in the future. Venancourt was one of the first to warn that this situation was disadvantageous to French trade and a potential source of dispute because it called into question the exclusivity of French rights there.

Gautier reinforces the case made by Venancourt about English settlers moving into the area of St. George's. The small number of families that had settled there when the French were absent during the wars with Napoleon grew rapidly, and at the same time others arrived from Cape Breton and other areas. The French outfitters showed little interest in fishing for cod out of St. George's, preferring areas to the north. So while French fishermen were deserting the area, a local population as well as an influx of outsiders was settling there. Gautier regrets the rarity of actions taken by commodores of the naval station to counter this development, but his conclusion is clear: St. George's was definitively lost to the French as a result of earlier laxity on the part of French authorities.

Gautier's description of the local population around St. George's is interesting. He uses the word "Jacotar" to describe them, one of the very earliest known uses of the word. For him, Jacotars were either deserters from the French fishing fleet (i.e., had jumped ship in Newfoundland to set up a new life for themselves) or incomers from Acadia (Nova Scotia and New Brunswick). The term was derogatory, describing those who lived a squalid, hand-to-mouth existence in extreme poverty with no will to extricate themselves from it. The attraction was that this area was not represented in the Newfoundland House of Assembly, and without representation there was no taxation. Law enforcement too was notable by its absence at that time.[12] Gautier's comments on the population provide a unique insight into conditions on the French Shore. He also includes a map of St. George's drawn by himself as part of his fisheries surveillance, showing the area known at Flat Bay.

Mer's report is very different. It is extremely comprehensive, covering his patrol of the entire French Shore as well as a presence in St-Pierre. Interestingly, anyone looking for major incidents between French and English will be disappointed. The most serious cases of corrective action he had to take occurred in St-Pierre and involved Banks fishermen going on a drinking binge when they put into port. He says of the Newfoundlanders with whom he came into contact, and there were many: "I have looked closely at this population, which practically everywhere I have found to be honest, industrious, well aware of our rights and obedient to the slightest command from us." It is true that around Flowers Cove some inhabitants proved to be somewhat obstreperous in their dealings with the French, but this was very much the exception. Mer's relations with the British authorities were extremely cordial too. The French had no fishing rights in Labrador and risked being turned away by the British naval ships. Mer was much amused that the British commodore made a distinction between fishermen from France and those from St-Pierre and Miquelon, treating the latter like Newfoundlanders and allowing them to fish there freely. Mer's calm objectivity is apparent on a number of occasions when an allegedly serious dispute turns out on closer examination to have no substance. He records the steady decline in the French fishery, with many harbours traditionally used by the French not occupied at all, and predicts, correctly, that the trend will continue. His comments on the proposals

---

12   See chapter 5, note 85, of Carpon's book for further details on the origins of the term *Jacotar*.

for amendments regarding the hiring of surgeons on fishing ships are as humane as they are forthright. And he too comments on the pockets of English inhabitants on the French Shore, which he, like Venancourt and Gautier, attributes to the practice of allowing English guardians to settle with their families in French harbours. As he says, "Today the evil cannot be undone." Given the number of disputes between the English and French over the fishery, Mer's most conciliatory approach is a pleasure for the English reader to discover.

The decline in the French inshore Newfoundland fishery was to continue in the years that followed, creating the conditions for an agreement with Britain to bring it to a close: the *Entente cordiale* of 1904, under which French rights to catch fish along the coast and dry it on land were given up in exchange for territory in Africa.

Notes on references to Indigenous peoples

We must comment on the understanding of Indigenous peoples in these texts. It is seriously flawed. This is not surprising, given the limited understanding of the subject in Europe at the time. Carpon believed that the Innu and Inuit peoples of the Newfoundland and Labrador were one and the same. He is not alone in this. Larrey says the same thing. Gobineau, in his *Voyage to Newfoundland*, repeats this notion. This was probably a common understanding in naval circles that was perpetuated in discussions among officers during the extended periods they spent crossing the Atlantic and the months they spent in Newfoundland. Carpon and others may have encountered Inuit hunters and fishermen who had come from Labrador to parts of the Northern Peninsula of Newfoundland, as well as members of the local Mi'kmaq population, but the two were distinct peoples.[13]

We would also like to add a few words on the terminology used to

---

[13] It is highly unlikely that he would have encountered any Beothuk: Shanawdithit, the last survivor of the Beothuks, died in 1829, and Carpon's first trip to Newfoundland was in 1826.

refer to Indigenous peoples in the texts translated here. It was standard practice at that time to use terms that would be inadmissible today. In the mid-19th century it was not at all unusual, for example, to describe Indigenous people as savages. This is not just a question of vocabulary: it reflects an attitude prevalent at that time. Rather than looking for language that would be acceptable now, we have preferred to maintain the English equivalent of what was actually written. To do otherwise would be to misrepresent what the authors said and thought.

VOYAGE TO NEWFOUNDLAND

OBSERVATIONS AND CURIOUS IDEAS LIKELY TO INTEREST THOSE WHO WISH TO HAVE AN ACCURATE IDEA OF ONE OF THE MOST IMPORTANT UNDERTAKINGS OF FRENCH AND FOREIGN SEAMEN

Gathered during several stays in those cold regions
by
C.-J.-A. Carpon,
Surgeon in the merchant navy, corresponding member of the Caen Agricultural Society

PROSPECTUS

When the navigators of the 15th century discovered the northern parts of America, they had no idea how important trade and industry in these areas would become.

People rushed avidly to this western continent, delivered by the genius of a great man as a prey to the cruel greed of the peoples of the Old World.[14] They wanted only gold, and all they asked of these lands that were so rich and fertile was this deceptive metal, which was to impoverish and ruin its rapacious conquerors.

---

14 This is Gautier's rather grandiloquent way of saying that this discovery opened the way for speculators to search for riches in the New World. (Translator's note.)

Already the Spanish had turned up their noses at the huge area along the shores of the St. Lawrence, which was for a long time a French possession: finding nothing there to satisfy their insatiable cupidity, they had chosen to debase this country with harsh winters but very fertile soil with the name Canada (*aca, nada! here, nothing!*). Returning to more sensible ideas, the peoples of modern Europe have recognized the value that these distant possessions might achieve as agricultural colonies and commercial settlements. So they have travelled there as farmers, merchants, fishermen, vying in sacrifices and efforts to procure for their respective mother countries the greatest number of advantages.

Among the major initiatives undertaken toward this end, there is none more important than the fishery that is carried out on the Grand Banks[15] or in Newfoundland itself. This is understood by all of those who are interested in our [French] naval power, and in the prosperity of our [French] naval trade.

However, with the exception of practical men, who is aware of how these operations are carried out, operations that are so lengthy, so repetitive, and so meticulous? In many respects, the results are of incalculable richness: the products of this fishery furnish the table of the rich and poor alike, but who understands how they are obtained?

This was the thinking of Mr. Carpon, or rather, which was suggested to him by enlightened friends, for it was only by yielding to their repeated requests that he finally agreed to publish his observations.

So the author does not in any way present himself as a writer: he shares with us, with no pretensions at all, what he has seen. This is a book for everyone, for all will find something useful in it. And do not imagine that it is just about the fishery: this work is full of fascinating details about the country, the inhabitants, ancient and modern, animals, and hunting. In addition, he provides us with a solid and authentic

---

15 Sometimes the word Banks is plural, and sometimes singular in the orginal. We have followed the choice of the author. (Translator's note.)

education, yet one that is at the same time amusing.

Furthermore, independently of its intrinsic value, it is, we believe, most timely. Even if it attracts just for a moment the attention of our French minds, which for too long have been distracted by sterile and impotent ramblings of our so-called promoters, on important operations, on a profession that is eminently useful and honourable, for this alone he is entitled to the support of worthy people and friends of good order.

So it with full confidence that we call upon the benevolence and the encouragement of the public for this interesting work, which Mr. Carpon has been anxious to make available to all by setting the price per copy at 2 francs 50.

E. GAUTIER
Teacher of literature in Caen

AVAILABLE AT:

PARIS:	LEDOYEN & GIRET, Quai des Augustins;
"	DAUVIN & FONTAINE, 55 Passage des Panoramas;
CAEN:	Eugène POISSON, 18 rue Froide;
LE HAVRE:	COCHART, bookseller;
CHERBOURG:	LEPOITEVIN & HENRY, booksellers;
SAINT-LÔ:	ROUSSEAU, bookseller;
COUTANCES:	DAIREAUX, printer-bookseller;
"	FOLLAIN, bookseller;
PÉRIERS:	GROULD, bookseller;
GRANVILLE:	MAHÉ, bookseller;
ST-MALO-DE-L'ÎLE:	CARUEL, bookseller;
SAINT-BRIEUC:	GUYON Frères, booksellers;
VALOGNES:	CAPELLE, bookseller;
ST-HÉLIER (JERSEY):	PERROT & HULIN, booksellers and typographers, Place Royale.

TO MR. V. MINARD
Pharmacist in Montmartin-sur-Mer

You, the best of my friends
Who gave me the idea
Of publishing my work,
In spite of all the jeering:
To respond to your wish,
You see how I make haste,
In a quiet moment,
To make the presses creak.
I dedicate to you
This fruit of my talent
On which all can pour scorn;
For my lack of learning,
My humble modesty
Must pardon me with you.
It is because of you
That this innocent work
Ventures to see the day.
If they say: "Foolishness!
The book's not worth reading!"
Then withhold your regard,
Because, like it or not,
It is now on its way.
If the reader likes it,
Then so much the better.
If, alas, he does not,
And it rots in the store,
Too bad for the author!

INTRODUCTION

Having been requested on a number of occasions by some of my friends to publish a small brochure on the manner in which fishing and hunting are carried on along the coasts of Newfoundland, I often promised myself to yield to their wishes, but never took things any further. Being exhausted day and night by the demands of a very extensive medical practice, it would have been extremely difficult, if not impossible, when I returned home in the evening to think of anything other than rest, which is indispensable to regain one's strength. Necessity required me to do this rather than scribble down anecdotes about Newfoundland and its boats.

Finally, I am leaving my native soil, for five months at least, and am returning to the east coast of Newfoundland as a surgeon in the merchant navy. This journey will provide me with the leisure to make good my promise to my dear friends.

I shall no doubt fall far short of their expectations; however, relying on their friendly disposition, I believe that I have their pardon in advance.

But there is another public, and it is the fear of this, just as much as my life of toil, that made me delay for a long time. I recall the condemnation of Boileau[16] on any mediocre writing:

---

16   Nicolas Boileau (1636-1711): poet and literary critic, His *Art poétique* was considered to be the definitive handbook on poetic composition at the time. (Translator's note.)

> An author on his knees in a humble preface
> Vainly asks for pardon from the reader he bores:
> He will gain nothing from this cross judge.[17]

However, I took comfort, as sometimes happens with even the most faint-hearted. I reflected that too great a severity toward me would be unjust, that perhaps I am entitled to some indulgence, and that perhaps people will see in my writing the work of a man who is a foreigner to the world of letters. I told myself that this publication might have a certain interest, especially in maritime departments. Young men intent on following the difficult career of seaman will find useful information there. And then how many families have one of their number, or at least someone close to them, whose fate is dear to them, and who is involved in these perilous expeditions?

Finally, those who have been on them in the past, and, due to age or loss of strength, which is quickly exhausted in so laborious a career, can no longer go on them, will no doubt recall with some pleasure the work and the pastimes of their youth and maturity, for as our life declines, memories become more important to us: *Forsan et haec olim meminisse juvabit*.[18]

These were the considerations that swayed me.

Being more accustomed to wielding the scalpel than the pen, I need the full indulgence of my readers, and I implore them to grant it. They will, I trust, be generous enough not to cast too critical an eye on this unpretentious book; they will reflect that by bringing my work into the full glare of publicity, I am simply yielding to the curiosity of fine fellow-citizens, on whose friendship I can count for life.

I am a surgeon; this is a state that differs considerably from the profession of writer, for, in the exercise of his duties, a doctor may make

---

17 From Boileau's *Satire IX*. (Translator's note.)
18 "Perhaps this too will be a pleasure to look back on one day." Virgil, *Aeneid*, I. 203. (Translator's note.)

discoveries or compose works based on his experience without necessarily rising to the heights of the talent of a historian. Moreover, this is simply a narration of facts of which I have many times been an eyewitness, and that I am now making so bold as to set down, with the thought that some may profit from it, and others may find some pleasure in it.

There is nothing beautiful but what is true; only truth is pleasing.[19]

Guided solely by this axiom from the great master, I aspire to no title other than that of honest narrator. Hence, I have no fear of ever receiving from anyone a refutation of the facts contained in this little work. The truth, as everyone knows, is of the highest importance in all circumstances. It is in vain that beauty of style delights us, or harmony of phrasing pleases us, if all these flowers of rhetoric serve only to embroider a lie. That is something that my nautical bluntness has always despised, and never have I travelled down that path. So, on reading what I have to say, you may rest assured of the accuracy of my accounts; indeed, these facts are such that, if they were to be controverted, they would expose me to frequent embarrassments, for cannot the reader at any time run into one of those men who, like myself, have travelled through those western parts? Well! Far from fearing the evidence of such travellers, I call upon it in support of what I set forward. I may be forgiven for insisting on this point, for it is on my integrity as a writer that I count to give my humble work whatever interest it may have, exposed, as it is, like many others, to the malevolence of critics.

I hope nevertheless to blunt the severity of censors with this dual consideration, which summarizes both the object of my work and the rightness of my intentions: my goal is to instruct and to entertain the ordinary reader, but especially to make myself useful to young men who are called to the noble and difficult vocation of seaman.

---

19   Boileau, "Rien n'est beau que le vrai; le vrai seul est aimable." From *Épitre IX*. (Translator's note.)

CHAPTER 1

*Crossing from France to Newfoundland—Advice to young seafarers—
General and particular facts—Attempts at narrative verse—Recollections
of shipwrecks—Health advice*

Since the departure and the crossing from France to Newfoundland offer nothing worthy of attention, I shall mention only the most notable events and relate them simply, in a few words.

Once we have said farewell to the fair land of France to make for these North American islands, we soon find ourselves cast into the middle of the Atlantic Ocean. What, then, can we seriously expect to find worthy of description? From morning to night, we observe the same things: a ship, fellow travellers, the sky, the vastness of the watery plain, criss-crossed by ships from all the nations of the world.

And so, leaving our ship to make its way on a sea by turns calm and rough, let us use our leisure moments to talk about details that may be of some interest to the reader. Since cod fishing is the primary objective of our journey, people may be curious to learn how this fishery is conducted and how the fish is prepared for transportation to practically every country in the world. I shall speak, then, of some principles of fishing and hunting, gleaned from my own experience, which will, I believe, be of great use to those who might wish to visit this region in whatever capacity. These documents may be of use to officers, travellers, and ordinary seamen, since, before leaving for any country, is it not always reassuring to obtain information relative to the expedition on which one is about to embark?

Many young men who hope to become officers embark as volunteers for the cod fishery; they receive no salary, but neither are they required to pay any fees. For their first season, the outfitter of the ship on which they sail receives 50 francs from the government as an incentive, and he receives this same sum for all those who go on any voyage whatever for the first time.

This reward is given in exchange for the benefit that accrues to the state's navy, for, in this way, it recruits daily new subjects whose courage and skill are assured if ever the dignity of the nation should be threatened.

In Newfoundland, these volunteers are given the curious name of *butter-eaters*, an indication that at least they were not reduced to eating their bread dry. In fact, both when they are on board and ashore, they are accepted at the captain's table with the other officers, and, like them, obliged to stand their watches[20] and lend a hand with everything relating to the fishery.

When the captain sees that they are intelligent and hard-working, he gives them his trust and makes them responsible for a variety of missions, which are quite frequent during the stay in Newfoundland.

For example, he puts them in command of a suitable number of men for the task at hand, transporting wood for heating or construction, building cabins, or setting up drying areas, etc.

The men who are assigned by the captain to a volunteer or an officer in this way owe their superior both obedience and respect, and, to prevent cases of insubordination, are subject to the same disciplinary regulations as sailors in the state's navy.

When these young men have reached the age of 20, they may, after two seasons at sea, be called up for service to the state. Indeed, this is

---

20   By *watch*, they mean the time that the seamen responsible for the ship's movements have to spend on deck, under the orders of the captain or an officer. The latter is known as the *officer of the watch* during his period of duty. (Author's note.)

the common fate of all sailors and citizens of the nation, to which all men should consider that they owe a debt of duty.

The volunteer who is given a travel warrant has an advantage over the ordinary seaman: if his talents have been cultivated by a good education, once he arrives on board a vessel belonging to the state, he quickly earns the respect of his superiors, who grant him special consideration.

The young sailor who has satisfied the requirements of conscription thinks he is free of any further service to his country. This is true, as long as he does not do two tours of duty as a seaman, to distant parts, after being demobilized from his military service. Otherwise, on his return from the second voyage, he is automatically listed, and a Commissaire[21] may give him papers for Brest or some other major port. To avoid receiving this warrant, anyone who does not intend to go into the navy has to have himself unlisted at the end of each fishing season, that is, if he wishes to remain free to do as he chooses and stay with his family. Travellers, passengers, and cooks do not fall into this category, since their profession is considered as being outside the navy.

The doctor in the merchant navy is also exempt from service to the state and cannot be obliged to perform it, unless there are special circumstances.

The doctor/author should remember, when describing the area he is travelling through, that his task will be incomplete if he fails to mention the customs of the inhabitants, the illnesses most frequently encountered in the country, the ways of treating them, and the means of preventing them.

So I propose to say a few words on these different matters from the point of view of the surgeon.

---

21   Following a system set up by Louis XIV, maritime departments in France had a *Commissaire des classes*, who was responsible for maintaining a register of men going to sea and their position. In Normandy and Brittany these men were divided into four classes, and the Commissaire was responsible for notifying each class when it was being called up for service in the navy. The men were not allowed to work in the fishery if their class was called up. (Translator's note.)

These sundry digressions may be of great use to young medical officers in the merchant navy and also to those who, although they do not intend to go to Newfoundland, may nevertheless wish to find out what goes on there; they will find in my book a depiction of the country and the work involved in the fishery.

In 1826 I composed a sketch of Newfoundland in verse. I did not publish it, because on my arrival in Granville I saw another, which could have been considered the twin of my own, and which was already being enjoyed by a large number of readers.

It did not deserve the title of poem any more than mine did, though this was how it was described. Though no more than a rhyming narrative, it was a little too clever. Mine was much more reserved, and, if I had given it to the press, it would certainly have had as many admirers as the other, for one should never overdo things.

I shall insert here and there throughout this journey a few fragments of my poor verse; this is a weakness on the part of the author for which, I feel sure, my readers will forgive me. I beg your indulgence in advance for the mistakes that these lines may contain. It will be readily understood that I am not including them as a model of poetry and that I am well aware of their true value. They are the poor product of a mind that has never felt the secret influence of heaven.[22] I have a passion for composing verse; if I was prevented from doing so, it would upset me greatly. Why would I not be allowed to add verse to my prose? *What harm can it do?*[23]

The memory of the 1826 season will remain with me forever. It was spent in Newfoundland on board the *Euphrosina*, under the command of Mr. Adelue, a master of ocean-going vessels who had the rank of ensign.

We had been in sight of the three-master *Belle Julie* from Granville for just a few hours when it sank around 6 p.m., pierced by a large block

---

22 Emphasis in the original. The phrase is a quotation from I.3 of Boileau's *Art poétique* (1674). (Translator's note.)
23 Emphasis in the original. This is a common phrase, but probably a reference to scene XVII of Molière's *Sganarelle* (1660), where Sganarelle reflects that there are worse things than being cuckolded, and that he would rather be that than dead. (Translator's note.)

of ice. We mourned the loss of many from her large crew.

The vessel *Nathalie* had suffered the same fate on 28 May 1826 at 8 p.m., with dreadful consequences.[24]

The port of Granville, from which both of these fine vessels had sailed, was plunged into the most terrible consternation, as were the smaller communities that were involved in this irreparable loss.

The pack ice that year, according to the accounts of the most experienced seamen, was unlike anything ever seen before. Some icebergs stranded on the shore were more than 100 metres from the tip to the base. And we remained for 40 days in the midst of the perils that had just given rise to these sad events.

The dreadful shipwreck of *Nathalie* has been described in a very touching manner by Father Daniel, Officer of the Legion of Honour and Director of Education for Caen.[25]

His work, which leaves nothing to be desired from the stylistic point of view, is unfortunately all too accurate in its account of what happened at that terrible moment. How I wept as it reminded me of the loss of several of my best friends, swallowed up in the abyss! Allow me to recall some episodes of this dreadful catastrophe, in which I myself was involved:

Quaeque ipse miserrima vidi.[26]

---

24   See Gaud Houiste, *Naufrage du navire* la Nathalie (Coutances: Voisin, 1827). A much briefer account of this shipwreck, also by Houiste, is found in the *Annales maritimes et coloniales*, 1826, part II, vol. 2, 481–87. This latter version was translated into English by Scott Jamieson and appeared in the *Newfoundland Quarterly* 87, no. 4 (Summer 1994): 5–7 ("A Hatful of Mussels–The Loss of the Sailing-Ship *Nathalie*"). The same volume of the *Annales maritimes et coloniales* also includes an account by the captain of the *Belle-Julie*, Clair-Désiré Letourneur, of the sinking of his ship. This too was translated by Scott Jamieson and appeared in the same volume of the *Newfoundland Quarterly*, 7–9, along with Letourneur's recommendations on how to deal with a shipwreck.
    One hundred and six men were lost in the sinking of the *Belle Julie*, while 31 were saved. Carpon notes that his ship, the *Euphrosina*, had earlier been close to the *Belle Julie*, but must have lost contact, since the men saved were picked up by the *Élisa* and the *Comte d'Estourmel*.
    The *Nathalie* had 74 men on board. Of these, 17 escaped in a boat (it could carry no more). Four reached the ice and were picked up by another ship, the *Louisa*. Houiste and his two companions survived 19 days on the ice, succeeded in reaching land, and were picked up by a passing English ship. The remaining 50 men were lost. (Translator's note.)
25   Abbé Daniel, *Naufrage du navire* la Nathalie, *de Granville* (Coutances: Voisin, 1827). Based on the account by Gaud Houiste. (Translator's note.)
26   A quotation from the opening lines of Book 2 of Virgil's *Aeneid*. Translation: "very unhappy things which I myself saw." Interestingly, the original continues, "et quorum pars magna fui" ("and of which I was a great part"), which would have been equally appropriate; perhaps Carpon omitted this out of modesty. (Translator's note.)

When we arrived in port at Cape Rouge, I was informed that three shipwrecked men needed urgent assistance; they had been brought there after miraculously escaping death, having remained on the ice for 12 or 14 days in bitterly cold temperatures with nothing to eat or drink.

These unfortunate men were Mr. Houiste, first mate of the *Nathclie*, and seamen Jeoret and Pottier, all three companions in misfortune who had been rescued by an English schooner.

As I was preparing to leave, I received an invitation from the most senior of the merchant surgeons to go to see Mr. Hélin, a shipowner from Granville, fishing at the head of the bay at Cape Rouge. I found three colleagues there, awaiting my arrival beside the sickbed of these poor survivors.

The loss of the *Nathalie*. The caption reads: "The ship was lost. With it alas, most of the unfortunate men on board were also lost for ever!!!" Frontispiece from *Naufrage du navire La Nathalie* by Gaud Houiste (Voisin: Coutances, 1827).

Mr. Houiste's face looked like that of someone whose features had been disfigured by a long and painful typhoid fever. He had retained the use of his limbs, numbed though they were, but their normal appearance gave no cause for concern about their ability to function in the future. This was not the case with Jeoret or Pottier: their toes were sphacelated from the effect of frostbite;[27] their faces were in a sorry state and their complexion was deathly: in short, their appearance inspired both horror and pity.

I expressed myself in favour of the immediate resection of the toes to the healthy joints, in order to assist nature in its efforts, and I offered to carry out the operation.

At first my two colleagues were not swayed by my opinion; but, a few days later, I had the satisfaction of having it favourably received by the chief surgeon of the naval frigate; he operated on these two patients with all the success that might have been expected from his skill.

Like my colleagues, I had put my bandaging material, my cotton waste, and my drug supply at the disposal of Mr. Hélin's surgeon. It would have been greatly satisfying for me to have contributed everything I possessed to the relief of such suffering, but these survivors were entrusted to the care of the chief surgeon, who had them taken to the naval station at Croque, where they received all the attention that their condition required.

Since those terrible misfortunes, navigation through the ice is carried out with much more caution than in the past, for it used to be a very unequal struggle. I recall having heard many times on board, in the old days: "We're going to slog our way through the ice." This is one of those old seafaring expressions that is no longer used in these icy seas, thank heavens! Why is it that men become prudent only as the result of the most disastrous experiences?

Before ships leave France, it would be wise for the health commissions, set up in ports that are major outfitting centres, to require that the shipowners supply the surgeon with at least two woollen blankets and two mattresses. These would be for the use of any poor patients unable to obtain them for themselves. Moreover, on board, the sick should be placed close to a hatchway or to sleeping quarters, so that

---

27 Freezing and burning, although diametrically opposite, produce effects that are exactly the same as far as tissue damage is concerned: sphacelation and gangrene. (Author's note.)

they can breathe air that is fresher than the foul and polluted variety found between decks. Once on land for any length of time, it would be beneficial to isolate the sick in a separate area, protected from the rigours of the outside air.

In Newfoundland the cabins built for the crews are inhabited by a large number of men at the same time. They make a lot of noise day and night, especially during the fishing season. The doors are forever being opened and drafts of cold, damp air can bring a sudden halt to a bout of sweating. This sweating can lead to the recovery of a patient if it lasts one or two days, and the patient would inevitably die if it were not systematically allowed to run its course.

Quite apart from this disadvantage, already serious enough, the constant moaning of those who are gravely ill and unable to sleep disturbs the rest of their companions who often greatly need it.

In fact, when the fishery is at its height, the sailor is only too anxious to spend the four or five hours' rest he is given out of 24 quietly in his bed. What is the end result of this unfortunate association of the healthy and the sick? A regrettable increase in the number of the latter.

If men who are wet through and exhausted cannot get a wink of sleep for several days because of the noise made by the sick, will they themselves soon not be unable to work because of that indisposition known as aches and pains, or other no less troublesome complaints?

What happens as a result of this? Enormous losses for the outfitter, for a good fisherman's working day is highly productive.

So I am not afraid to say, and this advice is intended for the outfitters, that there would be a real saving for them, quite apart from any patriotic or humanitarian considerations, if they were to have a small cabin built to serve as an infirmary for the sick. It would be located near the surgeon's, and this area, which would be of no great expense, would be intended only for individuals whom it became absolutely essential to isolate.

And since Newfoundland is such a healthy country, one rarely sees dangerous fevers there. So much the better, then, if the quarters intended for those with fever or injuries could remain vacant during the crew's stay on the island! However, what I am proposing is a precautionary measure, in the interests of cleanliness and hygiene. No serious objection to it can be feared when one is dealing with Frenchmen and Christians.

CHAPTER 2

Another departure from Granville—View of the Mont-Saint-Michel—Thoughts it inspires—Organization of duties on board—Order of personnel at mealtimes—Seamen's food—Religious exercises—Attractions of a life at sea—Coasts of Brittany—Lighthouses and lights—Fresh impression in the Atlantic—Storm—Seasickness, presumed causes—Persistence of certain indispositions—Medico-gastronomic prescription

On Tuesday, 11 May 1847, at 2 p.m. in Granville I went on board the ship the *Deux Sophie*, under the command of Captain Mr. L. Renaudeau, master, ocean-going.

The preparations for getting under way were carried out swiftly and skilfully, the first mate promptly calling the roll of crew members. When everyone had answered present, the hired labourers were sent ashore, and the outfitter was soon informed by one of his employees that the seamen who had been signed on were all on board.[28]

We were soon swept out by the tide, and its swift current, with the help of the easterly winds, quickly took us outside the bay. We watched the higher ground of Granville, the prosperous communities of Saint-Pair, Bouillon, Carolles, Saint-Michel-des-Loups, and Champeaux all fade from our sight.

Here the coast forms a point or a cape, beyond which we could see the huge Bay of Cancale. Beyond these shores, littered with reefs that are the curse of ships, rise the picturesque buildings of the Mont-Saint-Michel, as if they were built on an enormous pier. This was

---

28   The police is immediately called upon to arrest anyone who fails to show up on board after having been paid his advance. (Author's note.)

The *Sans Gêne* leaving Granville for the Newfoundland fishery. Postcard from a photograph by J. Puel, collection of M. Wilkshire.

once the refuge of pious monks. Today this mournful retreat has a sinister appearance and calls to mind only woeful memories and bitter thoughts.[29] Within its confines, which were previously devoted to the observances of the religious life, political and other prisoners bemoan their fate and, deprived of their liberty, expiate their crimes and their excesses under harsh discipline. My fellow travellers and I were unable to refrain from commenting on our own existence as compared to the miserable condition of those wretches. They are deprived of so many things that we enjoy, and especially sweet liberty which is, after a clear conscience, the most precious of blessings for honest souls. How many victims of treacherous advice are detained there! How many of those raging firebrands, for whom disorder is a need, were led by their political anger to crime and dishonour! Let us show our utter contempt for these

---

29   The abbey of the Mont-Saint-Michel has its origins as far back as the eighth century. In the 11th and 12th centuries, a Romanesque abbey was built on the site of the original Carolingian structure, then Gothic additions were made in between the 13th and 16th centuries. By the 17th century, the abbey had fallen on hard times, and in 1780 parts of it were demolished. It became a prison for political prisoners as well as common criminals, and continued to serve this purpose up to the second half of the 19th century, when it was taken over as a national historic monument. It is an extremely popular tourist attraction in 2020. (Translator's note.)

depraved creatures who find a kind of pleasure in dragging peaceful citizens with them into the abyss, men who were perhaps not born for crime, but who were made guilty by disastrous advice. Eternal shame on seducers, on selfish men of ambition, the dishonour of mankind, whom nature seems to have put in this world only for the misfortune of their fellows! *Opprobrium hominum, et abjectio plebis.*[30] Pharisees preaching in public places, hypocritically leading people astray, a thousand times more criminal than the foolish people who are beguiled by their subversive theories!

We remarked on the enormous gulf that exists between the life of right-minded people and that of creatures who are debased by vice! We enjoy the pleasures of a calm and respected existence, while the dissolute are deprived of all rest and have to be always on their guard. Forever preoccupied with troublesome thoughts, tortured by the painful remorse that their disgraceful conduct causes them, their life can be no more than an unbearable burden. This is why they gladly run the risk of losing it, either out of despair or out of hatred or envy of honest people. And yet, how many of these hopelessly lost men are led astray forever by the folly of one youthful misdemeanour!

> In crime, the first step is all that it takes;
> One fall is sure to lead to another.
> Honour is a rocky isle with no beach;
> Once you have left, you can never return.[31]

While we were indulging in these painful thoughts, our ship was headed to the northwest, and the captain gave the order to assign duties.

This is done by first designating the men known to be capable of keeping watch. For this task, they always choose the finest sailors,

---
30 "The reproach of men and the outcast of the people" (Psalm 21:7). (Translator's note.)
31 Quotation from Nicolas Boileau's *Avertissement à un futur mari (Warning to a future husband)*, 1694. (Translator's note.)

those who have acquired the most skill through continuous experience at sea. They can never be too experienced in critical moments, which often occur on the open sea, but especially along the coast. There are two main watches: the *starboard* watch and the *port* watch.[32] The man at the helm, or *helmsman*,[33] is given the course to follow. He steers on the compass bearing that he has been given, and if the winds should happen to turn against him, he advises the officer, who immediately gives the order for the manoeuvre that will allow the ship to sail as close as possible to course. This is so as to make use of precious time by taking advantage of every possibility likely to bring the ship to its destination without taking it too far from the path it is supposed to follow. On the darkest of nights, the steering compasses are lit by the lamps of the binnacle; one sees them shine out with great brilliance, protected from the inclemency of the weather by their reflective glass.

Whether it is pitch dark or bright sunlight, we sail on. On board ship, a small number of men are not required to stand watch: the captain, the surgeon, the officers' chef, the master carpenter, the storekeeper, travellers, and passengers.[34]

Perfect order must reign on board a ship, as in military quarters; it is for this reason that everyone knows his post and does not leave it except on the orders of his superior.

As for meals, on merchant ships each dish serves six men and a boy; the latter is considered the sailors' servant, and indeed he is. He is the one responsible for carefully washing the dish, slicing the bread for the soup, and putting a small piece of salt pork in the pot. The pork is tied with a piece of sail yarn to a wooden skewer, bearing the number of the dish and running right through it, and stays firmly attached to it. The cabin

---

32 When one is looking toward the bow of the ship, *starboard* is to the right and *port* is to the left. (Author's note.)
33 The seaman responsible for pointing the rudder in the direction the ship has to take, which is known in sailing terminology as being or not being on course. (Author's note.)
34 By *passengers* (*passagers*), Carpon appears to mean men from a different fishing vessel carried either to Newfoundland or back to France by arrangement between the outfitters; by *travellers* (*voyageurs*), he probably means those who are being carried on board for other reasons, probably for a fee. (Translator's note.)

boy plunges the skewer into the cook's (*coq*'s)[35] pot until the meat is fully cooked, or at least until it is time to pour the soup over the bread.

When the men are on board, they, like the officers, have three meals a day. At 8 a.m., they eat a breakfast of bread and butter, with one and a half glasses of cider to drink; at midday, they have soup and fresh meat from the day they leave until there is no more hanging on the stay. The meat ration is 250 grams per man and the drink allowance is the same at all meals; they are allowed as much bread as they want, but are strongly advised not to waste any. Bread and water are not denied anyone in the merchant navy unless the captain judges it appropriate to ration them because they are held up by bad weather. This rationing is the responsibility of the chief storekeeper. The dishes are laid out according to rank. The masters[36] eat together; they have half a glass of cider more than the others and certain special considerations.

When there is no more fresh meat, they serve 192 grams of salt pork and the same weight of potatoes per man per day. The evening meal consists of a soup and leftovers from lunch.

On Fridays the crew eat cod and potatoes at midday; it is the only day of abstinence. This, then, is the diet of sailors during the crossing to Newfoundland. Their meals are always served on deck, rain or shine; as is usual with seafarers, there is always plenty of good humour.

At 8 a.m., they ring the bell for the changing of the watch and for communal prayers. One of the crew members, known to be a good singer, is immediately installed as celebrant. In the morning he sings hymns to the Holy Virgin, ending with the *Angelus*; at 6 p.m., more or less the same thing happens. On Sundays and feast days he strikes up the *Dixit*, the *Magnificat*, and the *Nunc Dimittis*, as well as the *Angelus*, accompanied by a hymn for those at sea. When prayers are over, he

---

[35] This is the name given to the crew's cook; on land, his cooking is known as *coquerie*, from *coquere*. (Author's note.) In fact, this appears to be a simple corruption of the English *cook* and *cookery*. There was a cook for the crew and another for the officers. (Translator's note.)

[36] By *masters*, Carpon is not referring to senior officers, but to those responsible for a group of crew members–boat master, seine master, beach master, etc. (Translator's note.)

always addresses God with the following invocation: "May the Good Lord save the ship, the captain and the crew, and give us a safe journey!"

The crew always sit down to eat after prayers, and when they are feeling well, the officers eat heartily in the mess room, sheltered from the weather, while the men on deck are no less cheerful around their pot.

There is no need to speak of the officers' food: it is always good. The outfitter has to provide them with coffee two days a week, on Thursdays and on Sundays. If they have a fancy to indulge in this fine, aromatic beverage on other days, they are perfectly at liberty to do so, but they must then pay, though just for the sugar. The outfitter always provides their spirits.

Many people imagine that it must often be boring on board ship, but this is a mistake. After dinner, during the break known as the *gloria*,[37] you drink a good cup of coffee and smoke a pipe; you listen to a host of amusing little stories that help to pass the time. And remember that you are never alone at sea, for they are continually announcing other ships which you approach and speak to. They give you news of the place you have just left or the one you are going to, and there is nothing in the world that can give you such sweet satisfaction. The variety of conversation, the incidents, the manoeuvres, and especially the grand fellows who keep you company, make you look with absolute contempt on the deception of false friends that you have left far behind you. At the same time, the good men around you remind you, by their openness, of the true friends that you hope to see again.

While we are busy discussing these matters, our ship, forging ahead under full sail a short distance from the coast of Brittany, soon takes us out of the doleful sight of the Mont-Saint-Michel. And so the sad thoughts inspired in us by that house of criminals are soon replaced by the cheerful memory of the merry and unusual country fêtes of the Breton region.

---

37   The *gloria* is a drink of sweet coffee laced with spirits, popular in Normandy. (Translator's note.)

But let there be no mistake: if, from afar, the low hills that run alongside and overlook the shoreline have a pleasant enough aspect, the same is not true of the coast itself. It is strewn with reefs, a nightmare for sailors, and would frequently be the scene of many shipwrecks if a number of lighthouses scattered along the coast did not give warning of the dangers, pointing navigators to the course they have to follow.

The presence of officers who are trained, experienced, vigilant, and endowed with great caution is a fortunate thing indeed as we leave the waters of the Channel behind us.

Night and day, the captain and the officers keep their eyes glued to the charts, especially when mist and bad weather prevent them from discerning with the naked eye the course that they have to hold for their safety and that of the crew. Whenever they pick out a lighthouse, or any piece of land, they immediately take a compass bearing on all of these points, which can then be used as guides in recognizing others: in short, they neglect nothing in their efforts to pass successfully through the dangers that surround them and to arrive safely at their destination. On Wednesday, 12 May, the day before the Feast of the Ascension, we were tacking through all these perilous reefs, but the weather was fine and it allowed us to observe the awesome sight from afar and without any fear.

Among these terrible rocks are the Horaine, the Barnouie, the Gautier, the Minquiers, etc.

The Horaine, a short distance off the coast of Brittany, is an extremely dangerous rock for anyone going through the Raz de Bréhat. Between this main rock and the land are several other rocks that are just as treacherous. The Horaine stands 7 metres above the surface of the sea even when the tide is at its highest.

At midnight on the 12th, the St-Malo light was spotted to the south in the southeast quarter, and the Cap Fréhel light to the southwest.

That same day, at 8 a.m., the duty officer had spotted the Horaine to the west-southwest. That perilous rock is approximately 50 nautical miles[38] [c. 90 km] from the Île de Bréhat.

Barnouie Rock also stands 7 metres 30 centimetres out of the water, and Gautier Rock, to the north-northeast of it, rises 5 metres above sea level. Next there is a chain of rocks connected to the plateau of Douvres Rocks; these rocks are always visible, and there is only a narrow passage between them.

To the east of the Passage du Raz rises the huge and dangerous Minquiers shelf, greatly to be feared because of the power of the currents caused by the height of these countless rocks.

The lighthouses and lights are essential aids for navigators; this is why the general administration of the Highways Department, with the greatest consideration, has taken care to erect many lighthouses at the dangerous points.

On leaving Granville, on your way out of the Channel, you come to the Lihou Rock or Cape, a light that is of no use on departure, which often takes place in broad daylight. But the return journey can occur at any hour of the night, and the situation is then quite different: with its brilliant lamp, comparable to that of the lighthouse on the Île de Chausey, and visible for a distance of 15 nautical miles [c. 27 km], this fixed light becomes a beacon of hope for getting back into Granville.

The Chausey light, visible for 12 nautical miles [c. 21.6 km], shines its beam every minute.

The light on Cap Fréhel is intermittent and carries an average distance of 18 nautical miles [c. 32.4 km].[39]

On Les Héaux de Bréhat there is a fixed light which also has a range of 18 miles [c. 32.4 km].

---

38   A nautical mile is approximately 1.8 kilometres. In future instances, the distance in kilometers will be given in square brackets. (Translator's note.)
39   Although Carpon does not specify, one assumes that he is referring to nautical miles, as in the following references to the power of other lighthouses. (Translator's note.)

The one on Sept Îles is intermittent and has a range of 9 miles [c. 16.2 km].

Following the normal route for leaving the Channel, passing close to Sept Îles, you reach Les Feuillées, and even the northern part of the Triagons. But it is possible to avoid these reefs by making use of the intermittent light on the Île de Batz; it has a range of 24 miles [c. 43.2 km], but can sometimes be seen from between 33 and 36 miles [c. 59.4–64.8 km].

In order to avoid shipwrecks, which, unfortunately, would otherwise often happen along this extremely dangerous coast of Brittany, especially in the approaches to Aber-Wrac'h, they have taken the wise precaution of erecting a white light on a small island called the Île Vierge; every four minutes this changes to red flashes, preceded and followed by short pauses. This light has been active since 15 August 1845.

I shall not elaborate further on these details of our navigation; whatever interest they may have for sailors, they might seem tiresome to ordinary readers; moreover, they have been written about more than once. I must limit myself to those facts that are worthy of some attention.

As our sails were continuously filled by a good east-northeast breeze, we said farewell to French soil, with the Île d'Ouessant seeming to mark the end of it, and soon we could no longer see the splendid lighthouse built on the northeast tip of that island, with its fixed light that has a range of 18 miles [c. 32.4 km].

We were swiftly carried out into the middle of the Atlantic Ocean. The isolation that is then experienced makes a great impression on those who are not used to sailing. The fact of seeing themselves for the first time between the sea and the heavens, far from friends and relatives, throws them into terrible consternation at first, but fortunately, this feeling does not last long. If it were otherwise, they would doubtless fall victims to the illness known as nostalgia (*nostalgie*), or homesickness, or pain of leaving (*maladie du pays ou de retour*): these are the names by which it is known. But practical distractions come to their aid and either prevent them from being overwhelmed by an onset of the affliction or cure them of it completely. Young sailors, who are well used to this kind of situation, and are generally of a cheerful disposition, ask them if they can sing. And when they reply in the affirmative, together they strike up humorous couplets and joyful refrains. If the dejected passenger is unable to sing himself, at least he listens to the songs of these children of joy, whom troubles have never made melancholy. There is nothing more cheerful than seeing these sailors, happy at their fate, strolling around the deck, singing simple romances or lively songs. Nothing is more likely to drive out gloomy ideas and bring back joy and serenity to the soul. There is no exercise that is more salutary. Since it comes from the heart and acts on the heart, it is more powerful than any medication in the world for curing a condition that is produced simply by tedium, but whose consequences are often very dangerous and sometimes even fatal.[40]

We were treated kindly by the winds up to the time we lost sight of all the dangers of the Channel, but this fine weather was quickly followed by a violent storm. However, this did not oblige us to heave to, because of the excellent sailing qualities and sturdiness of our ship. On all sides the sea seemed to be nothing but yawning chasms ready to swallow us up; the angry waves rose to prodigious heights, and to the young men we had on board going out for their first trip, the imminent demise of the whole crew seemed inevitable. Repeated attempts to console them and give them reason for hope were in vain. They kept crying: "My Lord, save me! Farewell mother and father, I shall never see you again! Lord, forgive me! How wretched I am at being brought out here only to drown!" and other similar lamentations. For as soon as any real or imagined danger appears, all self-respect is cast aside, and

---

[40] At that time homesickness was considered a potentially serious illness. The entry under "nostalgie" in M.-N. Bouillet's *Dictionnaire universel des sciences, des lettres et des arts* (Paris: Hachette, 1857) also notes the possibility of dying from it. (Translator's note.)

we hear all that despair can tear from the heart of a man who believes he is at death's door.

But the storm finally abated, the fury of the waves was calmed, and minds were set at ease; the severe fright that had gripped our young sailors left them, and they would have been in a satisfactory state if other problems, of a physical nature, had not become apparent and lowered their morale.

During the rough weather, seasickness had been felt even by several experienced sailors, but especially by the young who were on their first trip on the high seas. I myself felt some uneasiness, even though I have been used to this kind of voyage for many years. In my case the sickness was no more than a mere indisposition, but this was not the case with many of our men, who were terribly ill. Several writers have spoken of seasickness as being a temporary indisposition. They do not know what they are talking about.

During my stay in Paris I had the honour of studying under Baron Larrey, who soon considered me one of his best friends and with whom I continued to correspond up to the moment when the world had to mourn the loss of that brave and learned man. Here is the opinion of the able doctor on this sickness that he, like myself, had the opportunity to study in his voyages overseas.

Woe to anyone who happens to be constitutionally susceptible to this ailment, for it is the most inconvenient and the most disagreeable one with which anyone who intends to go to sea can be afflicted.

The sickness affects, more or less acutely, those who are making their first ocean-going voyage. However, there are people who are hardly bothered by it, or who, having put up with a first attack, face all future storms with no recurrence. Yet there are others who, even after several trips, are constantly sick in heavy weather and are unable to keep this strange affliction at bay. We will attempt to give the reasons for these differences by discussing the causes of seasickness. The symptoms are generally known, but we have to explain their origin. As long as the vessel maintains its balance and has a steady and regular motion, however swift it may be, the man on board feels no indisposition. But if headwinds impede the movement of the vessel, or if, as a result of a squall, it is tossed by the waves, the sailor feels the effects of the two principal movements to which the ship is subjected. The first of these movements is known as rolling; this is what moves the vessel from starboard to port, with varying force. The second is known as pitching; it consists of the alternate raising and lowering of the bow and the stern. In the first case, anyone who is inexperienced is convinced that the ship is bound to keel over; in the second, he is afraid of going straight down into the depths. At first it is the mind that is struck by these unruly movements. Then, added to this first effect, which is emotional and absent in experienced sailors, there is another, which is physical. These unnatural movements produce shocks, the effects of which are concentrated in the brain, the most impressionable part of the body because of its mass, its softness, and its lack of elasticity. The molecules of this organ, after being shaken about, collapse upon each other. This is the cause of all the symptoms that characterize seasickness.

The greater the mass of the brain, and the softer its consistency, the more this organ is susceptible to these effects. This is why young men, whose brains are very large, are the most subject to seasickness. People of advanced years, whose brains have diminished in size and are, in addition, of a firmer consistency than in young subjects, are less likely to suffer from this complaint. Inhabitants of maritime coasts and cold climates, in whom the brain mass is less developed than in those who inhabit warm countries and the interior, adapt much better to the vicissitudes of navigation: they are less subject to seasickness.[41]

The first effect of this shock to the brain is sadness and a feeling of

---

41   It is impossible to determine precisely the reasons for this difference, but experience shows us that all animate beings, as well as plants, that are exposed to the influence of winds or gases coming from the sea, especially on coasts with a northern exposure, are generally limited in their development, either in whole or in part, and remain relatively compressed and reduced in size. (Author's note.)

panic-stricken fear that grips the individual. His face becomes pale and his eyes flood with tears; he cannot take any food; he remains silent, seeks out solitude and rest; he staggers as if he were drunk; he feels giddy, has ringing in the ears, and an unpleasant heaviness in his head; he becomes nauseated, and soon after has fits of vomiting, which become frequent, painful, and persistent until the cause ceases. This vomiting, the main symptom of the sickness, is sometimes accompanied by bleeding and by convulsive movements. They are no doubt produced by sympathetic irritation or a disturbance that is created between two nerve cords, the eighth pair of the pneumogastric nerves. It is at the beginning of these that the effects of the disturbance in the brain appear to be concentrated. And since they are distributed almost entirely in the stomach, this organ is the first to be affected by this morbid condition. It is then communicated sympathetically to all the organs of the chest and the lower abdomen. This results in faintness, a feeling of suffocation, the suppression of intestinal excretions, and persistent constipation of varying duration. The strength of the patient diminishes considerably to the point of exhaustion, his legs no longer support the weight of his body, and when the individual tries to walk, he loses his balance and falls over like a man who has had too much to drink. He huddles in the nearest corner and stays there motionless until the vomiting obliges him to move.

The patient receives no nourishment since he cannot keep down food of any kind.

Weight loss becomes increasingly pronounced and the intellectual faculties grow weaker, due to the stress on all the physical organs. This deterioration becomes so pronounced that, far from being afraid of death, as in the first stage of the sickness, most people would be glad of it at this point. Some even try to take their own lives, and we have indeed seen instances of this.

This sickness would doubtless have an unfortunate outcome if it lasted for any length of time, but it is rare for the causes that produce it to maintain the same degree of intensity beyond seven, eight, or nine days.

The more violent the storm, the more quickly it ends; calm follows almost immediately, and this moment of tranquility generally sets the sick on their feet again. They are cured as if by magic, and completely regain their functions.

Their strength returns rapidly, and they soon forget their troubles. At the first headwind, especially when lying to, the same thing starts all over again, and in some cases is just as serious as before, while in others it is not nearly as bad; then there are some who never have a recurrence.

The organs gradually get used to these upsets or shocks and end up by carrying out their functions without any disturbance or confusion.

But in some people, the condition is just as bad on their second or third trip as it was on the first. It is difficult to explain these differences. In all cases, it is the brain that is the most affected. The proof of this is in the relief that one obtains by getting into a hanging frame,[42] and covering one's head with a tightly wound bandage.

As long as you remain in this position, the seasickness is calmed. But it comes back as soon as you leave your hammock and come into direct contact with the ship again. This condition is doubtless very unpleasant, but it is rare for sufferers to die, unless there are other complications associated with it. However, the patient can be put out of action for a long time and fall into malnutrition. There are very few known ways to prevent seasickness, and none has been found to be effective in curing it. It is essential for the cause to cease in order for the problem to disappear. However, it will be less violent and less long-lived if, before its onset, your personal hygiene includes bathing with a strong solution of water and vinegar over the entire surface of the body; add to this great sobriety, take vegetable acids mixed into your food and drink, and smoke a pipe in moderation.

---

42   A kind of bed used on board ship by officers, passengers, and the sick. (Author's note.)

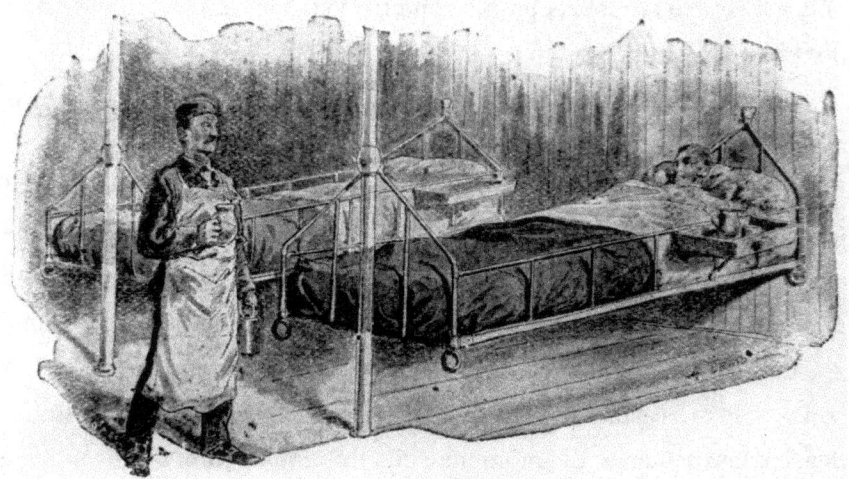

From Louis-Pierre-Marie Coquin, *Hygiène et pathologie des pêcheurs de morue à Terre-Neuve et en Islande* (Bordeaux: Impr. du Midi, Paul Cassignol, 1900), 147.

You should avoid coming into contact with cold, damp air at night and should stay as little as possible between decks and in the places inside the ship where breathing foul and polluted air will predispose you to vomiting. Here, you must follow the example of experienced sailors who, in their leisure time, stroll about on deck, where the air is purer, and where, little by little, you become accustomed to the motion of the ship and the waves.

Once seasickness has set in, you must eat very little, taking only foods that are easily digestible and able to fortify the stomach and absorb gastric juices, which become very abundant in these circumstances. Examples are biscuits and crusts of bread soaked in coffee or wine, in oxycrate[43] or in lemonade.

For those who do not like coffee or wine, tea and a light punch are also beneficial, but you must avoid fatty and sweet foods, salads, soups, and vegetables of all kinds. A little roast meat may be eaten, but

---

43   Oxycrate: a mixture of water and vinegar. (Translator's note.)

only a little. You must keep warm and try to take as much recreation as possible. This is the way to ease the ill-effects of seasickness.

Everyone has his own thoughts on this strange affliction, and forms a personal opinion. Which one should we adopt? The one, of course, that best conforms to good sense. I remember having heard a host of facts about seasickness by which people attempted to give an irrefutable explanation of the cause. A naval surgeon whose name escapes me attributes it to the loss of balance and explains it in the following terms.

Our fluids, especially the blood, acquire from the organs that contain them a certain balance, which gives rise to our normal condition. Seasickness occurs at the moment when this equilibrium or this normal condition is upset.

The immediate cause of this disruption of the equilibrium lies in what physicists have called the inertia of matter: when the body follows the swinging motion of a vessel, the fluids that are caught up in this general movement tend to continue their progress in one direction after the solid matter has come to a rest, or is already moving in the opposite direction. In this way the blood leaves the brain and moves to the lower parts of the body, when the body, having followed the ship in a downward motion, starts coming up again. The opposite takes place when the body, having followed the ship in a pitching movement, or in an upward movement, starts going down; then the blood starts to rush toward the brain in too great a quantity.

So, according to this explanation, seasickness is primarily caused by the first of these two movements of the blood, that is to say by the transfer of this liquid from the brain toward the lower extremities.

In support of this theory, our doctor points out that any large demand on the blood supply, in any organ whatever, at the expense of the nerve centres, produces the same indisposition and the same physiological effects as the rolling and pitching of a ship. The dizziness produced by a swing, by a circular movement, by the motion of a carriage, and especially by that of a camel, is due to the same cause. Bloodletting, and the current practice of applying enormous cupping glasses in order to free the central organs by drawing a large quantity of blood toward a limb, and the movement of blood to the uterus brought about by pregnancy also produce nausea and vomiting that cannot be distinguished, from a physiological point of view, from those that characterize seasickness.

After frequent and lengthy discussion of this subject with naval medical officers, I have found considerable pertinence and accuracy in their observations on the occasional causes of the sickness that is the particular subject of these remarks, but unfortunately I have never, anywhere, seen any way to prevent the onset in persons who are constitutionally predisposed to being affected by it.

Since constipation can often in itself prolong the problem to 18 or 20 days or more, it is crucial from the beginning to use mild laxatives such as syrup of peach blossom, the juice of stewed prunes, enemas, etc.; such treatment gives the most satisfactory results.

What a strange creature man is! Why is it that the organs that are most necessary for the preservation of our being are also those that are most susceptible to disturbances?

At the beginning of this voyage, several of our men were extremely upset in the stomach and in the lower abdomen. Since their internal organs were carried from left to right by the rolling, and then up and down by the pitching, they became feverish and constipated. And, in this condition, the stomach, being mechanically forced backward, set off a series of contractions of the diaphragm through this contact.

Fits of nausea and vomiting were the inevitable outcome of these uncontrollable movements. In order to avoid these problems by maintaining the intestines in a more stable position, I used a belt of heavy canvas held in place by three buckles which could be replaced with leather laces or strong cord.

This device covered an area that began at the xiphoid cartilage[44] and went down to two fingers' width above the navel.

Several of my patients tried out this procedure, which I knew very well to be quite harmless. They nevertheless paid old Neptune the due that he exacts for travel on the deep. Yet, as one can see, the theory behind it is entirely compatible with the general opinion of my colleagues, which I also share. They all have in common a loss of equilibrium, nervous irritation, and a rush of blood toward the centre and to the extremities. To conclude this subject, let me say that seasickness has existed since the creation of the earth, and will last as long as it does, unless the human constitution is greatly modified, which is scarcely probable. Let me add, finally, that many fine things may have been said about the reasons why it occurs, but no doctor has ever been able to prevent it in anyone who is constitutionally disposed to it.

If you would nevertheless like a palliative for this complaint, here is my recipe. Two hours before you embark, go to a restaurant. If you like oysters, eat a few dozen with bread and butter. Moisten this food with a good white wine. Then make sure that the kitchen serves up lamb chops, good-quality English-style roast beef, or some other dish that is more to your taste. Eat your fill of this succulent food, and wash it down with a good Bordeaux, which is well known for its digestive properties. After such a fine beginning, following the same principles to their conclusion, pull the bell-cord; a waiter will immediately run up the stairs as nimbly as a rabbit, and, casting his eyes around this temple of Momus where you are holding court, he will come straight to you. You will look at this gentle keeper of the cellar, with his eyes half lowered and a respectful air, full of admiration for your inclination to live well; he will quickly ask you, in those soft tones likely to touch the hearts of those most firmly opposed to loosening the purse strings: "What would you like, sir?"

---

44 The lower part of the sternum. (Translator's note.)

You will answer him, softly too, but in a tone that has an edge of superiority to it: "A coffee, waiter, and a glass of old cognac." The words are hardly out of your mouth before you are served, and you will lose no time in doing justice to this final element.

At the end of this pleasant gastronomic interlude, you will be well ballasted, like your ship, and ready to take on the pitching and rolling. Thanks to the moderate doses of tonic that you have taken, your blood will circulate freely in your veins. In order to maintain this balance, the absence of which is what constitutes seasickness, fill your stomach, before falling sick, with good food chosen according to your taste (*for you know the old proverb: a dish you fancy comes half digested*).

I repeat, you should then drink something good and fortifying; do not forget my advice. All of this is so that if, in spite of these wise directions, you happen to lose your equilibrium and pay the price for it, you will not, by a long way, be as upset as a person who goes on board without having eaten. Everyone knows that there is nothing worse than trying to vomit when there is nothing in your stomach. The food one takes cannot fail to absorb the gastric juices. Stimulating and fortifying drinks accelerate the circulation through their effect on the nervous system, and tend to prevent the loss of equilibrium (so important to maintain), to prevent an attack of seasickness, or at least to change it into a simple indisposition: a happy change indeed!

This culinary formula should, therefore, be put to use before you embark, for once you are on board and sick, there is nothing left to do except resign yourself to suffering all the consequences of the sickness. I can still hear our young sailors repeating in chorus: "That's one medicine at least that can be swallowed without too much difficulty, and it doesn't need to be sugared! Thanks to the inventor of this gastronomico-anti-Neptunian pill!"

You must at least agree with me, you whom I have saved so many times from a dreadful sickness by means of this powerful relief, that many scientists have taken out patents for discoveries that are not as useful as mine.

CHAPTER 3

*Drawing close to Newfoundland—First floating ice,
or loose pack—Various sights—Suffocation of fish: an explanation—
Birds and various animals on the ice—Hunting seals and
polar bears—Sighting of land—Arrival*

Despite the sickness of several of our men, who were unable for a while to put any proper ballast in their stomachs, our ship was keeping up its progress toward the island of Newfoundland. On 5 June, after wrestling with the sea for 25 days, we saw some of those birds that the sailors call turrs; they are black and white with a pointed beak. Their broad feet, being webbed and located on the sides of the rump, allow them to swim and dive with great speed. Dovekies are a smaller kind of turr; I recognized these birds as belonging to the guillemot family. When these are seen, the men on the cathead are told to keep a sharp lookout,[45] for when they see these web-footed birds they know they are close to the ice pack. In fact, the very next day we found ourselves surrounded by scattered pieces of ice of enormous size. One cannot imagine what an ice-covered sea is like unless one has seen it. Despite the fact that, even in its most northerly parts, Newfoundland hardly extends above latitude 51° north, this area of the island already has the appearance of the Arctic Ocean, an appearance that is quite different from our European seas at that latitude.

---

45 The name *cathead* is given to the two heavy pieces of wood that project beyond the bow of the ship and are used to suspend the anchors and haul them out of the water. This is the place where they put the lookout man, to whom they call from time to time "Watch out forward!" (Author's note).

So, for anyone who has not seen them, the movement of these huge floating piers[46] is almost impossible to imagine. They nearly always move toward the south. It often happens that, after leaving the pack ice to sail on the open sea, you find yourself surrounded by a mist so thick that visibility is reduced to 8 or 10 metres. Then, suddenly, the mist clears and gives way to the brightest daylight. When this happens, you are amazed, on returning to the same area to reconnoitre the pack ice, to find no sign of it in the spot where, a few hours before, you had come to an impenetrable barrier. These icy blocks of massive size resemble all kinds of different objects: one looks like a church with its bell tower; another seems to have two spires like a cathedral; here is a superb portico, resting on pillars that assume a crystal brilliance in the rays of a beautiful sun; there, in the distance, is another tableau looking for all the world like a huge principal dwelling capped with roofs and surrounded by smaller houses, making you think of a farm with all of its outbuildings, their roofs covered in snow. You could go on forever when describing the ice pack for, to a traveller's eye, it offers thousands of the most beautiful and amazingly varied sights.

Among the icebergs, on the surface of the water, one comes across large numbers of dead codfish; we salvage as many as possible, for they are all good to eat. I have never seen one that was spoiled, and I presume that this perfect state of preservation has to be attributed to the fact that the swim bladder remains intact for long periods; this organ bursts only when the fish decomposes, forcing it down to the depths when it is of no further use. I have also tried to find out why these fish die, and I believe I have found the answer. If you see a fish in a river or a lake, load your rifle with a bullet and aim just below and in front of the head, so that the bullet passes as closely as possible to the nose of the fish. The velocity with which the bullet is fired and the violence

---

46 Some navigators believe that the ice sinks, in other words disappears by going down to the bottom; others think that it is carried along by the force of the currents: this latter view is the only rational one. (Author's note.)

of the disturbance abruptly interrupt the vital air supply, and the fish is killed without having been touched. This death is brought about by sudden asphyxiation. Similar effects, although much more powerful, occur in the icefield. Icebergs of colossal proportions cover the surface of the sea, rising and falling with the waves, making a tremendous noise. It is easy to imagine how such a heavy fall can create a shock of indescribable violence in the water that is in immediate contact with these enormously heavy blocks. Acting as a kind of pneumatic machine, they must cause the sudden death of all the animate creatures that are in the upper layers of the water. I have carefully examined these fish and have never been able to find on them the slightest trace of wounds or bruises. I am firmly convinced that, given their healthy size, they die for lack of breathable air, which is cut off when the water around the mountain of ice is suddenly forced aside.

Icebergs vary greatly in size and shape. One often mistakes a piece of ice for land, when the tip seems to disappear, mirage-like, into the clouds. It is often in the lee of these huge blocks of ice that, in fine weather, the hunter finds the best game on the icefield, the ruddy turnstone. This bird has a plumage that is a mixture of rufous, dark brown, yellowish, and white, and is about the size of a thrush; it has a long, thin pointed beak. The turnstone found on the pack ice is extremely plump and feeds on small grasses that the icebergs carry with them when they break away from land; the meat of this bird is far preferable to that of all other seabirds, which are found in huge quantities in these cold regions. In addition, there are all kinds of kittiwakes, gulls, guillemots, divers, hagdowns,[47] sea parrots,[48] and all sorts of ducks,[49] such as the black duck whose beak has at its base, on the upper side, a handsome red membrane that stops just below the

---

[47] Carpon's term is *dadin*, a popular name for the shearwater, commonly referred to in Newfoundland as the *hagdown*. (Translator's note.)
[48] The term Carpon uses is *calculot*, which, like *sea parrot* in English, is a popular name for the Atlantic puffin. (Translator's note.)
[49] The names by which I am referring to some of these birds are doubtless not the ones given to them by natural historians, but those by which they are most commonly known among navigators of the northern seas. (Author's note.)

nostrils.[50] This bird is generally very greasy, and despite all the care the chef takes before serving it at table, he can never make a dish of any delicacy out of it. Nevertheless, it is eaten, usually with some salt pork, although one soon tires of it.

On the ice pans one finds seals and polar bears. Ship owners from the island of Newfoundland carry on a considerable trade in these animals. From 10 to 20 March, they send out schooners known as sealing ships from St. John's, Carbonear, Harbour Grace, Twillingate, Fogo Island, etc.

These vessels are covered on the outside with steel plate to protect them from damage and are crewed by a number of men in proportion to their tonnage. These men take them into the icefield, where they remain blocked. As the seals come out of the sea to go and sleep on the ice, the Newfoundland hunters, armed with powerful rifles loaded with fistfuls of powder and shot, run from pan to pan toward these amphibious creatures and kill them. When their rifles are discharged, they throw themselves on the animals that have not been hit and kill them stone dead with a blow on the nose from a stick.

Generally, the hunters have only one gun for every four men. But each one of them has his stick, or club, and another, longer one at the end of which a hook and a long metal spike are very firmly attached. In a sheath hanging from his belt is a case knife for skinning the animals. This operation on the seals is carried out so quickly that a man who is used to the hunt can skin more than 100 in a day.

This is how it is done.

With a single cut, he goes around the neck of the animal, slicing through the fatty tissues down to the muscle. He then cuts into the skin of one of the front feet, through the fat, continuing from the neck down to the tail flippers. It is the tail, together with the two feet, armed with long claws and broad webs, that gives the animal the ability to swim

---

50   The bird Carpon is describing is the black scoter. (Translator's note.)

as fast as lightning. After making a deep circular incision above the flippers and the tail of the animal, he takes hold of the skin on both sides, and the fat attached to it, with the hook. Since there is nothing to attach the fat to the muscles, the pelt can be pulled off with great ease. Once it is cleaned of its fat, it is traded with other skins.

The faithful Newfoundland dogs are there, wearing collars to which leads are attached. These end in iron hooks onto which the skins are fastened. The dogs go carefully back and forth carrying these products of the hunt to the ship that they came from, often 3 or 4 miles [c. 4.8-6.4 km] away.

The skin of these seals is used by the inhabitants of Newfoundland in the manufacture of shoes, coats, and caps. From the fat they make an oil that they sell at a very high price, and the carcasses of the animals are used as food for their dogs, together with the remains of fish that they keep salted, frozen, or dried for the winter season.

One often still encounters enormous polar bears on the ice pans. Many of them weigh between 600 and 700 kilograms. These vicious animals come mostly from the icy region of Baffin Bay and reach Newfoundland by moving from one floe to another. They feed on seals and fish that are available daily. The she-bear, accompanied by her cub, will confront any danger; she heads straight for the most formidable group of men with fearsome daring, and does not give up until she is dead. The male, when he has no family to defend, runs away from men, unless he is starving; if this is the case, he needs prey, and he will brave the fire of hunters to get one. The wounds he receives only make him more fearsome. If they are not fatal, he continues to pursue his prey to satisfy both his fury and his hunger and does not give up the attack until he is dead.

We may conclude from the above that if you want to be lucky enough not to tempt the appetite of those creatures, you must meet them when they are full from a recently finished meal. The sealing schooners generally have 18 or 20 men on board. At the first sight of a polar bear, every man arms himself with a long, high-calibre rifle loaded with lead slugs, and with a pike and an axe. To distract the beast, they set a few dogs on it; these know instinctively not to get too close. In the meantime, the hunters surround it and never fail to kill it. The ferocious quadrupeds often swim toward the fishing boats and attack them in an effort to take the men, but they pay dearly for this temerity. Since the first thing that the animal does is to try to climb aboard, the crew all have to go to the same side of the boat and leave the other side free for the bear. As soon as it has put its paw on the edge, they cut it off with an axe, and when it falls back into the water, they throw a rope with a slip knot around its neck. This allows them to kill it with axes and spears if they have no firearms. When the skin of these animals is of good quality and is removed properly, it sells in Newfoundland for between 80 and 100 francs. The meat has a nauseating odour and is fit only for the stomach of purebred Eskimos.[51] Not enough polar bears are killed for there to be a special trade in their fur. This is not the case with seals and other amphibious creatures of this kind. A schooner with 20 men on board can bring back 2,000 seals after a stay of a month or six weeks in the ice. At this point they consider that they have a full catch. Every man receives a share based on the oil that is obtained, which sells for a very high price, and on the skin, which makes handsome shoes of good quality.

It would be a waste of time to give a description of seals. Since every work of natural history gives a detailed description of their shape, I have limited myself to a short explanation of how to hunt them, something that I have done myself on the icefield. These migratory animals come down from Greenland and Baffin Bay to Newfoundland; I think they come to this island in search of a milder temperature in which to bring their young into the world. The ice pans, often swarming with them, offer the most convincing proof of this.

---

51 See Preface, p. 25.

When it is born, the seal is completely covered with long white fur. As the pup grows, this fur is gradually shed, and one can see it being replaced by a coat of short hair with patches of different shades, for these animals are never the same colour. They can be black, grey, striped, etc., and the price the skins fetch varies according to the diversity of the colours. The savages[52] make them into magnificent tobacco pouches for smokers, but the best are those that are made from the skin of the flippers; this has to be removed with care and the claws left attached.

On 7 June, to the delight of the entire crew, we heard the cry of "Land!" and at noon the officers sighted the northeast tip of Groais Island, to the northwest in the western quarter, 30 miles [c. 54 km] away. This island is about 9 miles [c. 16.2 km] from Cape Fox, which forms the entry to Conche harbour to the starboard and is about the same distance from Bell Island, which is why navigators say Bell Island and Groais.

These two islands were covered with snow at that time, and still looked as if they were in the grip of a harsh winter that was only just coming to an end. The mountains of the mainland of Newfoundland also had the same appearance. On the 8th, we were within sight of the high ground of Crémaillère, where we could see a ship under full sail hugging the shore of Goose Cove. We made our way along the edge of the icefield, which at first we had not thought was there.

A thick mist enveloped us and obliged us to go about, and we tacked for a few hours among the loose ice and growlers.[53] To avoid making contact with them, the crew was obliged to change course continually. Finding this ice pack did not dash our hopes of making land at the first opportunity. As the weather had become brighter, the captain ordered the ship to go about and to sail for the points that we had already seen.

---

52   See Preface, p. 25.
53   The term *loose ice* (*couailles*) is given to any area, large or small, of little pieces of ice that one can sail through without running the risk of damaging one's ship. This is not the case with *growlers* (*bourguignons*), which, although they are hardly visible on the surface of the water, are nevertheless of great size underneath, and consequently very dangerous. (Author's note.)

We soon noticed, just off the land, a long white strip that seemed to be attached to it. We thought that this brightness might be an effect caused by the refraction of the snow piled up on the slopes of the hills and on the hilltops, and we hoped to be able to reach Griquet, our destination, the same day, but we were disappointed in this expectation. With a favourable wind behind us, we soon saw that this brightness was an impenetrable ice pack, and that its enormous icebergs were blocking Hare Bay, St. Main's Bay,[54] St. Lunaire Bay, and the other harbours along the coast.

Seeing that it would be impossible to get through these prodigiously high mountains of ice without running the risk of imminent danger, the captain ordered the ship to go about in the other direction, and to run out to sea where there was freedom to move.

We were within sight of 10 other ships that, like us, were being cautious at the sight of these invincible obstacles; they followed our example and undertook the same manoeuvres.

On 11 June, the lookouts reported that the ice pack had moved. The helmsman received the order to sail through the path that had been opened up for us, and, in spite of a large quantity of ice that was avoided with great skill, we dropped anchor in Griquet harbour. The captain and I set foot ashore, and went to inspect the cabins that formed our living quarters, which we found in a fit state to receive both ourselves and our crew.

---

54   Carpon's text first read Martin, corrected to Main in an errata sheet added later. The Gazetteer of Newfoundland does not include a bay of this name. However, a number of early maps of the area show what is now St. Anthony Bight as St. Men or St Mein. All of these are corruptions of St. Méen, a Breton saint of the sixth century, and St. Main is simply another variant. He has been referred to at various times as Conard Méen, St. Méven, and St. Néven. (Translator's note.)

CHAPTER 4

The surgeon and his duty on board—Illnesses peculiar to sailors—Cures for scurvy—Landing—Cabins—Installing men and material on land—Seine fishing and jigging—Jigging with a single-hooked jigger—Hook-and-line fishery—Caplin—Mackerel—Herring—Squid—Various methods of catching them

The outfitter of a ship with a crew of 40 men, not including the boys, is required to have a surgeon on board, failing which the clearance papers cannot be collected from the naval office. In the port where a ship is fitted out for any kind of fishery, or for ocean-going voyages, a commission consisting of two doctors and a pharmacist is established. In accordance with a royal decree dated 4 August 1829, this commission is charged with examining young medical students who intend to go to sea, and awarding them, if they are considered worthy of it, a provisional licence to embark as surgeons on board a merchant vessel. The candidates pay 15 francs to the commission as a fee for the examination that they undergo.

Medical doctors and health officers[55] are exempted from this examination.

After he has signed his contract with the outfitter in the presence of a notary, the naval surgeon is informed by the outfitter of the date when he has to be present for the inspection in the presence of the Registrar General of Shipping. The surgeon makes sure that he is there so that, if he should see any men among the crew who are not

---

55 Carpon himself was a health officer. (Translator's note.)

fit to undertake the voyage, either because they are temperamentally unsuited or because of sickness, he can inform the outfitter, who would then be able to find a replacement. When the inspection is completed, the officers and sailors who have signed on for the cod fishery receive their advances, and, on the next St. John's day,[56] the sum they are owed for their shares and bonuses[57] is determined, working on the basis of one-fifth of the result of the previous fishery. This, at least, is the way it is done in Granville, unless there is a special agreement between the contracting parties. The day you receive your advances, you are told when your baggage is to be put aboard and the day of departure.

The surgeon has his surgical chest taken to a pharmacist so that it can be supplied with all the drugs and implements appropriate for the voyage, of which a list is provided by the commission. The latter inspects it and applies seals. The examiners receive a fee of 15 francs[58] for this task and deposit the keys to the chest at the naval office. The captain gives them to the surgeon when they leave, after he has presented his crew list and collected his clearances. The surgeon has to take care to have this little pharmacy placed in the best-lit spot on board, that is to say by the main hatchway, so that at any hour of the day or night he can take from it whatever he needs for the health care for which he is responsible.

Most ships have no surgeon, not having the number of men on

---

56 At that time the men who were hired were often in Newfoundland, but relatives or friends bearing a power of attorney could present themselves at the outfitter's office to collect the money owed to those who are away, or the latter collect it themselves on their return. (Author's note.)
 St. John's day falls on 24 June, at which time the French fishing fleet in Newfoundland would be in the early part of their fishing season. (Translator's note.)

57 By *share*, they mean the portion that anyone who has signed on is entitled to of one-fifth of the net product of the fishery. This share may be subdivided: there are half-shares, etc.
 They call *bonuses* the perquisite given to officers of a barrel of cod and a barrel of oil from the liver of this fish. This perquisite constitutes a *full bonus*, but there are also *half-bonuses, quarter-bonuses*, etc. (Author's note.)
 Here Carpon is referring to the system of remuneration used in Granville, where one-fifth of the net proceeds from the sale of the catch was reserved for the crew, with each member of the crew receiving a share, or more than one share, or a fraction of a share, according to the conditions under which they were hired. See also the table showing Carpon's own remuneration in the Preface, p. 15. (Translator's note.)

58 These 15 francs are charged to the outfitter. (Author's note.)

board to make the presence of one a requirement. These ships are nevertheless equipped with a surgical kit, for the inspection of which the outfitter also pays the sum of 15 francs every year.

The captain is given a booklet that is known in naval circles as the *Paper Doctor*.[59] In this little manual are listed all of the illnesses that are most common at sea, as well as the methods of treating them, so the treatment the men receive depends on the intelligence of whoever is looking after them.

The tasks of the surgeon on board consist of drinking, eating, and sleeping, caring for his patients, and maintaining a state of hygiene that is likely to preserve health. For example, throwing overboard all animal and vegetable refuse, the decomposition of which would spread noxious gases in the air, and could taint it; making sure the deck, the steerage, and the living quarters are washed frequently; removing foul odours with chloride; installing fans or ventilation ducts to refresh the air in areas that become insalubrious through being occupied by a large number of people; and making sure that the kitchen utensils and the seamen themselves are kept clean.

The seafarer, just like anyone on land, is subject to a large number of infirmities, but there are some sicknesses that are peculiar to sailors, especially after a long period at sea. The most common are scurvy, dysentery, and tenesmus.[60] For the treatment of these conditions, I refer captains to their paper doctors and surgeons to their medical works.

I shall simply say that there has never been a better antiscorbutic than porpoise blood, taken hot, and cod broth, as well as the flesh of that fish eaten fresh. I have been able to judge the favourable results of this medication many times, and I attribute them to the presence of a certain quantity of iodine in these species of fish.

---

59 The text of this *Paper Doctor* can be found in the *Annales maritimes et coloniales, Partie officielle*, 1844, 837–79. It includes a list of the contents required in the medical chest and provides advice to the captain on how to deal with a wide variety of complaints ranging from apoplexy to scurvy to sprains and fractures. (Translator's note.)
60 Tenesmus: an unproductive urge to empty the rectum or bladder. (Translator's note.)

The surgeon is, then, as one may judge from the foregoing, the only one who can share the tranquility of the captain's routine; he sits at his table, to his right, and is charged with doing the honours with the food, with carving the meat and serving it to the officers, always beginning with the most senior. In keeping with French manners, he must always serve himself last, which, indeed, can only be in accordance with his natural inclination to courtesy. My daily routine on board, insofar as it was special to me, was as follows.

At 6 a.m., with my captain, I would drink a good measure of very hot sugared tea into which I would put a little brandy and a few biscuit crusts. Then, when it was fine, I would go up on deck, and smoke a pipe in the open air.

This was the way I prepared myself for prayers, and for the first meal of the day, which, since it had started out so well, could have only a happy conclusion.

The use of hot, aromatic drinks, with a moderate amount of alcohol, is most salutary in cold countries. It keeps the skin properly warm and prevents many indispositions. I recommend that such drinks be taken in moderation, but I exhort seafarers above all to refrain from excess, the effects of which are always terrible for anyone who goes to bed cold in a state of inebriation. I could quote unfortunate examples that have occurred both on land and at sea, in temperatures that are to be found where cod fishing is carried out, but this digression is perhaps already too long, and is making us forget our ship, the *Deux Sophie*.

The captain and I were already on land when our men jumped from the chain-wale[61] into a boat that had been put into the water to take them ashore. The old hands rushed to inspect their shelter from the previous year and to put it in a fit condition to be lived in, for the first task of a seaman who is going to stay any length of time in a country such as Newfoundland is to make sure that he is properly settled

---

61 Chain-wale: a plank attached to the side of a sailing ship abreast of the mast, used to attach the shrouds. (Translator's note.)

in. He must protect himself from the cold, damp air, which at night would be extremely harmful to his health. Those of our young sailors who were seeing Newfoundland for the first time seemed astonished, and one could read in their eyes their unease at seeing nothing that could provide them with a shelter. In fact, the first wharf that they set eyes on was the stage ... But I can hear you asking already, "What is a stage?"—Patience, friendly reader; the time will come (in the not-too-distant future, I hope) when I will see to it that you have an idea of this structure, which requires nothing of the architect's art, or even of the mason's skill, and yet has its importance, I assure you. Yet let us admit that these walls of thin sticks with no roof do little to inspire the hope of being comfortable there the day after arriving.

Nor do the living quarters or cabins look very inviting: they are huts built on the shore with trunks of fir trees that are pointed at their lower end and sunk into the ground with a sledgehammer; they are placed as close to each other as possible and caulked with moss or poor-quality oakum. These huts are covered with angled boards with paper placed over them, or tarred canvas, which makes them waterproof. In times gone by they were covered with the bark of fir trees;[62] this method, now forbidden because of the enormous damage done to the trees, which were completely dried out because of this procedure, was completely ineffectual, for the barks were never free of a few knots, and these knots often had holes, leaving a free opening for water to come in; this put you in the unenviable position of being in the dry only in fine weather. Since the fishermen's cabins are not always properly caulked with moss, there is a large gap between each log and the next. To solve this problem, they nail to these logs a number of horizontal crosspieces onto which fir branches are attached; these are piled up one on top of the other and arranged so

---

62   These barks are known as *rinds,* and in Newfoundland every day you hear the expression *rinding* to denote the action of peeling the bark off fir trees. The inhabitants of Newfoundland have the sole right to remove the bark from standing trees; the French can do it only to those that have been taken to their premises. (Author's note.)

that the outside air cannot penetrate. On the inside, there is a sort of corridor formed by tree trunks which serve as supports for a quantity of small beds set one over the other up to the top of the wall. Their base is a strong net with a large mesh on which the bags of straw and mattresses are placed. The way these frames are built allows those who sleep on top to climb up as if by a ladder, and nothing is made more quickly than a sailor's bed on the coast of Newfoundland.

In France I can think of only one dwelling that is of a design comparable to the Newfoundland cabins: the clog-maker's shack in the forest where he works.

The main building, that of the officers, consists of a huge kitchen, with a fireplace made of clay and black granite stones that are unaffected by fire. Near the hearth there is a large stove of artistically arranged bricks; it is destined to receive many a saucepan simmering with a misty vapour that delicately titillates the senses. A partition separates this kitchen from the dining room, and it is in this mess room with four long, narrow benches, set around a table of the same shape, that the officers take their meals.

A large room connects with the kitchen: this is the storeroom, a mysterious depository for liquids, whose care is entrusted to the chief cook. Next to this precious depository is the bedroom of the captain, whose presence maintains order and prevents certain abuses.

The chief cook, or chef, sleeps next to his barrels, and makes very sure that his liquids are not of a strength that could make people overexcited. An attic under the peak of the roof is used for storing the fishing implements, the ship's rigging, and sacks of biscuits.

This main cabin is used only by the officers, and the men go there only on business. As for their rations, a small window at the end of the storage area allows them to be passed through when the person requesting them has managed to make himself heard by calling out in a loud, clear voice *Ave Maria*! To indicate that he has been understood, the reply *Gratia* is given and he is immediately served.

Since the primary purpose of the voyage is cod fishing, on which the fortune or the ruin of the outfitter often depends, the first thing they do on landing is to go and look at the boats[63] that were hauled up to a dry place the previous year, to make sure that they are all fit to be sent out. After any necessary repairs have been made, they put them to sea, and load on board everything that is of use for the expedition. Each *fishing boat* is manned by three men, who, in the language of the Newfoundland fishery, are known as the *master*, the *foreshipman*, and the *midshipman*.

The *seine skiff* has a crew of eight: the *seine master*, the *foreshipman*, and six men known as *seine men*.

After they have loaded their skiff with the seine and a supply of food, they make for the grounds where they suspect the cod to be. There these interesting fish make their presence known either to the naked eye or because of an instrument known as the *jigger*.

This device consists of two large fish hooks set back to back, so that the hooks stick out in opposite directions; once they have been put together in this way, they are placed inside a cast-iron mould that is filled with molten lead. When one opens the mould, in the same way that spoon makers do, one sees an admirably formed shiny fish with its tail pierced by a hole, through which the end of a long line is passed.

After they have sounded the depth of the water, the fishermen, armed with this instrument, drop the jigger overboard, keeping it suspended so that it never touches the bottom. While it is in this position, they move it by pulling it up rapidly and then dropping it down. The cod, being curious and hungry for prey, take this lure for the real thing and, playing with this artificial fish, are hooked in any part of the body; very often, two are caught at the same time. Before the arrival of the caplin, a fish that is used as the preferred bait for cod, it is not unusual to see fishermen take 25 louis'[64] worth

---

63 These boats are of two kinds: fishing boats and seine skiffs; usually the latter are simply called skiffs. (Author's note.)
64 The louis had a value of 20 francs. At that time a loaf of bread cost around half a franc. (Translator's note.)

of fish in a day by these means alone. This, then, is the process known as *jigging*.

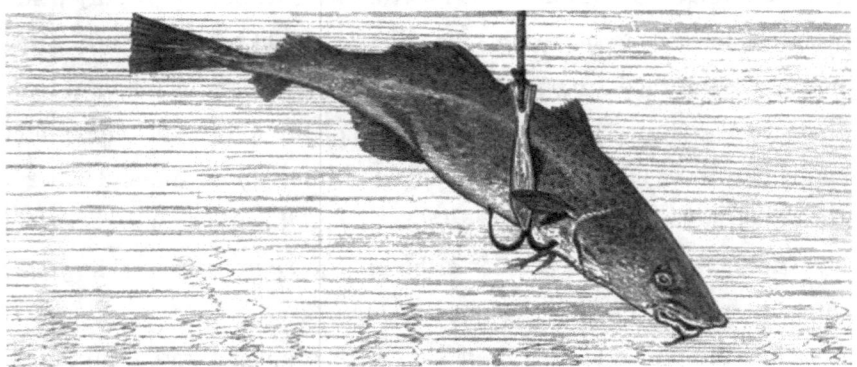

Cod hooked with a jigger. From *Harper's Weekly*, 9 January 1875.

When the seine master has taken a few cod from the water by this process, he can put out his net with the same confidence as if he had seen a large quantity. He gives the order to anchor with the aid of a long rope and an iron grapnel that the Newfoundlanders call a *creeper*.

There are numerous large pieces of cork floating on the surface of the water attached to the creeper; they are known as *floaters*, and to these is attached another rope, which has to be anchored almost on the shore with the aid of another grapnel. When the seine is fixed in this manner, the men row strongly with long oars, making their boat move swiftly. This causes the net to be paid out very quickly, while the other end, after it has been spread out in a circle, has to be brought back to the floater, which is placed there as a marker. Before the seine is completely closed, they repeatedly hurl out a piece of iron with sliding rings.[65] This apparatus is held by a length of rope, the rapid movement of which creates a ringing noise. The fish are terror-stricken at the sound of this clanging, which is probably something they have never heard before. Since this terrible din is coming from the one escape route open to

---

66 This device, known in Newfoundland as a douser, was used by both the French and English fishermen. (Translator's note.)

them, they retreat. In a flash they are helplessly confined, and become the property of the outfitter and his crew.

The boats used to help with the seine then approach the net, which is gathered aboard the seine skiff with the lead weights, as well as aboard those boats that have come to lend a hand in setting the net and then in hauling it.[66]

During this hauling-in process known as *reeling in*, the seine master estimates the size of the catch simply by looking at it, and if he thinks he does not have sufficient space to carry it, he signals to the boats in sight, or tells people back at the room. In the meantime, in order not to lose his time or his fish, he puts the excess of his catch in net bags made with heavy twine, anchors them in a safe spot, and continues his successful fishery.

Once the cod are piled together into the net, they are not taken out by hand but with a long, thick metal spike shaped into a curve and firmly attached to the end of a small pole cut from a fir tree. With the help of this tool, known in the area as a *pew*, one can fork three or four medium-sized cod at the same time.

This rapid process is the only one that can be used where the fish are found in such abundance.

Jigging with a *single-hooked jigger* is done with bait, but, as with the two-hooked jigger, it still has an artificial element to it. They use a small lead fish, with a hole in its tail to pass a line through. It is admirably cast on a large hook, covering the shaft. The mouth, which is at the bend of the hook, seems to be open, ready to swallow the real caplin threaded on to it in a semicircle. It looks as if the two little creatures are struggling to devour each other. At first the cod plays the role of the cat Minagrobis in La Fontaine's fable *The Cat, the Weasel and the Little Rabbit*, but with this crucial difference: it ends up becoming the victim of its own greed and credulity. Before beginning

---

66 In fishing terms, by hauling the net, once it has been cast overboard, they mean pulling it out of the water by hauling up, one after the other, the lead weights that are brought into the boat, while always leaving in the water the pieces of cork that keep the net afloat. (Author's note.)

this fishery, the master of the boat sounds the depth, to find out how many fathoms there are.

He shakes his baited lines, first 1 fathom from the sea bed, and always manages to take some fish; then he sets his line 1 fathom higher; the cod follow, still attracted to it; he continues this manoeuvre until he reaches the point where he has paid out only the minimum possible amount of line.

One can readily see why the fisherman acts in this way. If he sets his line with a variable quantity of lead for weight, according to the currents, in a depth of 40 fathoms of water, it will take a certain time to reach the bottom; it will take even more to haul it up again, especially when a fish weighing 20 or 25 kilograms is hooked on to it; so the shorter the distance between the fish and his boat, the greater the advantage to him in getting it aboard.

For the *hook-and-line fishery*, the method is the same, except that the shaft of the hook is not covered with an artificial fish. And the hook is larger; instead of putting a single caplin on it, they put two, facing in opposite directions.

When they are going out to fish using one of these various methods, the captain, the chef, or an officer wake the men at daybreak. They have been given their day's provisions the evening before, and they will return to the room around sunset, bringing back the fruit of their skill. This is how things are done during their stay in Newfoundland.

Caplin make up the regular diet of the cod; this little fish draws the cod to fishermen. The length of the caplin is between 22 and 23 centimetres. The skin of this fish is greenish along the back; there it has two fins, one large and one small, and about halfway down the sides there is a ridge beginning at the upper part of the gills that gets thinner as it carries through to the tail. The belly is a pearly colour; two fins stick out from it a little below the nape, two more between the nape and the vent, and the fifth, semicircular, starts at the vent and ends practically at the start of the tail, which is forked and vertical. On top of the head in the occipital region, one can see in a transparent area three small lobes criss-crossed with tiny blood vessels; another smaller lobe, pink in colour, is attached to the others, and with them forms a kind of cross. This organ constitutes the brain, which, as far as one can tell through the skull, seems to be speckled with a multitude of small grey dots. The head, semicircular in shape, is strongly depressed on the sides and looks like mother-of-pearl, especially around the eye socket.

The pupil of this friendly little fish is dark blue, giving it an expression that is full of vivacity and making the strikingly white cornea stand out very prettily. The lower jaw, which is a little longer than the upper, ends in an obtuse point, and these two parts, as well as the tongue, have very small teeth that are almost imperceptible. The meat of the caplin is very good when it is fresh; sometimes it is salted so that it can be dried.

The caplin come to Newfoundland to spawn at the beginning of July. The cod follow them, and this bait that they find such a delicacy causes them to be hooked or to fall into the nets. They take caplin with a net that is a large seine, and it is set as for cod. There are such great quantities of this little fish that in a single wave the sea sometimes casts up a mound of them 1 metre deep, over a very long stretch of coast. Boats run aground on these fish as if they were on a sandbar.

We have just said that the caplin is a choice dish for cod. But these little fish are not always willing to keep the cod company for the duration of their stay along the coast. They go out into the open sea after spawning, toward the end of July or in early August. People say that they go south and into the Mediterranean, where they are in fact not unknown. It may be assumed that the cod follow them, and that one could definitely fish large quantities of them on banks in more southerly parts, if they were known as well as the Grand Banks of Newfoundland. Even after the caplin have gone, there are still very fine fish along the coast known as late-season cod. They are fished then with bultows[67] or by the other methods that we have described, but with a different bait.

Nature in its admirable wisdom knows how to provide for the needs of both reasonable and unreasonable creatures. The caplin are off on their travels, but the cod still have to find something to satisfy their voracious appetite; well, nature, excellent mother that she is, then drives huge quantities of mackerel, herring, and squid from the depths of the ocean toward the coast of Newfoundland.

Although the cod are fond of the smaller population of the watery element, they do not disdain any larger species that present a little more volume to their greedy eyes, and go after them with particular pleasure, for they need far fewer of them to fill their bellies.

The men take herring and mackerel by setting across the entrance to the bays and harbours nets with a mesh that is the right size to take the head of these fish; once they are caught, there is no way they can be set free except by the hand of the fisherman.

The mackerel have the same shape and taste as in Europe. The herring are much larger than the ones that our Dieppe fishermen and others take in such enormous quantities off the coasts of Iceland, but in general the herring found in Newfoundland are not as valued as those on our European coasts, for their flesh is generally oily. But they can be enjoyed either grilled or boiled and then served in any kind of sauce, although a piquant sauce is best.

Squid, which are much like the cuttlefish in our country, are caught in two ways, with *jiggers*[68] and with fires.

This is how to go about making the device known as the jigger. Roll a playing card into a cylinder that is about half the thickness of a no. 6 candle;[69] plug the lower end with a piece of cork and maintain it in a cylindrical shape with a small tie; take some brass wires with very sharp

---

67   Bottom lines that are set and left overnight, with a large number of hooks on them. (Author's note.)
68   The means of fishing for squid is known as jigging. (Author's note.)
69   This refers to the diameter of a standard size of candle available in France at the time. (Translator's note.)

Bultow or trawl (long line with many hooks ready for baiting). French Shore Interpretation Centre, Conche, Newfoundland. Photograph: M. Wilkshire.

points and pass them right through the base of the card from one side to the other; surround this little mould with salt and then fill it with molten lead; then bend the brass wires into the shape of a hook; put a hole in the upper part of the lead to pass a small line through it; then scrape it to make it as shiny as possible.

When you are in your boat, you pull this little hooked grapnel through the sea in jerks, and the squid rush to put the membranes of their tentacles on to it; they are freed only when they get to the open air.

If, while amusing yourself waging war on squid, you do not want to find yourself looking like a black man, take care not to put your nose anywhere near the parrot's beak of this nasty little fish, for when it comes out of the water it blinds you by squirting a substance as black as ink in your face, as if it were coming out of a syringe.

Huge quantities of them are caught by lighting fires on a dark night along a shore where there is a rocky beach with a gentle slope; the squid come in and are washed up, and they can then be taken by hand.

One final piece of treachery practiced on squid![70] They cut different fish into small pieces and bait lines with them; the results are most satisfactory.

The meat of the squid is in my opinion very good, especially with a pepper sauce.

---

70   This fishery that is carried on toward the end of the stay in Newfoundland is known as the large bait fishery. (Author's note.)

CHAPTER 5

Surgeon's duties in Newfoundland—Proposal for reform in this area—Hanging gardens—Seasonal horticulture—Preparation and salting of cod—Verse on the practice of medicine in Newfoundland—Warning to young doctors—Case of infected finger with complications: strange cure—The stage—The header—The splitter—The salter—Income and distribution of the season's catch—The wash house—The oil vat—Extraction of cod-liver oil—Thoughts on the medicinal qualities of this oil—Salter's victory celebration—Humanitarian appeal to the government—Urgent necessity of reform in the merchant navy health service—Unsuccessful efforts of the author in this connection

We saw above what the duties of the naval surgeon are on board, duties which, in normal times, are certainly neither too extensive nor very difficult. Perhaps you would like to know what exactly his responsibilities are in the harsh climate of Newfoundland and during the season of arduous labour there.

A ship's surgeon in the merchant navy is also the pharmacist. Since he is given particular care of the sick in his room, for the honour of his profession he has to carry out his duties scrupulously toward these people and cure them as rapidly as possible. This is in his own interest, and in that of the outfitter, who provides him with food and payment. In exchange, he is obligated to carry out the work with which he is charged, unless he is excused from doing so by genuine cases of illness.

Perhaps it is fitting here to warn my colleagues of the necessity for them to take certain precautions if they wish to be reimbursed for the medication that they supply.

Let naval medical officers be fully warned, before they liberally hand out expensive medication to sailors they do not know, that no deductions can be made from their wages, except for their food, board, and clothing.

If the sailor has any real estate, he can be obliged to pay through the legal system, but if he is not a property owner, financial claims made against him are useless when one finds oneself in dispute with a man who is not acting in good faith. Unfortunately, I have been a witness to this all too often. To avoid any dispute, it is best to require a note written or at least signed by the debtor, payable at the outfitter's office, or, in case of death, at the Marine Office. In addition, it is important to make sure that this paper is properly signed by the captain.

It often happens, when there is a great deal of work to be done, that you hear men complain of being no longer able to bear the pains they feel throughout their limbs.

These complaints are often groundless, but it also often happens that, if the doctor tells the officers that the men should be made to continue to work, the complaints become well founded. Without allowing oneself to be taken in, it is best to proceed tactfully, keeping the workers free of aches and pains by means of a short rest. One should make clear to them that, in France, nobody can be admitted to a hospital unless they have an injury or a fever, and that since they have neither of these conditions, they can be given only a very brief relief from their duties.

After they have been given some soup and a quarter litre of wine, they fall into a deep sleep and wake up completely cured of the troubles of the previous day, ready to go back to work in good spirits and with all of their energy.

Medicine in Newfoundland is certainly not practiced as it is in France. There are, in the merchant health service, a number of extremely misguided practices on which I shall make a detailed report to be submitted to the appropriate authorities. But, while awaiting improvements in this area, one must try, as far as possible, to make up for this lack of proper rules and hygienic procedures and do everything one can in the circumstances.

As long ago as 1831 I tackled this problem and sent a memorandum on it to Baron Larrey, with whom I had the honour of being particularly well acquainted. He received my work most favourably, promising me that he would send it on to his colleague Mr. de Kéraudren, Chief Inspector for the Naval Health Service, and to the minister responsible for that department.

Portrait of Kéraudren. From Paul Brau, *Trois siècles de médecine colonial*, (Paris: Vigot, 1931).

The death of Larrey, that learned military surgeon, brought to a halt my attempts to bring about an improvement, and things remain as they were until further notice, but the following letter is sufficient proof of both the sincerity of my efforts and the importance that was attached to my observations:

War Ministry
Paris, 22 December 1831

I received your letter, my dear Mr. Carpon, and I read with interest the observations you made in it on the manner in which doctors entering the merchant navy are recruited. These observations are a tribute to your philanthropy and your humanity. Rest assured that I shall explain them fully in a letter that I shall write to the Minister for the Navy and to my colleague, the Chief Inspector of this department. If my observations are favourably received, no outfitter will be able to take on board his ships any doctor, young or old, who does not have proper qualifications or certificates that guarantee both his capacity and his skill. The examination or verification of these documents would be done by the health commission of the seaport where the doctor intends to embark; this commission would in all cases be authorized to set any examination it sees fit to determine whether full confidence may be placed in him. Finally, I believe that, insofar as their salary and discipline are concerned, doctors or surgeons in the merchant navy ought to be subject to the regulations of the health service of the Royal Navy, etc.
signed BARON LARREY

Let us hope that the plans for reform that I had the honour of putting forward at the request of the chief inspector of the military health service are soon fully and completely put into effect!

The adoption of these preventive measures would be a prudent and humane step for the nation; they would benefit all our merchant seamen, who show themselves to be the devoted servants of our country when they are called upon to defend its honour or its interests.

The ships that carry on the cod fishery on the coast of Newfoundland stay there approximately three months, and the aim of sensible people is to spend the time as agreeably as possible. In order to do this, they take care to make the most of their resources. This is why they take with them a large number of young cabbages planted in baskets filled with soil; these baskets are hung from the top so that the plants are not damaged by freezing spray; they survive and grow perfectly well. The crew would not give up these gardens for those of the great Semiramis.[71] They keep all the cabbage stalks in this way after the leaves have been used for making soup during a part of the crossing. On arriving in Newfoundland, they plant them in the ground together with potatoes. They also sow turnips, peas, lettuce, chervil, spinach, garden cress, celeriac, and radishes, which they have the pleasure of watching grow rapidly, for there are few countries where plant growth is more active.

These tasks are a useful and agreeable pastime and are carried out under the direction of the surgeon. It is an advantage, then, if he enjoys the sweet pleasures of horticulture because of the services rendered to the kitchen by these fine vegetables. After one has made free use of them in Newfoundland, when the time comes to leave, one lifts what remains of one's enormous cabbages; one hangs them by the stalks from the stern of the ship, and everyone says repeatedly during the crossing: "Thank heavens for the cabbage soup bubbling in the pot!" Potatoes

---

71 Semiramis: Queen of the Assyrian Empire, famous for ordering the creation of the hanging gardens of Babylon. (Translator's note.)

and turnips, if they are stored in good condition in a cool, dry place, are excellent for giving flavour to the cooking on board, just as they did in the main cabin on land. Are we not repaid a thousand times for our trouble? But there is a task that is even more essential, about which I shall say a few things in verse of my own on the subject of our skilled practitioners in the crucial task of *splitting the cod.*

By the way, in Newfoundland everyone has a hand in the cod fishery! Some catch the fish and others prepare it. Everyone works happily together, for it is in everyone's interest to see the piles of this fine fish increasing rapidly day by day. Splitting is the responsibility of the senior officers in the room. The captain, the first mate, the lieutenant, and the surgeon are not last in line when there is work to be done, when a hand is needed. This is a job that is vitally important for the outfitter as well as an opportunity to reward the officers and men, whose shares and bonuses depend on the catch.

Cleanliness is absolutely indispensable when one is preparing and splitting the fish. Often the cod is not as fresh as it might be, but it is still good for salting.

The blood or reddish liquid of this fish is extremely acrid, to the extent that it would cause excoriations if one did not take the wise precaution of carefully washing one's hands with soap every time that one stops work, even if it is just for five minutes. This way one keeps one's fingers supple, avoiding anything that might hinder their movement. So the surgeon, like all the other officers, takes part in the major task of the preparation of the cod, and it is to this that I allude in the following reply to the questions of some of my colleagues:

> You who ask me how the art of medicine
> Is practiced here beside a sick man's bed,
> The explanation is not difficult.
> One or several deaths cause them little grief

In these distant lands; there, fortunate men
Become doctors caring for seafarers,
After two months' study as assistants;
Though little skilled, they try to appear so.

What weight is given to these grand titles!
For they hear themselves called *chief* or *doctor*!
A soul transported by these giddy words
Is no longer bound to narrow confines;
All these lofty terms, as if by magic,
Make the ignorant overconfident.
Humble deference paid to witless minds
Seems to transform them into men of science,
Even though standing covered in fish blood
They scarcely know how to skin a rabbit.

There, medical skill does not go beyond
Being able to split a cod swiftly;
So rest assured you'll be a fine doctor
As soon as you're an excellent splitter.
When practicing this art, make sure that you
Neglect nothing: it is more important
Than any real skills that you may have,
And without this, you would have no knowledge.
We have seen this art elevate a doctor
To lofty heights, despite all his mistakes.
Had he any rivals in ignorance?
Listen! And you can judge from these few words.

Once, a poor sailor, fearing for his life,
Asked for his doctor's help with an illness

That was already causing him distress.
The doctor had been fooled by lead-swingers
And was afraid of being tricked again.
Being about to do his doubtful duty,
He sees the captain arrive, who asks him:
"Tell me, doctor, if this man here is sick.
Should he be sent to bed with tea or lemonade?"
Our careless doctor says that he is not!
They put the man to work—or to his death!
The illness gets worse, the poor man expires.
At last the healer is obliged to say:
"We cannot say he was wrong to complain;
He must have been ill, because now he's dead!"

You can well imagine how, after this,
The crew all start to complain quite loudly.
They then all shout: "Killer! Murderer!"
Which gives the poor doctor some food for thought.
His soul is plunged into dread torment.
This mishap is why more than one idler
Is able to taste the pleasure of rest.
Pretending to suffer when they are well,
They shout, thrash, and twist, and then try to bite,
Saying farewell to all their family.
The whole performance is quite disturbing.
The timid doctor, breathless, in a rush
Opens his pharmacy, takes out a bottle,
Saying: "What caused this plague to descend here?
If the outbreak does not come to a halt,
We shall all have cause to fear for our lives!
Tell me where it is you can feel the pain,

I'll let some of your blood straight away."
But the crafty fox, in a clever move,
Easily escapes the sharp instrument.
"For seven or eight days I've been feeling faint,
Stumbling about like someone who is drunk.
Last night," he says, "when I was in my bed,
I was perished with cold the whole night long."
"It's an upset stomach," says the doctor,
"I have just the thing you need to treat it.
Keep warm; tomorrow morning you must take
A measure of wine with some cinnamon.
If that's no good, you'll have an enema
That might pull you through, at least I hope so.
It's a mixture of heavy oil with nails[72]
Boiled in it to make it less harsh.
Soon after, picking up this instrument
(Let us call it 'the treasured cannula'),
We'll administer it without delay,
And you will see how much good it does you."

"Doctor, I trust your treatment completely.
I fully hope to be entirely cured.
I think I shall sleep much better tonight.
I feel much improved, doctor: I beg you
To save me completely, if possible."
"Don't worry my friend, I'll pull you through
This pretty pass, I know the situation:
Your urine is clear, and that's a good sign,

---

[72] Experienced surgeons on the coast of Newfoundland used to have very good results when they promised this treatment, if they were just dealing with malingerers or with men who were tired. A couple of hours' rest was sufficient to cure them, for they were persuaded that the doctor intended to put flat-headed nails inside them to make sure their intestines were properly cleaned out. (Author's note.)

In just a few days I'll have you cured."
The patient gives thanks and sleeps a deep sleep.
The doctor goes to see him the next day:
"Thank God, with the help of my skill, I see
That you are on your way to getting well.
There is your final proof that misfortune
Cannot forever plague the doctor's work."

Other idlers need not be very smart
To profit from this rank incompetence;
They watch the actor in his deathbed scene,
Then copy it all, and have the same treatment.
Such successes, claimed as fantastic cures,
Finally reach the ears of our sailors,
And the poor man they called a murderer
Is praised by all as a great physician.

Indeed, it is most prudent not to rush into declaring that this or that man is well enough to carry out his duties. For in many cases it is impossible, even for the most experienced doctor, to give an opinion that will cover him against any unfortunate and reprehensible errors. Moreover, given a modicum of wisdom, one cannot be fooled for too long by these fraudulent complaints from malingerers. And in any case, is it not better to relieve an idler of his duties for a few hours than to run the risk of making the kind of error of judgment that is unfortunately all too common among several of our colleagues, who cover themselves in shame and confusion when they make them, if they have any sense of decency at all? In fact, every day, we see cases where a simple indisposition at first shows no sign of developing into a serious illness, but if we try to dismiss this malaise, which a single sweating fit is often enough to cure, we can lead the patient to a premature death. The fateful accident recorded in the few lines of verse that you have just read is unfortunately absolutely true; I witnessed it with my own eyes.

So I advise young doctors to act with caution and circumspection to avoid finding themselves out of their depth as a result of irresponsible and careless behaviour. In this way they will also avoid the unpleasantness of being seen as ignorant by those around them. Generalizing on the basis of a particular incident, the latter will show only contempt for other doctors or health officers, instead of the respect with which our profession is treated when it shows the skill that one is entitled to expect from a man who is daily entrusted with another's fate.

A surgeon on the coast of Newfoundland is always busy dealing with cuts, boils, and, more than anything else, infected fingers. This latter affliction, which is very common there, is no doubt caused by the sudden transition from a very warm temperature to excessive cold, and by punctures from fish bones, hooks, etc.

On the subject of this kind of complaint, I am going to relate briefly an incident that seemed to me quite remarkable. A man came to consult me one day with an infection on the index finger of his right hand. I applied a poultice of linseed meal to the affected part, and repeated the application of this emollient until the skin took on a yellowish colour with a scattering of a few small suppurating spots. I removed the dead skin and found three small centres of suppuration. After probing these areas, I observed that the first joint was decayed as well as along practically the entire length of the bone. I informed the patient that amputation was the only course available. He accepted this, even though he regretted the necessity of it, for the loss of a finger would have made him unable to carry on his trade of cobbler when he returned to France. I thought about it and deferred the operation until the next day. Sleeping on something allows one to see it in a fresh light. By the time the patient came to see me, I had thought of another approach, and set about trying to extract the bone while preserving the flesh, which I found to be sound. I extended the incision for the affected joint in a longitudinal direction. I gripped the bone with ligature forceps, and with the help of a narrow-bladed and pointed scalpel, held perpendicularly, I quickly cut through the joint. Once this bone was extracted, it was immediately dissected lengthwise and separated from any fleshy part.

Since the bone of the second joint was also necrosed, I cauterized the wound for several days with lunar caustic and dressed it with yellow ointment to which a small amount of camphor had been added.

A few days after this operation I was pleased to see a healthy scar forming. Apart from a slight reduction in length, the finger is the same shape as before. The nail has remained fresh and intact, and the patient uses his finger as he did previously; he now considers the accident as something insignificant.

Preoccupied as I am with my subject and carried along by the pressing memory of so many details, I may lose sight of the order that I had first intended to follow. I trust the reader will forgive me a slight lack of organization. I am counting on your indulgence to be enable me to reach my goal, that of both informing and entertaining. I recall that, in the previous chapter, I referred to the stage. Now that we are properly settled in and busy with our halieutic[73] occupations, as a learned man would say, it is appropriate to give a description of the stage. It will be brief since the structure has nothing very complicated about it. Trunks of fir trees, set close to each other and laid out horizontally, form the base or the floor, and other similar trunks, set vertically, form the sides and the gabled ends as well as supporting the peak. The front section, facing the sea, is known as the stage head or gallery. At the edge, it has a platform with more fir trunks laid lengthwise on top of each other to a height of about 1 metre; this is to prevent the cod that is thrown on to the floor from falling back into the sea.

---

73 Carpon is deliberately using a somewhat pedantic term. Halieutic simply means related to fishing. (Translator's note.)

A MIXED MARRIAGE 97

Photograph of the interior of a French stage taken by Paul-Émile Miot, 1857. Library and Archives Canada, PA-194630. Acquired with the financial support of the Ministry of Heritage under the Cultural Property Export and Import Act.

Overhead there is a large piece of sailcloth[74] that is furled or unfurled as desired. It is arranged both to protect the people who work in this kind of shed from the wind and the cold, and to prevent the lamps from flickering when they are working in the dark.

Back about 5 or 6 metres from the stagehead are the tables for the *headers* and the *splitters,* and between the two is a passage about 1.5 metres wide which serves as a walkway for those working at the fishery.

Approximately in the centre of this large rectangular area is an enclosed space reserved for the salt. Above this space, in some rooms, they put the beds of the shoremen. These are the workmen who do not go out to fish but whose job is to ensure that it is in a fit state to be loaded on board dry and properly processed.

This sort of large cage has one or more entries, and very much resembles the other cabins, except that, instead of planks, it is covered with a huge piece of sailcloth pulled tight with straps that are fixed in every direction to the uprights on the sides.

Long poles opened up into an inverted V[75] are placed a short distance from each other and laid over the peak; the lower ends are tied down so that the wind can have no purchase on the canvas roof.

The table on which the cod is prepared is set up in the following manner: it is about 1.5 metres wide, and on the splitter's side it has a gap where the heads and insides of the cod fall into the sea; to his right there is a notch, below which there is a basket set on a small table to receive the livers.

The header stands in a half-barrel into which a large opening has been cut to allow him to step inside it easily. On his front he wears a well-tarred apron which is like an extension of this half-barrel.

The splitter sits on a wooden chair of a suitable height for the table; its seat, below the level of the table, is covered with tarred sailcloth

---

74 In Newfoundland, this is known as a windbreak. To *furl* and *unfurl* signify rolling up and unrolling. (Author's note).
75 They are known as *pincers*. (Author's note).

forming an apron; it is nailed on to hoops and is hung up every time the splitter leaves his work. The header also observes the same rules of cleanliness. To stop the cod that is being handled from slipping, a block[76] is fixed onto the table at an angle, coming to a point at an open notch on the right of his working surface. Below, there is a barrow to carry the split fish to the salter. To the left is a slit through which they drop the backbones or sound bones that have been removed from the cod.

Above the table there are supports on which they hang the lamps, nowadays lit only in case of dire necessity—for example, when they are afraid of the fish decomposing rapidly. In times gone by, however much fish there was, it was split and salted without delay, as soon as it came in.

Beneath all of this there is the continual rise and fall of the tide, which is essential for washing the remains of the split cod out to sea, and preventing the spread of putrid and noxious gases.

Imagine now that you are face to face with two individuals in the gear that I have just described.

The header is armed with a pointed, double-edged knife and wears a mitten on each hand.

The splitter has his left hand wrapped in a glove that has no fingers, and in his right has a knife with a broad, square blade. Young boys are standing on the stagehead, and there are haulers there too, to the right of the splitters. With the men organized in this way, the only thing missing is the fish. Then comes a boatload of cod. The master ties up his boat to the stagehead; the midshipman or the third hand goes ashore to prepare his superiors' meal; and the master and the foreshipman, each at their end of the boat, spear the cod with pews and toss them up onto the stagehead. The boys take them by the eyes[77] and line them up to the left of the header.

The latter also takes hold of the cod by the eye; he cuts its throat

---

76   In Newfoundland this block is known as a *cleat*. (Author's note.)
77   The only effective way to take hold of these large fish is to push your middle finger right into the eye socket. (Author's note.)

and in the same movement of the knife opens its belly down to the vent. With his right hand he removes the liver, which he puts in the basket placed to the right of the table, and with the same hand tears out all the intestines at once, pulling them toward the fish's nape. Then, with the fish on its back, he gives its neck a twist and breaks it, tearing the skin with his left hand, which holds the head on the edge of the table, while with the right he pushes the cod so that it is lined up on the splitter's cleat at the same moment as the insides are falling into the water.

The splitter takes it by the left flap,[78] places the fish up against the cleat, and opens it with a single cut from the left side, from the nape to the beginning of the tail. Then he moves it to the notch in the table, and with a second movement he removes the entire backbone of the fish from the vent to the upper extremity, cutting the medullary substance down the middle. Once the cod has been prepared in this manner it slides into a barrow which, when full, is immediately replaced by another. And the barrow men, each of them looking after two or three tables, race to put these flattened fish into the hands of the chief salter.

This summary, brief as it is, suffices, I believe, to explain the process involved in trimming and flattening cod, but what is really amazing is to see 10 or 12 of them, and even more, picked up by the boys, headed and split in less than a minute.

The ship's officers, including the surgeon and others who are signed on as *splitting officers,* carry out this work with surprising dexterity.

I have summarized, in a few technical lines of verse, the initial preparation of the cod as soon as it has been removed from its watery abode:

> A sailor throws it, a boy picks it up,
> And swiftly passes it to the splitter.
> Standing in a barrel, gripping its eyes,

---

78   The term *flap* is used to describe the piece that is created when the belly of the fish is cut open up to the point where it meets the lower jawbone. (Author's note.)

He opens it to the vent with his knife.
Two right-hand fingers remove the liver;
He quickly sends it without head or guts
To the waiting splitter armed with his knife.
In two strokes, he drops it in the barrow.
The crew of haulers, in their filthy clothes,
Move it when they hear "The donkey's farting!"[79]

The salter is also responsible for both the solid and liquid stores, and in Newfoundland plays one of the most important roles in the preparation of the cod. The fish is brought to the salter's feet; he begins the first pile at the end of the stage, laying the cod flat, with the flesh facing upwards and the flaps spread out. The bottom layer lies on a bed of salt, and each one receives the amount required for preservation from his experienced hand. An excess of this mineral would burn the flesh of the cod and make it much less saleable.

Each pile is 1 metre 60 centimetres wide, the same height, and of variable length.

The stage is not always of the same dimensions, and its shape also varies according to the number of men. According to the rules of the port of Granville, a room with 100 men on the coast of Newfoundland has to provide its outfitter with 4,500 quintals of dried cod, or 45 quintals per man. When they reach that point, they have a *full catch*, and one-fifth of it is shared among the crew according to their respective rights, for some have no more than an advance, while others have a quarter share or a half share; others again have a double share and their bonus.[80] If the catch is not full, that is to say if they do not reach the figure I just mentioned, they are paid on a pro rata basis, still based on the price for which the cargo is sold.

---

79   A coarse expression, indicating that the barrow cannot take any more fish. (Author's note.)
80   The bonus (*pratique*) is a barrel of cod-liver oil and another barrel of 5 quintals of dried cod. (Author's note.)

The storage area intended to take what the fishery produces has to be much larger than a living area where there are only 40 or 50 men. In addition, because of its size, the stage needs two pieces of sailcloth instead of one to form the roof. In that case the two drip edges meet in the middle and lead into a wide gutter from which the water flows into barrels, or is taken away from the stage by a series of troughs.

Each piece of sailcloth is tied down separately with the kind of pincer I described as an inverted V, but overall, the construction is the same.

When the fishery is plentiful, a pile[81] reaches the normal height in one or two days and then settles considerably, but first of all they begin another, then put more on the first one, carrying on in this way until the salt is completely used up, its space taken up by piles of fish. It is not unusual to see the piles come into contact with the tables of the splitters, who can then pass the cod straight into the hands of the salter. The latter continues giving the fish the same treatment, along with his spreaders.

When they have had the good fortune to use up all their salt, they put the chief salter on a chair and carry him in triumph around his domain, asking him if he has anything with which to salt a few more cod, and what he has done with all the salt that was given to him? The questions and answers that they exchange in this ceremony make up a series of jocular speeches which throw them into fits of laughter, and the triumphal procession concludes with a little party full of gaiety that strikes me as too unusual to let the details be passed over in silence. I shall say a few words about it when talking about the blubber barrel.

The wash house, like the stage, is made of fir logs of average size that form a floor; it is next to the stagehead, built separately on piles. The surface is raised a little above the level of the sea, the exact height depending on the rocks that may be in the way, or on the total or partial

---

81 The shoreman responsible for building the pile must always take care to make the central part domed so that the fish drain completely, without the water being able to settle in case of a rainshower; for there is nothing more harmful than *breachy* water that settles in the middle of the piles of fish. In fishing terms, the word *breachy* is given to water that is a mixture of salt and fresh. (Author's note.)

absence of water at ebb tide. This sort of bridge, leading directly to land, can be used by wheelbarrows and hand barrows for carrying fish over its entire length. At the end next to the sea there are barriers, and 1 metre 70 centimetres from these, they make one or more square openings that they call *wash house openings* (*lanternes du lavoir*). In each of these squares there is a large stake sticking up, 5 or 6 metres high, including the end set into the stony part of the seabed. These pillars are called *wash house ladies* (*dames du lavoir*).[82] The tops are all held together by strong poles nailed horizontally, and by two others in the shape of an X that cross over above the middle of the opening, where a pulley is attached to them. Attached to two of these posts or ladies are two other posts, nailed directly to the floor and coming up to the top of the ladies. They are designed to receive the ends of the axle of a windlass or reel used to raise and lower the baskets, the handles of which are held by an iron hook.

The floor of this deck is made very solid by several stakes set and fixed in a perpendicular fashion on the sides of the openings; they call these *supporting stakes* (*piquets d'attente*).

In the area that I have just described to you, they require a piece of equipment needed for the washing of the cod.

For this they use the *ram's horn*[83] with a *stirrer*. The ram's horn is made from small round bars, attached at the bottom in an upright position to a solid base, and at the top to solid, squared crosspieces. The bars and the crosspieces are hardly more than 1 metre in length; they are bound by means of ropes arranged like the mesh of a net. This is to

---

82 No doubt this name comes from the fact that on the top they have a head that looks a little like the wooden dolls that countrywomen use to arrange their lace bonnets. (Author's note.)

83 *Dictionary of Newfoundland English*, 2nd ed., s.v. "ram's horn," quotes Banks: "[The French] Method of washing their Fish out of the Salt is very Different & much worse than ours they do it in a square trough the sides of which are secured with Lattice work this is set between 4 poles raised up in the water always where I have seen it close by the side of the stages on the tops of these poles are blocks by which the Trough is easily hoisted up or Let Down into the water into this they Put their Fish & Letting it down into the water Poke them with Sticks till they are Sufficiently washd some of the People also getting into the trough & moving them about with their hands & feet." The same entry also has a quotation from Lewis A. Anspach, who speculates that the term ram's horn (washing vat) may well be an anglicized form of the French rinçoir. (Translator's note.)

prevent the fish, in the various movements it undergoes when it is being stirred, from passing through the openings. This ram's horn is lowered into the water with the aid of four double blocks, and as there is a gap between the opening and the ram's horn, a net is spread between them. This is to prevent fish that fall into the water from being lost. This can happen when the men tip cod from the pile into the ram's horn from a barrow that they hold on one side only, by the end of the handles.

Armed with a stirrer or long pole onto the end of which they sleeve at a right angle a piece of wood of convex shape, about 25 centimetres long, the washers stir and turn the cod in all directions; the fish is held suspended in the water by the rapid and continuous movement of this tool. When it is properly washed, which happens very quickly, they haul up the ram's horn to let the fish drain; a man who, for the purposes of this operation, is called the *Parrot* (*Perroquet*)[84] goes down and, with his hands or a wooden shovel with a number of holes in it, puts the fish into baskets that they immediately take to the beach in hand barrows or wheelbarrows. There they make a fresh pile, known as a faggot.

The piece of equipment used for the preparation of cod-liver oil is called a blubber barrel. It consists of a square frame, 3 or 4 metres high, built with supports which are set both horizontally and vertically and they are fixed with blocks and pegs. The length is about the same as the

---

84   This is quite possibly the derivation of the French term *Jacotar*, in Newfoundland English *Jackatar*. *Dictionary of Newfoundland English*, 2nd ed., s.v. "jackatar," lists the variants *jackie tar, jackitar, jack-o-tar, jackotaw,* and *jacky tar*. The word is defined as "A Newfoundlander of mixed French and Micmac Indian descent; the speech of such a person." The common nickname for any parrot in French is *jacquot,* corresponding to *polly* in English. It would be natural to refer to French fishermen by a characteristic aspect of their work. *Le Petit Robert* notes that the suffix -ard has a pejorative or vulgar connotation and gives *froussard* and *revanchard* as examples. In his *Histoire de la pêche française de la morue dans l'Amérique septentrionale,* 3 vols. (Paris: Maisonneuve et Larose, 1966), Ch. de la Morandière includes a *Dictionnaire terreneuvier* or vocabulary of terms used in the fishery. His entry under *Jacotar* reads: "Renegades who have deserted to avoid military service and taken refuge among the English on the west coast of Newfoundland in the nineteenth century. The Jacotars had a poor reputation" (3:1380; our translation). The -ard suffix may stem from the way these people were commonly perceived. Moreover, those involved in the English fishery generally had a very unfavourable view of the French method of washing salt cod, a further reason to look down on those who practiced it. This use of "perroquet" to describe the person carrying out the washing of the fish is unusual in documents relating to the French Shore, although Carpon uses it as a term in common use at the time. *Jacotars* were a marginalized group, generally living in squalor and showing little inclination to rise above it. The main attraction of such a life was the absence of taxes and law enforcement in the area at the time. The true French form ought, then, to be *jacquotard*. The fact that this form has not been recorded is of little significance: the spelling is a written approximation of an oral tradition, both in English and French. (Translator's note.)

height. This little structure is built on the water's edge so that all of the effluent from it can be washed away by the sea.

In the lower part, the uprights are connected to a floor, the edges of which are covered with strong boards up to a height of about 50 centimetres. This area, which is just like the collecting basin of a fruit press, is caulked with oakum and pitch. From the top of the structure, small, very straight fir poles, with the larger end squared off so that they touch each other only at the base, go down at an angle to the centre of the container, so that a little further up, there is a slight gap between them, gradually widening toward the upper part of the square, where they are nailed on to the top. The upper side of the poles is lined with cheesecloth or coarse cloth, through which the blood and oil from the cod livers run and drain into the collecting basin. Two drainage pipes are fitted to this basin, one of which is intended to draw off the blood or bloody water, and is located 6 centimetres above and to the side of the other drain, which is used to draw off the oil.

First, they unplug the drain intended to draw off the blood, and when the oil starts to flow, they put the plug back in; then they draw off the oil from the other drain and put it into barrels. The cooper, after having rolled them under a lean-to,[85] stacks them up and fills the bung so that there will be no spoilage as a result of fermentation.

The arrangement of little poles covered with cheesecloth is called a vat; where they meet, they form a kind of square funnel and, at their base, they are about 33 centimetres from the edge of the vat.

On the outside, and at the base, a piece of coarse cloth is nailed all the way round, as for the sticks forming the vat.

The object of this procedure is to prevent the frothy scum that covers the oil from being parted by the wind and rain, which would cause the oil to evaporate on contact with the outside air. A ramp built

---

85 Carpon notes that the term used in the context of the French fishery is *vaugeard*, which has no equivalent in English. (Translator's note.)

Photograph of the interior of a French stage taken by Paul-Émile Miot, 1857. Library and Archives Canada, PA-194630. Acquired with the financial support of the Ministry of Heritage under the Cultural Property Export and Import Act.

on piles and with handrails made of fir trunks, because of its gentle slope, allows people to climb easily up to the top of the vat, into which they throw the cod livers. Once they are decomposed by heat, they produce a lot of oil. The quantity that the cooper obtains from them is indeed considerable when the fishery is plentiful—when, at the end of the trip, they have as many barrels of oil as there are crewmen.

A few days before leaving Newfoundland, they bring what is left in the blubber barrel to the temperature of boiling water. This is the way it should be done, although it is not followed by the master of every expedition. To begin with, from the top of the vat, they throw onto what is left of the cod livers first warm water, then hot, and then boiling, stirring it all thoroughly with a stirrer.

They repeat this process for several days, taking care to increase the heat gradually, so that the oil is extracted naturally as if by the effect of sunlight. After this treatment there is only a very small quantity left in the sediment, and this sediment is sold to curriers for the dressing of leather. They also use it to coat the surface of the fishing boats, mixing in with it a small quantity of tar; this serves as waterproofing for caulked seams as well as for cabins covered with planks to which they stick sailcloth or tarred paper.

Since there has been tremendous success in the treatment of scrofulous diseases and other similar complaints with cod-liver oil, if experience shows it to have definite therapeutic value, we should advise rich patients of sluggish disposition to go and stay in Newfoundland to drink this restorative oil, in all its purity, to their fill. They can then return to the bosom of their families fresh as daisies, with their temperament changed for the better.

Having gone over the work required for the preparation of cod, we will surely be allowed a moment's relaxation for an account of the triumphal procession of the salter. This is a most unusual festivity, the celebration of which makes those involved split their sides with laughter. First, they bring a barrow, on which they lay a crown woven from a mixture of birch, fir, and juniper branches. Once the salter is crowned, they grab hold of him and lie him down on the barrow that has been covered with greenery. Then four men each put one of the handles on their shoulder. Up to this point, this farcical ceremony would seem to be reminiscent of a Merovingian[86] inauguration. They put the national flag on the handle of a stirrer and the flag-bearer approaches the procession. Soldiers in different uniforms, mostly consisting of tailcoats gaudily decorated with wildflowers, cod fins, and caplin woven into ornamental braid, stand there waiting for the signal to begin. Each of them has on his head a tricorn hat adorned with flowers, which he has previously moulded into the required shape.

The captain of this troop is chosen from among the headers; he steps forward, wearing his uniform and with his head covered by a long, pointed hat with flowers on it. He has two swabs[87] as epaulettes and, at his side, you can see a long wooden sword hanging from a canvas bandolier. He casts severe looks at his men as a reminder of the respect that they owe their leader. The second salter and the spreaders armed with stakes are situated behind the barrow. Behind them there are four headers armed with wooden sabres and bandoliers of tarred rope.

One of them carries a barrel strung around his neck to serve as a bass drum; the three others have mess tins as smaller drums.

At the command "Shoulder arms!" you see a forest of stirrer handles and salt shovels being raised, and at the order "Forward march!" they make a terrible noise with the mess tins and the barrels, until they reach the wash house, where an unholy din gives way to the deepest silence.

Then a harsh and authoritarian voice, addressing the salter who is being carried in triumph, says sternly:

---

86 The Merovingian dynasty ruled most of what is now France from the middle of the fifth century to 751. (Translator's note.)
87 A kind of broom made from ropes. (Author's note.)

"What have you done with your salt?"

"It was stolen from me."

"Who stole it?"

"The captain."

A detachment of soldiers break away to go and look for the captain. When he arrives, the leader of the troop tells him in the following terms of the accusation that has been made against him:

"The salter accuses you of having stolen his salt; we ask that justice be done to the thief, and it is our intention to punish the guilty parties severely. As for the salter, we shall drown him if he cannot give a proper account of the use he has made of the salt …"

"Ah! My friends," says the captain, "I ask your pardon on his behalf; I shall show you what has become of the salt. The poor salter is not guilty, and neither am I. Come with me to the beach."

The procession moves off to the same accompaniment as before, and the captain, with a long stick of whitewood in his hand, gives the sign to halt in front of the door to the main cabin. The troop forms a semicircle, and then they all swallow a glass of brandy presented to them by the chef.

And the drums sound again for the chief salter's justification. The captain, pointing to the piles of cod with the end of his stick, cries out: "My good men, there is the salt!" Cheers are heard all around. They walk around the beach, to the accompaniment of songs, mess tins, and barrels, and then carry the exonerated salter back to his quarters. The latter hastens to offer his friends refreshment, and this little Newfoundland carnival concludes with a sort of feast that verges on excess.

I have talked about the way cod is caught, headed, split, salted, and washed. I said that when it comes from the wash house, an apparatus whose structure I have attempted to describe, the cod is put into piles,[88] laid flat, with the skin uppermost; it quickly dries out, since the moisture drains off easily because of the way the fish are laid out in a gentle slope.

The beach is an area of seashore of variable extent that they cover with small rocks. It is on these that the drying is carried out, or, in places where there are no stones, on branches that are piled up. It can also be done on a structure of alder and fir branches made into a rack about 1 metre from the ground; this is called a *flake*.

When it is fine, the cod are carried to this platform and spread out with the flesh uppermost, and they stay there all day exposed to the action of the air and the sun. In the evening they are picked up and set in a pile of seven or eight one on top of the other, in the same direction. The skin of the first faces downward, and that of the others upward: this is what they call *faggoting up*.

The next day, if the weather is suitable, they set the fish out to dry again, and they build quite a substantial pile, still using the same method, except for the shape. The tails of the fish are placed next to each other, and the flaps or napes are on the outside; this rounded little heap with its marked dip in the centre allows the rain to run off, preventing it from getting inside. These heaps of fish are known as balls. When they are put back in a dry place, the cod can then be put in piles.

Bearing in mind the quantity of fish taken, the captain or master of the operation indicates the circumference to be given to the pile,[89] and once the outline on the ground has been marked out, the officers responsible for arranging the pile place themselves around it. The

---
88   This pile is exactly like the one made when the cod is salted, but much smaller. (Author's note.)
89   The instrument used to describe the circumference is known as a measuring stick (*semelier*). This is a kind of long, flat ruler, on the end of which is a nail that is pushed into the ground; this ruler has different marks that are known as *semelles* and is used like a compass to draw the circle. The number of *semelles* indicates the size or diameter of the pile. (Author's note.)
     The literal translation of *semelles* is soles; it seems the measurements were in feet. (Translator's note.)

men bring them their loads of 20 to 25 cod, carefully laid out in the same direction, carried on their left shoulder. The officers take these loads of fish and lay them out all at the same time in a spot they think is suitable. They build up the pile in the shape of a circular pyramid, which looks just like the top of a dovecote. The cod placed on top to protect all the others cover these fish like slates on rafters that have been prepared to receive them.

Beach used by French fishermen for drying fish, showing original walkways, New Ferolle, also known as Darby's Island. Photograph: M. Wilkshire.

It has often happened that, after a plentiful fishery, piles of fish have spent the winter on the beach in Newfoundland, and the next year the men could only congratulate themselves on their perfect preservation. All that was necessary was to set the first layer close to the ground on a wooden platform and cover the whole thing with tarred sailcloth.

When the cargo is sufficiently dry, on fine days they give the fish that they want to load on board its final exposure to the sun, which they call pre-loading exposure (*soleil d'embarquement*).[90] Then it is transported to the country where they think they can make the best possible sale for the outfitter from whom the captain received his orders before the ship left port, and for the crew, who receive one-fifth of the net value of the

---

90   Adolphe Bellet notes that each of the phases in the drying process is known as a soleil (sun, or exposure to the sun). He distinguishes 10 different drying phases; see *La Grande Pêche de la morue à Terre-Neuve* (Paris: Challamel, 1902), 72. (Translator's note.)

proceeds, according to the custom in the port of Granville.

Most of it is sent to St-Pierre in Martinique and to Pointe-à-Pitre, French colonies in the West Indies. Since the bounty given in those countries to ships arriving laden with salt fish is quite lucrative, very large quantities are taken there, making them one of the best markets.

A huge trade is also carried on in France, in Marseilles, on the Île de Ré, in La Rochelle, Bordeaux, Havre de Grâce, and all French ports where fishing ships are fitted out.

So these voyages to Newfoundland, besides training sailors for the state, have as their main goal the catching and sale of cod, but, like all of men's occupations, and more than many others no doubt, this one too has its accidents and its dangers. Apart from the indispositions that can occur at sea, a man can be injured or fall ill. What a terrible position it is for the sailor, if the crew he has signed on with is without the services of a good doctor, especially when the ship still has to struggle against the sea for a long while before reaching land! Does not the poor patient run the great risk of dying a victim of lack of foresight and properly administered care?

Here I call upon all of you who are naval veterans! On you who have once more become peaceful residents of the mainland, and enjoy on land the fruits of your honourable labour! You can add your voice to mine and help me to render an important service to poor sailors, perhaps to those with whom you may have fought for the honour of your mother country, or in whose efforts to achieve prosperity you have shared.

In the past, even when a ship had a crew of only 20 men, it had to have a doctor on board. But look at the law today! Note especially how it is enforced! What guarantees of experience and competence are required of young men that some make so bold as to call doctors, and who even usurp that title themselves? What proper training have they undergone to merit their accreditation? Most are good for no more than putting into practice that saying from the ancient satire: *faciamus experimentum in anima vili.*[91]

Does not the mere thought of such regrettable abuses make anyone with the slightest feeling of humanity tremble with horror? I have often taken up the cause of the improvement of health services in the merchant navy, but in vain; perhaps my efforts would have met with success if the Lord had preserved my venerable master Baron Larrey for science and humanity. But, as everyone knows, he suffered an untimely death on his return from his African campaign, where King Louis-Philippe had charged him with the mission of organizing the surgical and health services of the hospitals and armies in that region.

My hopes dashed, I still did not give up my attempts to achieve such a useful reform, and one so worthwhile for our sailors. In 1850 I sent a request to the president of the republic. Here are the exact words of the answer I was honoured to receive:

"Since it falls within the jurisdiction of the Ministry of the Navy, the petition sent to the president of the republic by Mr. Carpon was forwarded to that ministry on 3 June 1850."

"The General Secretary of the Presidency has the honour of so informing Mr. Carpon."

My petition reminded the president of the eminent service that Baron Larrey, a close friend of the emperor, had given to the army with the application of his ingenious pieces of equipment, resulting from a wealth of experience of surgery, and by the admirable invention of his flying ambulances which, since they allowed the wounded to be picked up right under the enemy's fire, spared the nation precious blood.

---

[91] "There is a marvelous story from the Seventeenth Century about the humanist scholar Muretus, who was a fugitive from France. He fell ill in Lombardy, and because he looked like a street person, the physicians who treated him were going to experiment on him. So they spoke to one another in Latin, saying, *Faciamus experimentum in anima vili* (let us try an experiment on this worthless creature). Then, much to their surprise, this worthless creature replied to them in Latin *Vilem aninam pro quo Christus no dedignatus est mori?* (Will you call worthless one for whom Christ was willing to die for?)." "The Paradox of the Cross," sermon, Dr. William P. Wood, First Presbyterian Church, Charlotte, North Carolina, 4 April 2004. https://www.firstpres-charlotte.org/wp-content/uploads/2017/04/4-4-04wood.pdf. (Translator's note.)

Next, I made known the noble intentions of the famous surgeon regarding sailors, for the mission of this fine soul had not yet been realized. He wanted, before the end of his glorious career, to apply the wealth of his experience to the merchant navy by setting up an irreproachable health service for it. But, unfortunately, death did not wait for his fine projects to be brought to fruition.

Despite such regrettable setbacks, I cannot abandon the hope of seeing these humanitarian reforms become a reality. This proposal was received with charitable enthusiasm by a man whose soul could not remain insensitive to anything that touched on the well-being of his fellow men, on honour, and on the prosperity of his country. His noble intentions will not go unnoticed.

In the current state of affairs, for the presence of a surgeon to be required on board, the ship has to have a crew of 40 men, not including the cabin boys. Note carefully that these poor children, whose number varies according to the wishes of the outfitter, are not allowed to be counted as men, no doubt because of their tender age. Their presence on board is considered as null and void. Now there is real philanthropy for you!

In nearly all cases, any man who falls ill on board a ship where there is no surgeon is at great risk.

The poor man often expires, whereas the slightest intervention, if it had been carried out in an appropriate manner, might have saved him from a premature death.

Is it not then urgent for the government to at least ensure that no captain takes command of any ship without first being able to carry out a bleeding when it is necessary, or introduce a probe into the urethra in a case of urine retention, or extract a tooth, or understand sufficiently the skeletal structure to be able to set a broken limb and put the extremity of a bone back in its socket?

This instruction, which would not require more than a day's work under the supervision of a surgeon, would save the lives of a host of excellent servants of the state who die in their prime, often leaving behind a family reduced to poverty.

In addition, merchant ships should never leave port without being provided with lightning conductors, and lifebuoys placed so that they can be thrown out almost immediately when a man falls overboard. How many times have I witnessed this cruel and terrible sight! How many fathers have I seen disappear forever into the deep, crying out in the most dreadful despair, before it was possible to go about and launch the lifeboats! All we could do was pray to God for the repose of their soul.

Should not these deplorable facts arouse the concern of a solicitous government? Let us hope, for the honour of mankind, that the administration that presides over the French navy will take measures to prevent these dreadful accidents, the very memory of which is heartbreaking for those who have witnessed them.

CHAPTER 6

Discovery of the island of Newfoundland—Beauties of nature in these parts—Swordfish and whales—Whales and caplin—Inhabitants of Newfoundland—Their trade—Their temperament—Marriages—Climate—The country's appearance—Crops—Brief comment on birds of various kinds—Aboriginals—Their past and present state—Their customs and habits—Their good faith—Griquet Bay—Tides—Temperature—Fine summer days—Mosquitoes—Ways to protect oneself from their bites—Spruce beer

Not all of our readers will be equally interested in our work of catching and preparing cod, despite its importance. But nature, infinite in her variety and inexhaustible in her bounties, will provide us with the means to occupy the minds of those who delight in contemplating her wonders. If we cannot flatter ourselves that we are providing constant entertainment for superficial minds, we hope at least to be able to procure some moments of satisfaction for those who wish to learn.

And first, let us say a few words about the discovery of this huge island of Newfoundland, which has become a training ground for the French, and perhaps even for the European navy.

To whom does Europe owe the discovery of the island of Newfoundland? This is probably something that cannot be ascertained definitively even today. Here, however, are the facts with which biographies provide us on this subject.

According to the most commonly accepted opinion, Sebastian Cabot, an Englishman born in Bristol, visited the east coast of the island of Newfoundland. An old map in the palace of the queen of England indicated that John Cabot and his son Sebastian had discovered land on 24 June 1497 at approximately 5 a.m.; it was named NEW-FOUND-LAND in English, or *Terre-Neuve*.

After a successful voyage, Jacques Cartier, who was born in St-Malo, landed on 10 May 1534 on the east coast of Newfoundland. The account of his journey tells us that Cartier had navigated according to an extremely well-conceived plan that he carried out with courage, skill, and perseverance.

Sir Humphrey Gilbert, a brave English officer and navigator, caught sight of Newfoundland on 30 July 1583. He entered St. John's harbour, and received gifts of provisions from all the English and foreign vessels, particularly the Portuguese. On 5 August, Gilbert, having set up camp on land, convened all the captains, read letters patent from Queen Elizabeth and was able to explain the sense of them to the foreigners. As a result, he formally took possession of the harbour and of 200 leagues[92] in every direction.

Having examined the area, they found it to be most suitable for a settlement, and they made the preparations necessary for reconnoitring the surrounding territory.[93]

It is far from our intention to make any claim to write a learned work on a matter that would require a specialized and perhaps lengthy treatise to produce a conclusive answer! We shall simply point out that these notes, as erroneous in substance as they are in form, seem to take no account of the expedition of the Portuguese Corte-Real, to whom the discovery of Newfoundland in 1500 is attributed.

We shall add that John Cabot was a Venetian in the service of Henry VII, and that in 1497 he discovered certain shores of North America between latitudes 56° and 58° north. He may also have visited the eastern shores of Newfoundland in the company of his son Sebastian

---

92 A league is an old measurement of distance roughly equivalent to 3 miles or 4.8 kilometres. At sea, a league is 3 nautical miles (about 3.5 miles or 5.5 kilometres). In future uses, the equivalent distance in kilometres is given in square brackets. (Translator's note.)

93 I owe these few pieces of information to my honourable teacher of rhetoric, Mr. Julien Letertre, member of the Caen Academy, presently librarian for the city of Coutances. (Author's note.)

Cabot. We have his account of his voyage published in Venice in 1586, a few years after his death, under the title *Navigazione nelle parti settentrionali*.

So, since we admit that our island was among the lands visited and explored by John and Sebastian Cabot, the honour of its discovery belongs to these Italians who arrived long before all the others.

However, we cannot forget Jacques Cartier, the navigator so honoured for his discovery of Canada, whose memory is perpetuated to this day in Newfoundland in the names given to some localities. For example, in Quirpon harbour, 6 miles [c. 10.8 km] from the Sacred Islands, on the starboard side going in, there is an island called Jacques Cartier, and the channel leading to it also bears the name of Jacques Cartier Passage.

In the waters around Newfoundland, so much feared by navigators during the pack-ice season (for the coast is generally quite safe), periods of flat calm can be delightful moments for anyone in good health. In these moments, he can gaze to his fill on the beauty of the most charming or the most curious sights that nature has to offer. And so, since I am lucky enough to suffer no stomach upsets at sea and consequently to maintain a healthy appetite, I took great pleasure in enjoying the magnificent vistas to which we were sometimes treated on days of at least partially clear and calm weather.

There is nothing as admirable as sunsets for the infinite variety of reflections and the way the light is diffracted. On the approach to the Grand Banks, weather like this sets cetaceans in movement: whales, swordfish, sperm whales, blowers or bottle-nosed dolphins, porbeagles, and porpoises.

The swordfish is the sworn enemy of the whale; as a result of this relentless hatred, they become locked in mortal combat whenever they meet. In this desperate and furious struggle, the swordfish leaps out of the water at lightning speed and falls back down again just as quickly to plunge its saw into the body of the whale, which dives and somersaults to counter the terrible blows of the adversary that is attempting either to kill it or to die with it. Soon the whale comes back up to the surface, noisily spurts water from its blowholes, and, in an effort to save itself, performs a variety of instinctive movements, sometimes succeeding in ridding itself of its enemy.[94]

People claim that after it has pierced the whale, the swordfish stays stuck inside it, and that the two perish after a length of time that is determined by the gravity of the injuries. They also say that the whale often puts its enemy out of action by crushing it with a blow from its tail.

The whale found along the coast of Newfoundland is the finback;[95] it is not nearly as large as the one found in the southern seas, and it is also much swifter in its movements, hence very difficult to catch. I have seen fruitless attempts at this fishery along the coast of Newfoundland where the whales escaped from the fishermen with only a few slight scratches. As the caplin arrive in the bays, one can see them pursued by huge pods of whales whose tail-slaps to stun and kill these fish often prevent one from sleeping.[96] The terrible din produced by the violence of the commotion created in the water and echoed by the mountain chains is repeated in a hundred different places, in such a noisy manner that in the dead of night it sounds for all the world like a rockfall from a large mountain.[97]

On a voyage to Newfoundland you frequently find yourself on a part of the Grand Banks in calm weather. You are sure to catch cod there.

---

94   This passage on whales is strongly reminiscent of the one in Larrey's account of his voyage to Newfoundland, which Carpon seems to have read. Both Larrey and Carpon were probably writing under the influence more of legend than factual observation. (Translator's note.)

95   The name that Carpon uses in French is *fine bague*, apparently quite unaware that this is simply a French rendering of *finback*. (Translator's note.)

96   Carpon is probably confusing two kinds of whale in this paragraph: swiftness of movement is characteristic of the finback, while the humpback would be the only one the author would have observed slapping the water with its tail to stun caplin. (Translator's note.)

97   Among the mountains in Newfoundland I shall point out in passing the Aiguillettes chain, which has limestone of excellent quality, and there is no doubt more elsewhere. (Author's note.)

If you cut one open and put your hand into contact with its intestines, you will find that they are ice-cold. With the aid of a thermometer one could determine the approximate temperature at the bottom of these seas; it must be similar to that of the cod and other fish of this kind, varying according to the depth. But as for the large animals I mentioned earlier, their temperature hardly changes when they are in northern waters, however cold the sea is. The marine monsters of the cetacean family have blood that is just as warm in Newfoundland, Baffin Bay, Hudson Bay, and the Davis Strait as in the southern seas.

Seals, those amphibious creatures that are destroyed in huge numbers in Newfoundland, also have very warm blood, even though they spend their entire life among mountains of ice and in the coldest of seas.

Later, we shall talk of the other animals in Newfoundland itself, but before that, let us say a word about the European population and the aboriginals on this island.

The Newfoundland settlers are almost all of English and Irish descent; they work mostly at the fishery. Their main trade is in furs, fish oil, seals, and lumber.

Many inhabit the coast, in the bays where the French fish. They are tolerated there as a goodwill gesture, for, according to the treaties, we have the exclusive right to fish on the east coast of Newfoundland and to prevent any Englishman from doing so in the areas that are granted to us for that purpose.[98]

But mutual interests and natural kindness have overidden these harsh rules of diplomacy. Not only do we tolerate the presence of settlers, we also provide them with all the means to earn their living, by obtaining for them all the equipment they need. In exchange

---

98   Whether French fishing rights under the Treaty of Utrecht were exclusive or concurrent was a much-vexed question right up to 1904, when the French ceded their rights in exchange for other compensations under the *Entente cordiale*. (Translator's note.)

for these services, the inhabitants repay us with many more. After our departure, they look after the maintenance of our cabins, living quarters, and stages and prevent them from being vandalized by a few ne'er-do-wells who could at any time ruin an operation, the failure of which could easily bankrupt the outfitter.[99] When we have singled out guardians who can be trusted, we leave them all kinds of provisions before our departure: butter, fat, salt pork, flour, biscuit, cider, wine, spirits, lines, and nets. This major source of supplies, along with what they get from their daily hunt, puts them in a position to survive the winter comfortably. In this season, when the weather is suitable, they put on snowshoes to be able to walk on the snow and go far afield to cut large fir trees that they carry to their houses on trains or sleighs with metal bands on the runners, hitched up to a number of their large and powerful dogs. They also push these trees down from hilltops, where the snow forms a smooth slope; in summer it would be impossible to get the logs out of there. In summer, they go off to find trees, which they mark with a few blows of an axe. These trees immediately become their property in the eyes of their neighbours, who would consider it a crime to take them for themselves. This rule of decency and honesty is generally well respected. These settlers are naturally lazy, and when they have enough to eat and drink, work becomes a burden to them; this is why many of them make plans to build a cabin, put together the frame, and 10 years later have still not covered it. It requires some vital necessity, such as the collapse or the destruction of the house they are living in, to impel them to do it. If it were not for their extreme indolence, many of these easy-going people could become very rich if they wanted to, and, happily, there

---

99 "By the late 1700s English migratory fishermen began moving into the area and the French were soon hiring *gardiens* for their premises, (usually English fishermen, since the French were forbidden to stay year round). Local tradition maintains that La Scie received its first English resident in 1826 when a Daniel Duggan was engaged to ensure 'the thievin' English on the other side of the peninsula couldn't get their hands on' French property during the seasonal absences." Article on La Scie in the *Encyclopedia of Newfoundland and Labrador*, s.v. "La Scie." Available at http://collections.mun.ca/PDFs/cns_enl/ENLV3L.pdf.

are some who, indeed, do want to. The settlers who are guardians for rooms[100] in the harbours are at the mercy of a number of merchants, to whom they are indebted for considerable sums; the merchants acquire valuable goods from these poor people at a very low price, in exchange for which they give them clothes, food, and drink.

The main warehouses are in St. John's, the capital of Newfoundland, situated in a favourable location on the southeast of the island, with a fine port, the entry to which is defended by a tower and forts bristling with guns. The town has a population of between 18,000 and 20,000 inhabitants and spreads out to the west in the shape of an amphitheatre. A dreadful fire broke out a few years ago in the centre of this town during which as many as 1,000 to 1,200 houses were destroyed by the flames.[101]

Since then they have rebuilt the houses with stone, using lime and sand. The women there are attractive; some of them have dark hair and eyebrows in striking contrast to their blue eyes; the complexion of both sexes points to a healthy and robust constitution; and, as in Russia, one sees surprising examples of longevity.

Those settlers who become rich as the result of hard work own their own schooners and leave to sell their goods and to bargain for all that they require for their domestic needs. They often have large families; I have seen very young women with 12 or 15 children.

In this country, when a daughter gets married, she and her intended are made to swear on the Bible to observe faithfully the laws

---

100 "A tract or parcel of land on the waterfront of a cove or harbour from which a fishery is conducted; the stores, sheds, 'flakes,' wharves and other facilities where the catch is landed and processed, and the crew housed ..." *Dictionary of Newfoundland English*, 2nd ed., s.v. "Room." (Translator's note.)

101 Carpon is referring to the fire which has been described by Melvin Baker in "The Great St. John's Fire of 1846" (*Newfoundland Quarterly* 79, no. 1 [Summer 1983]: 31-34). Also available at http://www.ucs.mun.ca/~melbaker/1846fire.htm. The fire started in the workshop of a cabinetmaker on 9 June 1846 on George Street; he was boiling a pot of glue on a stove when it boiled over and caught fire. The flames quickly spread because of windy conditions and lack of water for the firefighting equipment. The governor, Sir John Harvey, ordered a house to be dynamited to enlarge a firebreak, but the explosion caused embers to be sent flying, thus spreading the fire even further. Vats of seal oil on Water Street contributed to the blaze. Two thousand buildings burned, and 12,000 people (57% of the population) were left homeless. There were three deaths directly related to the fire. As a result of this event, a plan was developed requiring that streets be wider and buildings in the central core district be built of fireproof materials (brick or stone). Fire has always been a serious threat in St. John's, with its mostly wooden houses packed close together. The worst was in 1892, when the whole of the east end of the city was destroyed. (Translator's note.)

of marriage. The details of the agreement are recorded by an authorized representative carrying out the functions of an officer of the state.

The wedding is later blessed by a religious celebration when a priest passes through.

On leaving the parental home, the daughter receives as a dowry her clothing, two dogs, a small boat, a sled with its harness, and a net for fishing.

As for the other events that have to be officially registered, they keep a precise record of births and deaths in the harbours that are too remote from the city to be in daily contact with it. Delegates of the English administration are responsible for regularizing these records. The authorities in St. John's are aware of the state of the population along the entire coast by the collection of records from local registers

In the harbours on the east coast, the inhabitants are unable to use horses because of the nature of the terrain, which is made up of virtually inaccessible mountains and ravines, succeeding each other in an endless chain. On the hills and in the plains, there are excellent pastures which could provide the coastal inhabitants with abundant winter provisions for the large herds of bulls, cows, sheep, and goats that they could have available to them. But looking after animals, cutting hay, drying it, baling it, all this constitutes work, and anything that smacks of work is fundamentally repugnant to these wretched people, who are governed by an irresistible penchant for consummate idleness. But every rule has its exceptions. I can quote up to three examples: Master James, in Croque harbour, owns some delightful houses, and runs an inn and a café; everything about him indicates comfort and even affluence. Pierre Jais, like several others in Conche harbour,[102] is also an exception to this torpor and apathy in which the majority of the settlers vegetate. These people, at least, have animals of all kinds and poultry, but in the winter they keep only what poultry they need for breeding when spring comes. In fact, it would be folly, in

---

102   This harbour is better known under the English name of *Sit Down*. (Author's note.)

a country where every day you can kill partridge and wild duck by the hundreds, to waste food supplies for the sole pleasure of having barnyard fowl alive on your property. They are useful only in summer, when one can eat them while fishing for cod. This fishery is essential for survival when there is scarcely anything else on which to depend.

Industrious settlers grow cabbages, carrots, turnips, and especially potatoes, of which they lay in great supplies. I doubt whether one could grow cereals in the part of the island where we fish; the temperature there is mild for too short a period. But I have been informed that these last few years in the St. John's area they have harvested wheat of excellent quality, and that the land is cultivated there, as in France, by harnessing horses and oxen to the plow. Their manure, mixed with seaweed, helps to fertilize the ground and make it highly productive.

In the west, around Cape Norman, the coast of Newfoundland has flat areas of considerable extent. These could eventually attract the interest of speculators who would surely derive products from them that would be especially profitable since the land would cost them nothing. For undertakings of this kind, real workers are needed, not those poor sluggards in the harbours who regularly come to beg their meals as soon as the bell rings during the season in our rooms.

Among the lovely sights that nature has to offer in Newfoundland we should mention the frequent northern lights, popularly known as puppets[103] because of their strange variations.

The surface of the sea in the harbours also frequently offers striking effects of light that can be observed at night, especially when it is hot, around oars or paddles, or in the wake of ships. Naturalists attribute these lights to the presence of innumerable tiny phosphoric animals and also of animal substances that have putrefied and been dispersed in the water. Enclosed areas, where these lights are most common, could certainly pose a health hazard if one were to stay there too long.

---

103   The term Carpon uses is *marionnettes*. (Translator's note.)

The climate of Newfoundland is extremely cold and damp despite the fact that the island is located at a latitude between 46° and 52° north.

One finds small apple trees, pear trees, gooseberry bushes, raspberry canes, and a very large number of climbing and aromatic plants. Majestic mountains of great height ring the harbours and bays and offer extremely beautiful sights. In many places you see these steep hills fanning out in a host of different shapes and merging into gentle slopes that descend to a flat beach, carpeted by a magnificent covering of fine grass, clover, and vetches.

These high mountains are covered with pine trees, fir, spruce, birch, alder, and larch. But all the plants there are generally less healthy and more stunted than in Europe.

In the middle of the densest of thickets one finds a variety of large deer to which Europeans have given the name of *caribou*.

I shall discuss them in greater detail under the heading of hunting.

Several species of bird have remarkable varieties in these parts. A red partridge that is very common (ptarmigan, the *Tetra lagopus* described by Linnaeus) is different from the European one in that it is larger. The eye ring has a fleshy ridge that is scarlet in colour, the beak is rufous, and the tarsals are covered to the claws with a silky grey hair that is very thick. These partridge are red with brown, white, and black blotches in summer. In winter they are as white as snow. Everything leads me to believe that this colour change occurs without the birds losing their feathers. The thrushes too are also reddish brown in summer, and whiter in winter. This change no doubt takes place in the same way as with partridge. For a part of the winter the latter, who are virtually tame birds, live in holes without any light, where they grow pale. Provident nature has endowed them with this power of metamorphosis to save them from the voracity of foxes and birds of prey.[104] In the forest one comes

---

104 Carpon is mistaken: these birds do indeed moult. (Translator's note.)

across many birds of varying sizes, but they are not found in flocks as they are in France.

The rivers and lakes are teeming with fish, which for the greater part are salmon, salmon trout, and eels.

Some harbours are full of salmon that are much larger than those in Europe, and they are caught in great numbers. In these parts they kill many waterfowl. These do not taste very good, except for the Canada geese, black duck, and teal, whose meat is delicious, especially in August, when they have eaten the local fruit that grows everywhere, on the mountains and in the plains.

The native inhabitants of the island of Newfoundland are of the same race as the Eskimos in Labrador. Today they trade with the Europeans; in the past they practiced cannibalism.[105]

Their dress consists of a large hat in the form of a helmet, a very ample short coat, loose-fitting trousers, and short sealskin boots with soles of very thick leather, which they tan beautifully themselves. Over the coat, a long strip of skin serves as a belt. Before they had dealings with Europeans, they always used bows and arrows, the tips of the latter being made with pieces of bone, but now they use this hunting weapon only in exceptional circumstances.

When they leave to go hunting, they take with them bows, arrows, and rifles, as well as a canoe covered with sealskin or birchbark; they use it to cross ponds and lakes. As the people of this race live solely by their hunting and fishing, they take great care to ensure that both are fruitful. So, in order not to frighten large animals, such as wolves, caribou, bear, fox, etc., if they come across partridge or other birds in

---

105 See Preface, p. 25. In *A History and Ethnography of the Beothuk*, Ingeborg Marshall writes: "The consumption of human flesh in rituals connected with war has been recorded in Inuit as well as Montagnais, Eastern Cree, and Abenaki, and it is possible that at some point the Beothuk observed a similar custom" (Montreal: McGill-Queen's University Press, 1996), 427. As noted in the Preface (p. 25), Carpon wrongly conflates Innu and Inuit peoples. Carpon's book was written around the time of the fruitless search for survivors of the ill-fated Franklin expedition sent to search for the Northwest Passage through the Arctic, but the rumours of cannibalism did not begin circulating until after Carpon's book was published. It later became clear that it was not the Inuit who had practiced cannibalism but those survivors themselves, who stayed alive as long as they did by feeding on the remains of their companions who had died. (Translator's note.)

the plain, they kill them silently with their arrows, reserving gunpowder explosions for major strikes.

These men are quite well built. They have muscular bodies, dark brown or black hair that is flat and long, and sparse beards. Their eyes are small and deep-set with a sinister expression, and are shaded by black eyebrows that are short and frowning. Their noses are straight and flat, their mouths large, their ears long and pointed at the top, their lips fairly thick, their teeth are yellowed and often not at all regular, and they have a tanned complexion. For cord and thread, they use the sinews and tendons of the animals they kill. In summer, these Indians, like the settlers, supply themselves with provisions for the winter, since during that season, it is not easy for them to get out of their huts. They are very well able to bear the cold, if one can judge from their physique. Their skin is thicker than ours, as is the bone structure of the skull. Add to this the application of oily lotions over the entire surface of the body, together with clothes with a thick lining of fur, and you will readily understand that they can withstand the inclemency of the harsh winter season.

Before Newfoundland became an English colony, the huge forests of this island, which is 150 leagues [c. 812 km] in length by about 50 [c. 240 km] wide, were filled with these fierce, thieving creatures. In La Scie, after the peace of 1784,[106] a band came down from the mountains and, after shooting all the men in the settlement with their arrows and stunning them with their tomahawks, they decapitated them and carried away all that they could steal before the boats came back from fishing. One cabin boy was saved from this horrible massacre; he had cowered in a corner of the stage when he saw the carnage begin.[107]

---

106   The Treaty of Paris of 1783, which put an end to the American Revolutionary War, was ratified by Congress on 14 January 1784. (Translator's note.)
107   Details of this incident are not known, but Ingeborg Marshall writes of theft by the Indigenous population: "Pilfering goods and equipment from Europeans, a widespread habit among native people, was frequently commented on by early explorers" (*A History and Ethnography of the Beothuk*, 111). She also notes that the destruction that accompanied these thefts was likely a way of exacting revenge for injustices suffered and for deprivation of territory (112). (Translator's note.)

From then on throughout the island, these creatures, who are by nature impossible to deal with, were pursued to the death.

Seeing themselves hunted and exterminated in this way when the settlers laid hands on them, they moved from Newfoundland to the coast of Labrador via the Gulf of St. Lawrence, travelling in their canoes during the fine season and over the ice in winter.

Many of them surrendered, and good use was made of them, once they had been civilized a little, in finding and destroying the tribes in the interior.[108]

Those who still live on the coasts of Newfoundland are not to be feared today. Almost all of them have been converted to the Roman Catholic religion. They know a little English and French and among themselves have a social convention from which they never stray; they also have a chief or king, whose authority they respect. A few years ago, it was the illustrious Michel Aga, a resident of Bay St. George, who held the reins of government. His Majesty was very obliging, and one of my friends, who was fishing near the palace of this mighty monarch, often invited him to give a hand in drying the cod, stowing it on board ship, etc.

Following these small tasks, His Majesty and the captain would dine in style. After coffee and a good measure of liqueur, the king eagerly received as a token of gratitude a few litres of strong alcohol to enjoy with all his court.

Modern savages use the familiar "tu" to practically everyone with whom they come into contact. They have learned from the priests of our religion that we are all brothers in Jesus Christ, so the term "brother" is quite familiar to them.

In 1827 I met two of them, one of whom spoke passable English and French; the other knew only his mother tongue. According to the first one, they had been sent by the English government to explore the

---

108   In Newfoundland they were given the name of red savages because of the tattoos of this colour with which they covered their face and limbs. (Author's note.)

interior of the island where families of red savages were reputed to be still living, and he told me how he had killed one of them, the only one that he had seen during his travels. Here are the exact words of the story he told me:

"As we were beginning to run short of game, I saw from afar a large plain, in the middle of which was a pond surrounded by countless thickets."

"I thought this area looked good for caribou and we lost no time in going there. Soon I saw a herd of these animals. My friend lay in wait, and I went downwind from them so that they would not be aware of my presence. I picked out one very large one, and was soon within range, when suddenly I saw it fall and struggle; a red savage had just shot it with an arrow. I took several more steps and killed the savage on top of the body of the caribou."

"We took all that we could carry from the animal and we did not see any other savages during the course of our journey, but we found places where they had camped and feasted only a short time before. In the middle of these deserted places we were constantly on our guard, even though, with a rifle, one can keep a score of them at bay, and we had two rifles in perfect condition."

I would have gone hunting with these half-civilized savages if the demands of my calling had not kept me at our room. They left on their own, and brought back two caribou and a multitude of partridge. The rifles with which they were armed were single-shot flintlocks of very small calibre with no trigger-guard, approximately 1 metre 60 centimetres long; a piece of sealskin was nailed to the housing of the firing mechanism to cover it and to protect it from the damp.

Nowadays they use percussion rifles or flintlock muskets like us, and all the members of the family have their own gun, when they are old enough to carry it: father, mother, boys, and girls eagerly vie with each other to bring home something to eat.

Because they are accustomed to this kind of exercise from their earliest years, there is nothing about hunting or fishing that they do not know; these are their sole means of existence.

If they hear that there is much more game in one area than in others, they immediately leave with their whole family to go there, and in spring or summer their shelter is quickly built.

They cut three small fir trees that are tall and very straight and trim them, leaving the ends of the main branches sticking out to serve as hooks on which they can hang whatever they want. They place these three trees together like a stack of rifles and cover them with sealskins sewn together with animal sinews or with birchbark made to fit in the same way. On the lee side of the structure they leave a hole through which to enter. It is in this circular enclosure that they do their cooking and sleep, on moss, around a fire from which the smoke goes up through the top of the roof.

If there are very small children, they put them in bags made of skin or bark from trees, filled with moss. With the aid of thongs, they hang them from the hooks on the frame; these poor little children say not a word, bundled up as they are, either in rags or skins of hare or wildcat.

You may well think that these Indians are the most lowly of wretches, and that nothing can equal the privations that they have to endure. Well, it is exactly the opposite! They would not exchange their nomadic and adventurous life for all the opulence of the richest of monarchs. And if they were housed in a palace, they would die of boredom were they not quickly given back their freedom, which they consider the most precious possession in the world.

These men are skilful by nature, and, with materials and pelts that they prepare themselves, are now able to fashion a number of items of clothing. They also make musical instruments, flutes, violins, flageolets, etc. Their cords and bows are made from the sinews, gut, and tendons of animals, and they make an excellent rosin from the gum of fir trees.

The savage of these parts is second to none when it comes to keeping his word. During the present season (1847) I again found myself in a position to confirm this. Having exchanged gifts with a number of savages, I led them to my cabin to offer them liqueur and brandy. Two of them accepted my offer with marked satisfaction but, when the third one refused, I insisted that he accept. He instantly showed me a medal suspended by a small string on the left side of his chest.

This brass medal bore the stamp of the sacred hearts of Jesus and Mary. He explained that, about five years previously, after a drinking bout, he had flown into a rage at his father and mother, and, to atone for his error, he had made a vow to drink no more strong liquor for 10 years. He said that he had made this promise to God on his blessed medal and that he would rather die than break his oath. I was full of praise for the sincerity of his beliefs and gave him a number of different objects to show what an excellent opinion I had of him.

Then I went with them on board an attractive schooner that they had built and which they owned, and there I drank a small glass of a good liqueur that they make from spruce (*abies canadensis*); they gave me a small flask of it, for which I thanked them with a good bottle of Armagnac.

These bronzed Indians, purebred Eskimos,[109] now fully imbued with religious principles, have become very honest, humane, and hospitable, but they have an uncontrollable tendency to take revenge on those who have wronged them and who have not redressed that wrong.

One of the men from a ship close to our room recently witnessed a scene which proves the accuracy of this observation in a most convincing manner.

The savages in the area of Pistolet Bay had been ill-treated by men from a Breton room. The captain had promised these men an indemnity

---

[109] As noted in the Preface, p. 25, Carpon thinks that the Innu and Inuit of Newfoundland and Labrador are of the same race. (Translator's note.)

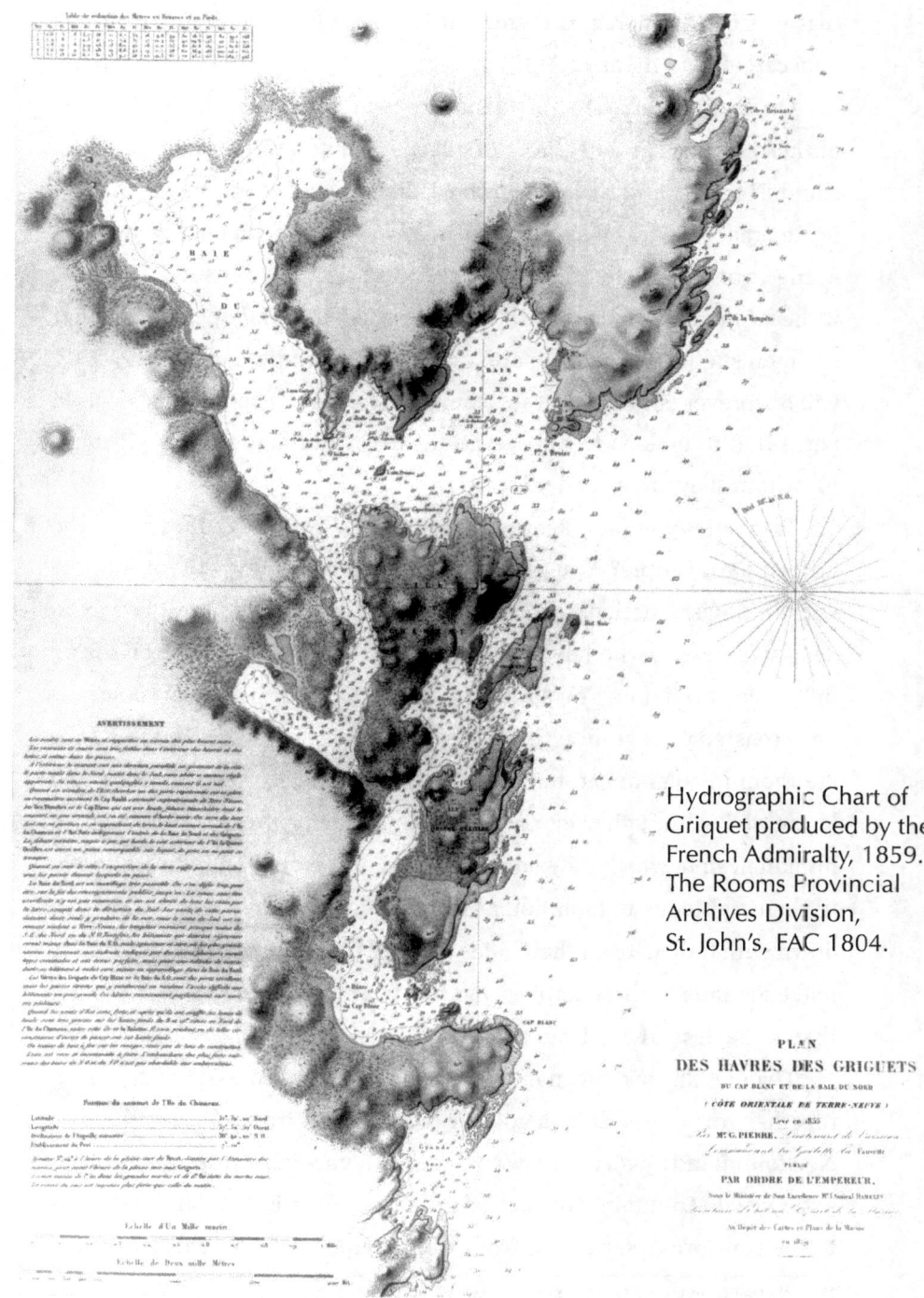

Hydrographic Chart of Griquet produced by the French Admiralty, 1859. The Rooms Provincial Archives Division, St. John's, FAC 1804.

that was certainly due to them. But he broke his promise, and that is unacceptable to them.

On seeing a boat a short distance from her cabin, the wife of one of these savages grabbed hold of a large rifle and ran off as fast as she could. Her husband rushed after her, not knowing what was the matter. Seeing that his wife intended to fire on men who were in no way involved in the wrongdoing, he tried to stop her and a struggle ensued. It was as if the woman was crazed with fury, yet she was finally persuaded that the men she wanted to take aim at were not members of the crew that will be forever cursed by these people. May a man of good conscience be permitted to make a few observations here, and may they reach those for whom they are intended!

Why did you not keep your word? Why did you mock these unfortunate people? You put your men at risk: they will answer for your ill-advised actions, perhaps with their life. This is not the way to deal with people who have become our brothers through the civilizing influence of religion. You should be aware, sir, that people of their race once roasted your grandfather and several Breton officers, and that they ate them in solemn ceremony at the head of Ha Ha Bay, which we all know well. Although they now reject with horror those awful feasts of human flesh in which they once delighted, this would not prevent them, in their righteous indignation at you and your crew, from mowing you down with bullets from their rifles. Believe me, you should immediately make amends to these natives and pay your debts, if there is still time; that is the best advice I can give you.

Griquet Bay owes its name to a series of islands, the Griquets, which together form an archipelago that is separated from the mainland of Newfoundland by very narrow passages. They are known as Camel Island and Camel Mountain, Griquet Island[110] and Four Ears Island, which is to the southwest, separated from White Cape by a very narrow arm of

---

110   The term Carpon uses is Admiralty Island, now known as Griquet Island. (Translator's note.)

the sea. These islands are all extremely close to each other, so much so that without shouting very loudly, one can carry on a conversation from one shore to the other. Griquet Island, where I was, is only 1,000 metres long, and of variable width to a maximum of 400 metres. It is surrounded by steep rocks and there is nothing on the higher parts but a few little bushes of fir and alder, some juniper and crabapple trees and a few climbing plants, such as black crowberry,[111] vetch, wild tea, various mosses and grasses. I have nicknamed this island the Rock of St. Helena, for from every direction it offers nothing but a picture of gloom and desolation.

To the north-northeast, Camel Mountain looms majestically over a stretch of hills and plains covered with greenery and conifers: it presents a delightful scene to the eye of the beholder. From the top of this mountain you have one of the most magnificent views that nature can offer. With the naked eye you can see the passage leading to the Gulf of St. Lawrence, where Great and Little Sacred Islands, Belle Isle, and the Straits contrast admirably with the land mass of Labrador, and seem to all belong together. Add to that a multitude of capes of prodigious height, and enormous bays, surrounded by green plains and charming groves, and you have in front of you one of the finest sights in the world.

To the south-southwest of Griquet Island you can see Four Ears Island, which is nothing much to look at; like Camel Island, it has quite a large number of shrubs, but they are not as well developed.

One point only on this island is worthy of attention: the top of Crow Head, where one can see for quite a long way and which serves as a barometer in forecasting good and bad weather.

To the southwest of Griquet Island rise the highlands of White Cape, near which a passage of the same name opens up. It was in this harbour that the ship from Granville, the *Mars*, went down.

---

111 It is on the slender branches of this plant that the little fruit known in Newfoundland as the curlew berry grows. (Author's note.)

Opposite the place on Four Ears Island known as Augustus Point, there is a very small passage known as the Gut, a name that is quite appropriate, for it is hardly wide enough to allow a boat to pass between the two huge pieces of rock, and even then the sea needs to be high for the boat not to touch bottom. Once one has gone through this narrow opening one comes into Southwest Bay, where I have had magnificent hunting and fishing trips.

Tides are felt very strongly on the coasts of Newfoundland, and sometimes strike with extraordinary violence and irregularity. One can get an idea of this from the frightening event that was witnessed by the crews of the *Deux Sophie* and our ship one year after the voyage which is the main subject of this work.[112]

On 24 September 1848 the ship *Deux Sophie* left Griquet harbour under full sail on its way to Marseilles. The ship that we were on was about to make ready to leave for Granville when suddenly there was a tremendous upheaval in the water. The tide was high and, in the space of five minutes, it fell so low that we could see the pebbles on the bottom that are normally covered by 2 or 3 fathoms of water at the lowest tide. From the reversal of currents, one would have sworn that the huge bay of White Cape was about to be drained dry. But, turning about on themselves, these fast-moving torrents instantly brought a high-water level 4 or 5 metres above the point rarely reached by the sea in the highest of tides.

The stages and wash houses were submerged. Ours especially would have been washed away if it had not been for the tremendous weight of rocks piled onto the stagehead to prevent it being broken up by ice in winter. This phenomenon was repeated three times in 15 minutes. The wind was blowing strongly from the southwest. We anchored our ship solidly, after having stowed the topmast and

---

[112] In 1847 and 1848 Carpon sailed with the *Deux Sophie*, then in 1849 with the *Abeille*. See microfilms F-1883, F-1879, and F-1881, Library and Archives Canada. He appears to be confusing his records here. (Translator's note.)

topgallant. That night, however, was perfectly calm, and the next day at 9 a.m. we were moving past Camel Mountain under full sail. By evening, the highest points of these western regions were scarcely visible on the horizon, and soon we were left with only the memory of them.

The climate of Newfoundland is extremely cold in winter and damp in spring due to the effect of the thaw and of the almost continual fog that, early in the fine season, reigns along the coasts and especially in the area of the Grand Banks.

Anyone who sails to Newfoundland should be sure to take along two types of clothing: one for the cold and the other for the heat. The sudden changes of temperature often give rise to scurvy. Vegetables cooked with fresh cods' heads make an excellent broth which will completely cure people suffering from this condition. In the month of July, the prevailing winds are from the north-northeast; at this time the cold gives way to fine weather and heat, and one of my friends who has a thermometer assured me that around the end of that month the temperature had gone up to 27 and 28 degrees above zero. When the sun is under the tropic, the nights disappear, to the point where the evening twilight shakes hands, as it were, with daybreak. I have often come back from my hunting expeditions at 11 p.m. or midnight, firmly convinced that it was only 7 or 8 p.m. But it has been written that paradise cannot exist even momentarily anywhere on earth.

In spite of the harshness and the long duration of the frost, as well as the great quantity of snow, the forests of Newfoundland which, by the way, are very numerous, are full of insects, especially mosquitoes. This is the name given in Newfoundland, as in many other places, to a small winged insect with a slender body set on long legs. On the front of its head it has a pointed sting with ridges that serves as a suction pump, and with the help of this sting it obtains its food. This insect is extraordinarily greedy for blood and is much like the one that we in France know by the name of *cousin*,[113] but the bite of the former is much more harmful, and sometimes, as soon as the skin is pierced, blood streams out over it.

If you find yourself in the woods in calm, sultry weather, among the trees that serve as a shelter for these harmful insects, it is not at all easy to prevent the cruel torture they subject you to. In some cases, facial bites cause very considerable inflammation and instantly blind those who are affected, making them unrecognizable for several days. They recover their sight only as the swelling of the eyelids subsides.

> You call in vain on the doctor for help,
> Or for soothing ointment from the captain:
> It's useless; the effect is immediate,
> And your face puffs out in a strange swelling.

Indeed, there is nothing more comical or unsightly than a person whose face is ravaged by mosquitoes: his features are so distorted that the only way to recognize him is by his clothes.

The bloodstains scattered here and there, the transparent red colour of the skin, the multiple blisters, weeping heavily, make the face look quite repulsive.

> In thundery weather, never visit
> The gloomy trails in a thick, dark forest;
> In the firs, the relentless mosquito
> Stings you deeply with his poisoned arrow.
> In these distant parts, this is without doubt
> The cruellest fate that man has to endure.
> Turn your face away from his painful barbs?
> He will always get at you somewhere else;
> In spite of your clothes of wool or cotton,

---

113 *Cousin* is a term often used in France to refer to the common mosquito. (Translator's note.)

> He pierces your skin with a single jab.
> In vain you attempt to shelter your head
> From the wretched beast's unwanted attacks,
> Despite all you do, the swarm buzzes, grows,
> Wreaks the most dreadful havoc on your eyes.
> Both eyelids suddenly become swollen ...
> For two or three days you lose all your sight!
> At that dreadful moment, you are lucky
> If one of your friends, whose eyes have been spared,
> Can lead you, blind from your experiences,
> To the modest lean-to that is your home.
> On a bed as austere as the lodging,
> Deprived of your sweet sleep, you firmly swear
> Never to walk in the forest again,
> Save in a nor'easter, and thus stay well.

If, during your stay in Newfoundland in the short summer season, you feel like going hunting, fishing, or looking at the sights, make sure you take your excursions when it is cool and there is a strong northeasterly breeze. If the coolness is followed by calm and heat, take the wise precaution of going back to your room as quickly as possible in order to avoid the dangers that I have just mentioned. This advice is of the greatest importance for travellers on the coast of Newfoundland, and I cannot urge them too strongly to follow it.

> These cursed creatures are kept prisoner
> In little shrubs by high wind and by cold.
> Coming back out when it's calm and sultry,
> The only thing they want to drink is blood.

Toward the end of August, night frosts and cold days kill the mosquitoes or drive them away, and one experiences the sweet satisfaction of being able to move around without exposing oneself to their unbearable persecution.

The cruellest and most painful torture that could be inflicted on a criminal would be to tie him naked to the trunk of a tree, with his hands and feet bound so that he is unable to defend himself. One hour of exposure to the wounds of these insects would be enough to bring about his death.

Their bite causes swelling of the affected part and a slight fever; however, this fever is only temporary. Cool lotions, applied locally, and rest are sufficient to cure these unfortunate conditions. It is better to prevent the problem than to have to cure it, so it will be of help if I indicate here the means of keeping mosquitoes at bay.

Take 128 grams of olive oil; boil a pinch of absinthe leaves in it for five minutes, then strain, squeezing out the leaves, and dissolve in this oil 8 grams of camphor.

Rub your face and hands with this mixture from time to time. As soon as I had put this to the test, the mosquitoes took an aversion to me and came close only to beat a hasty retreat. I now enjoy the indescribable pleasure of going about my business without being subjected to their painful harassment.

I have never seen frogs, toads, lizards, vipers, grass snakes, or any other snakes on the coasts of Newfoundland. I do not think that they could survive in such cold temperatures. And I do not think that the mosquito can bear the rigours of a winter that lasts nine months any better than reptiles. But the reproductive process of this insect provides it with the ability to perpetuate its pestilential species by laying its eggs under the bark of fir trees and inside pine cones, where the outside air cannot penetrate because of the depth of snow that covers them. When the snows melt, the warmth of spring hatches out the mosquito eggs, and they quickly reach their peak in size and viciousness.

They are most frequently found in spruce trees.

When the young buds of this plant are mixed with oats or crushed biscuit and sweetened with molasses, they make a refreshing and intoxicating beer.

This beer and tea are the main drinks of Newfoundland settlers, who are also able, insofar as their means allow, to savour the pleasures of good, old-fashioned wine, cider, brandy, and rum.

CHAPTER 7

Be prepared for all eventualities—A hunting trip becomes an embarrassing situation—False alarm—The situation turns to tragedy—Near-comic outcome—Notice to travellers in Newfoundland—Rare example of "economico-paternal" affection—Advice to hunters—On hunting in general—Abundance and conservation of game—Black bears: how to hunt them—Caribou: various ways of hunting them—Wolves and their wiles—How to hunt them—Beavers and their marvellous works—Hunting them—Otters and how to hunt them—Choosing hunting dogs—Newfoundland dogs—Their qualities and faults

Yes, you should be prepared for all eventualities. In calm, clear weather, four of us left the harbour of Cape Rouge to go to Bell Island (Grey Islands), on a full-scale hunting expedition.

Bell Island is about 18 nautical miles [c. 32.4 km] from the mainland. After sailing for a few hours, we came ashore on the southeast part of this wild and uninhabited piece of land.

The master of the boat had explained that we had to go only 3 miles [c. 4.8 km] by land from there to a place called The Islets. We merrily set out for that spot, where he was to pick us up and take us to the harbour to the southwest. I took off my jacket and waistcoat for freedom of movement, put my gamebag on my back and armed myself with my double-barrelled rifle and a hatchet. I slung a string-covered bottle full of brandy around my shoulder and off we jogged.

We had hardly climbed the first mountain when a flock of 18 or 20 partridge landed in front of us. They were instantly dispatched; several others suffered a similar fate, and in no time we were loaded down with them. Finally, after walking for five or six hours without straying from our course, our leader announced that we had reached The Islets. We were greatly surprised at not seeing the eagerly expected boat already moored there. The master had been obliged to raise anchor and make for the southwest on account of a very strong northeasterly breeze that would inevitably have driven him on to the shore. Subsequently, we fully understood that it had been impossible for him to keep to the plan, but we were nonetheless greatly disappointed. It was beginning to become cold and dark; we were hungry and needed rest and warmth.

I had fortunately had the forethought to put in the bottom of a large horn full of caps a lighter, tinder, and some matches. In our precarious position, these objects were of vital importance.

All four of us stretched out on a bed of moss, lichen, and climbing plants in the shelter of a hill, near a huge rock under which bears had spent the winter, and where they still came for shelter, for there was every indication that this cave was still a frequent haunt of theirs. However, we did not encounter any of them there.

There were about 40 or 50 bales of forage in the cave, which led me to believe the settlers and savages in Newfoundland when they say that, in winter, bears do not live exclusively on their fat but on whatever supplies they have gathered to survive for as long as the snows last, a period of nine months.

Moreover, it was very easy to see that the litter had been well grazed, and by them. Their footsteps stood out clearly on the boggy trails and in the mud along the shore of the ponds where they went to drink. But this is a question for naturalists to decide.

I greatly intrigued my comrades in misfortune when I told them to light a fire. We have only our rifles, they replied anxiously with an air of annoyance. Well, I said, take out the lead, load with balls and slugs, change your caps; we will have be able to defend ourselves in case of a nocturnal visit. As for the fire, I'll look after that. In five minutes, I had a fire burning in front of their noses that was big enough to roast an ox, and everyone set to work plucking the game, the only thing we had. From a string over the fire, and on rocks that we had heated until they were red-hot, we roasted 12 partridge and a duck. We devoured them eagerly and drank what I had left of the brandy, mixed with some water, out of a leather cup that never left my gamebag.

We agreed to keep watch, and the luck of the draw had it that I would go to sleep at the same time as one of my friends, while the other two stood guard, for fear of being surprised by wild beasts. It was cold and I was very lightly dressed; we had to find some means of compensating for this lack of clothes. With the axe I cut down some flat, bushy branches from fir and spruce trees. I made a blanket of them and fell asleep in front of the fire just as I would have done in France on a good feather bed.

My sleep was soon disturbed by one of my companions who started calling out in a very loud voice: "Pick up your guns! There's a bear! There's a bear! Duchesne has been eaten!" I have never got up so quickly, leaping into the bushes, rifle in hand, shouting out at the top of my voice "Where is it? Where did you see it?"

A voice replied from a distance "Look out! Mind you don't take me for the bear!" I recognized Duchesne, and I gave my friend a good scolding for having given us such a scare. But the poor fellow did not deserve it; he was pale with fear, and his senses were so numbed with fright that the next day he was unable to walk because his limbs were so paralyzed!

Duchesne had slipped away to get a drink of fresh water from a small stream that cascaded down from the top of the mountain. He was also looking for some good-sized wood to provide a plentiful supply for our campfire. One false step had caused him to stumble, and, as he fell, he had noisily cracked a half-rotten tree that he was carrying: *indè male labes*.[114] This, then, was the sole cause of so much fright. After the storm, calm: the man who was supposed to have been devoured turned up, axe in hand, with the trunk of a large tree on his shoulder, in fits of laughter at this nocturnal scare.

---

114   "This was the beginning of the misfortune." Virgil, *Aeneid*, 2.97. (Translator's note.)

"My friends," he said, "I am afraid I did not have any such luck. Coming across a bear would be very useful, if we have to spend a few days here; at least we would have had something to eat. I would happily take on the task of treating you to a feast of the meat of the most ferocious black bear in Newfoundland, as long as my axe did not lose its head during the encounter. Anyway, you would have been there to lend a hand. We are all well armed, and we should be no more afraid of a bear than a muskrat." These words, though reassuring, were not enough to calm the effects of the fright suffered by our unfortunate companion; I think that, on the contrary, they only served to increase them. But only one of the four of us was likely to retreat, and even with one man missing the battle would still have been won.

After spending a night[115] whose rigours were tempered by a blazing fire, we saw with great pleasure

> Dawn with its smiling face,
> Scattering flowers and rubies in the east ...[116]

and bringing us the comforting promise of a fine day. When we could see well enough to fire, we changed the charges in our rifles, said goodbye to our bivouac, and made our way, like true pilgrims, toward the southwest harbour. There all of our troubles would be forgotten at the sight of our boat, our bread, and our liquid rations, of which we were feeling sorely deprived.

From early morning on we fired our saltpetre continuously at partridge and occasionally at Canada geese. As everyone was by now feeling quite hungry, we got down to business in the shelter of a tall mountain, and in order to move things along more quickly, instead of plucking them, we skinned 12 game birds. This was done in a flash, one

---

115   In Newfoundland the nights are always extremely cold, even when summer is at its hottest. (Author's note.)
116   From a poem by Pierre Baour-Lormian, *Veillées poétiques et morales (sixième veillée)*. (Translator's note.)

of us taking care of the preparation while another was lighting the fire. The birds were soon cooked and eaten. A few cups of water concluded this rather primitive meal, and we set off again in search of the lifeline that the practiced eye of our guide was leading us to. At last, at 1 p.m., our leader, who was an experienced man, placed us at a distance of about 3 miles [c. 4.8 km] from the place where we would be once again safe and sound.

The need to eat caused us to call another halt: we feasted again on tasty partridge, which, prepared in the same way and served as before on small pebbles in lieu of plates, provided the one and only course. However, our poor colleague, exhausted by the present circumstances and fearing the future, was overcome with fatigue and weakness. He found himself suddenly completely deprived of the alcoholic beverages to which he was accustomed and his condition was becoming a cause for genuine concern on account of the discomfort he showed. He dragged himself around with difficulty, no longer had the strength to fire his rifle, and was holding us up considerably. He often lay down and begged us to go away and let him die. The scene was turning to tragedy when we saw a man in the distance making signs at us. We answered with shouts of joy, for it was the master of our boat, waiting for us like a new Messiah. He was coming to meet us, and already our privations were no more than a dream to be forgotten. Our boatman appeared to be carrying a bottle to restore our exhausted energy, and this sweet hope gave back a shred of strength to our friend, whose one thought then was to refresh himself thoroughly. But what a shock we had when, drawing close to this wretched sailor, we saw that he was zigzagging along in a way that betrayed his drunken state! Instead of a full bottle, all he had left was the handle, a silent witness to the misfortune that had befallen him. "My friends," he said, stumbling over his words, "I nearly lost my life, but luckily I only lost the contents of the bottle. To prove that I was coming to your assistance, I am bringing you the handle."

We were completely exhausted, and this doltish behaviour on the part of a man who had become intoxicated at our expense made us indescribably furious; we had great difficulty in seeing reason. Soon we were on board the boat, where we had an excellent meal, and we immediately gave the order to get under way and make for our room.

We gladly said goodbye to Bell Island and, like La Fontaine's crow, we swore, rather belatedly, that we would not be caught out again.[117]

Besides, every cloud has a silver lining. This accident confirmed what long experience had already proved to me: that one cannot take too many precautions against swift changes in weather in Newfoundland.

The temperature varies more on this island than anywhere else, and these changes from heat to cold often occur several times on the same day. For the sake of one's health, which could otherwise be at risk, one has to be prepared for such sudden variations. One should have some warm clothes as well as other lighter ones, and waterproof garments, to be able to change as required. This precaution is of the greatest importance both for those who are visiting the country out of curiosity and for those who have a particular duty to perform. If he sees what promises to be a fine day in the morning, a seaman in the service of an outfitter may not take along a change of clothing; the unexpected happens, our man is soaked to the skin, he gets cold and falls ill. The fact that he is in bed causes the outfitter a considerable loss, which would easily have been avoided with an oilskin jacket and a pair of trousers of the same material. In addition, once he has set sail, he should always wear woollen shirts and underwear next to his skin.

If we did not have numerous examples to the contrary, we should be tempted to believe that a harsh climate and a sometimes-excessive poverty must ingrain into the inhabitants a certain harshness of character. The following account would seem to lend support to that

---

117 An allusion to the fable *The Crow and the Fox*, where the fox uses flattery to trick the crow into singing, which causes it to drop the piece of cheese in its bill and let it fall for the fox. (Translator's note.)

view, but we must take care not to make generalizations on the basis of isolated facts.

In 1833 at the head of the bay in Great Brehat there lived an individual of Irish parents whose first name was John. On arriving from Europe, we make a habit of visiting isolated people like him to inquire about their health and how they have come through the winter. After the usual compliments, I learned from John that his wife had had two children who had died two hours after birth, but had been baptized by himself; that one of his other children had suffered greatly from the cold; and that his wife was very sick. The poor woman had scurvy; her child was suffering from gangrene as a result of frostbite in his toes and a part of the lumbar region!

My colleagues and I gave them all the care that their condition required. The mother and child were cured, but the latter remained greatly handicapped by considerable loss of bone and tissue that had been affected by gangrene. Decay of the vertebrae resulted in a hump.

Since I could not see any grave in the area around the cabin, I asked Master John what he had done with the children who had died. His reply made me shudder with horror. With incredible single-mindedness, he had cut the bodies into pieces, which he had then put on the pans of his traps to serve as bait for foxes; this, he added, had been extremely successful.

As he could see great indignation in my expression, he asked me: "How is it, Sir, that you are surprised at my behaviour? For my part, I can see nothing blameworthy in it; these children were baptized; whether they ended up in the belly of an animal or in the ground, they are still with the Good Lord."

I should never have gone back to the house of this unnatural father if humanitarian sentiments toward his wife and son had not made it a duty for me.

The sequel to the story of this interesting family is worthy of its elevated beginning!

Some while after this, soft-hearted John and one of his sons passed away on the same day. Two hours after the death of his masters, their faithful dog True Boy also expired. The good wife dug a hole in the ground and buried these three beloved creatures all together.

While he was alive, if Master John had had a premonition of this, he could have sung as the lyric poet did:

"My poor dog never leaves me!"[118]

But let us turn our attention to more cheerful subjects which, I feel sure, will not be without appeal to anyone who can handle a hunting rifle or a line.

However, before discussing hunting and fishing, which are great means of recreation, allow me, dear reader, to give you some advice which you will be glad you have followed if your star ever leads you to this country.

Never leave your room to go deep into the forests without being well armed, and carrying with you a lighter, tinder, matches, good powder, lead, balls, shot, iron slugs, caps of the best quality, a pocket compass, and a hatchet slung around your neck.

You should carry provisions for however long you wish to stay out of doors, and select a cave in the shelter of a mountain to set down your baggage. Once you arrive at the hunting area, you spend the night there in front of a good fire, a source of alarm to all wild animals, and you can be quite sure that they will not pay you a visit as long as there is a flame burning in the fireplace. Wherever you are, that is also the best thing to do when there is mist. It never lasts long, and trying to travel in that kind of weather is foolhardy, for you are sure to become lost, even in the areas that you know best.

When hunting alone, it would not be wise to attack a polar bear, for which lead balls are not very suitable because of the thickness and toughness of its skin. This is confirmed by what happened some time ago in Great Islets.

---

118 This is the refrain from a traditional song *Le Chien fidèle* (*The Faithful Dog*). Anonymous. (Translator's note.)

When a polar bear appeared there, the men armed themselves and ran toward it, the settlers taking their heavy rifles, and the death knell of destruction sounded all around. More than 30 shots, with shot and balls, were fired at it from 20 paces. It grunted, shook its ears and yawned, but, at first, it did not move from the place where it was sitting on its rear, on a rock surrounded by water. Then it threw itself into the water and started swimming. The English pursued it, and after a variety of charges of heavy lead slugs had been fired, it was wounded. Then, in a terrible fury, it turned on one of its aggressors, who blew a hole in its chest at point-blank range.

It stood up on its hind legs, howled, and fell down stone dead.

Here is what I think about this adventure: the powder was useless, as is often the case in Newfoundland. I have seen some that would not be sufficient to pierce the skin of a partridge at 10 paces. How can you expect powder like that to damage the thick skin of a polar bear?

I admit that long, coarse, thick hair presents in itself a considerable obstacle to a ball, but at such a short distance, using our reliable extra-fine powder of 17 or 18 degrees of strength, if the projectiles had not found an easy entry into the stomach or the chest, they would have flattened themselves on the bone. Then the bear would have yawned in a very different manner.

The settlers who, in the case in point, succeeded in killing the animal, put quadruple charges in their guns, and no doubt had better-quality powder.

I was not at the scene of the incident, but according to the explanation I was given by the main participants, their rifles were loaded with sulphurated charcoal rather than with saltpetre, which was included simply to give a little flame, and, thereby, put their lives in imminent danger.

Good powder is often the only thing that your life depends on; make sure that your horn is always well supplied with it. Have a bag of iron slugs rolled into cartridges so that, in a second, they can be put into the barrel of a large calibre, double-barrelled rifle. If a bear comes toward you and it is not possible to run, your calm will save you. Keeping full control of yourself, take aim at the chest or the mouth, and by firing at point-blank range you are certain to render it harmless. Shot is also the best projectile to use for shooting wolves and caribou.

In a fishing boat crewed by brave men there is absolutely no need to be afraid of the polar bear, one of the most ferocious amphibians. If it swims toward the boat to attack it, as has been seen many times, the men resolutely wait for it, and they all station themselves on the side opposite the one where the animal intends to upset the boat; as soon as it comes and hooks its broad feet on to it, they cut them off with axes. These initial wounds only make it more fearsome and it charges back. Then they throw a line with a running knot around its neck and render it senseless with blows from the head of an axe. It would be most unwise to use the cutting edge; once it is forced inside the skull it is difficult to extract. The animal could drag you into the sea if you were to hold on to the handle, or at least tear it from your hands. If you are deprived of this useful weapon of defence, the pews that all boatmen have at hand to fork the cod are of great help in encounters of this kind. And these powerful creatures with long, thick hair, stubbornly trying to eat anyone at sea, almost always pay for their fierce audacity with their life.

Before going into specific details, let us say a word about hunting and game in general.

Not all harbours are equally suited to the pleasures of hunting, and the amount of game varies in places along the coast.

The areas that I have found to be richest in game are the Grey Islands. On Groais one finds many caribou, foxes, otters, and often polar bears. Sometimes one also finds beaver there, and partridge and waterfowl are quite common.

On Bell Island, caribou and other quadrupeds are much rarer, but feathered game of every species found in Newfoundland is extremely abundant there. The ptarmigan seem to me to have multiplied to such an extent that an experienced hunter could take 150 of them in a single outing.

In the curlew season, you have to be on the southwest of the island for this hunt; you take cover at the edge of the seashore, opposite Green Island, and all you have to do is fire and pick up the game from morning till night.

The reason for this abundance, in partridge especially, lies in the fact that, because of their distance from the mainland, these islands are not visited as frequently in summer as in winter by the inhabitants of Newfoundland, or by the savages who kill all the game, depending as they do on hunting and fishing for their livelihood.

In winter, when the first snows start to fall, hares and partridge leave the dense thickets and come into the bays in large numbers. Since the majority of these are inhabited, the game is no sooner spotted than it is felled by rifle shots. Around the middle of August, I was with an inhabitant of Newfoundland to whom I was complaining of not being as lucky in hunting as I might have been in a spot that was as favourable as this. He told me that the harshness of the winter had forced all the game from the neighbouring mountains into the bay, and that when the first snows came, from the front door of his cabin, he had killed more than 1,000 partridge and at least 50 hares. He explained to me how they preserve the game, a process that is quite simple. Once the large quadrupeds are skinned, cleaned, and cut into pieces, and the birds are plucked and cleaned, they are placed in layers in piles of snow. They freeze very quickly and keep until the thaw. When the snow is blowing like dust or when excessive cold prevents the hunters from going outside, they cut off whatever they need with a blow from a pick. They always take from the oldest piles, even though, as long as the freezing temperatures last, there is no danger of this meat spoiling. If they have any left when the thaw comes, they preserve them by sprinkling salt over them. This is a true case of putting something aside for a rainy day.

During the winter the ptarmigan of the Grey Islands do not run any danger. There are no inhabitants, a most important condition for the preservation of game, and from which hunters derive enormous benefits, not enjoyed elsewhere. To my mind, this is the finest hunting area in the whole of Newfoundland.

Let us begin our explanation of each type of hunt with the black bear. There is no doubt that it is much less fierce than the polar bear; one must nevertheless use great caution on going through areas frequented by this animal. It is both herbivorous and carnivorous according to necessity, but the former of these two states is more familiar to it. To say that the black bear always runs away from men, and that it takes flight when it becomes aware of their presence, is nonsense. The two incidents that follow are sufficient to prove the contrary, and 50 others could be provided if necessary.

A short distance from Pistolet Bay, a young man washing some clothes in a brook winding through a small plain, close to the sea, was killed by a black bear, which, with one stroke of its paw, tore open the whole of the lower part of his chest and abdomen. The poor boy uttered only a single cry. On hearing it, people rushed to his aid, but it was too late. The bear had abandoned its prey and was making its way calmly back to the mountains when, after being surrounded on all sides, it was killed with its mouth still covered in blood.

In Great Islets two black bears of enormous size came down from the mountain and ate the supplies of some men busy cutting wood, without these men, whom the bears could see quite clearly, daring to stop them.

When they are hungry, black bears will face any danger to obtain food. It is not unusual to see them come into a fisherman's cabin at night to eat scraps of bread and the soup left in the dishes.

According to the settlers, a bear with young that are still too small to be able to defend themselves will brave the worst peril and will not give up until it dies.

While these animals sometimes attack man, it is also true that they generally do what they can to avoid him, and take to their heels when they are aware of his presence, unless they are unduly driven by hunger.

Black bears are hunted with a rifle and with traps.

When an aboriginal[119] finds himself in an area frequented by a bear, he takes cover, hiding himself with care at the edge of the plain where he has seen the animal coming to graze. He shoots it from as close as possible in the most vulnerable spot, that is to say in the chest or at the base of the ear. If the bear is not killed outright, its adversary, without showing himself, reloads his rifle, and if the animal's wounds prevent it from getting up, he finishes it off or lets it die before he approaches it.

To reach the plains, bears have well-worn tracks among the trees. Along these tracks the hunters set traps that are frightful to look at, and are attached with huge chains. Digging a hole so that there is nothing to prevent it from swinging shut, they cover the trap with moss so that the animal will not notice anything. They set another a short distance away, so that if it struggles, it is likely to fall into this one, thus ensuring that it is unable to free itself.

Along these trails, instead of traps, heavy rifles with their firing mechanisms covered in skin are also used. These are loaded with balls and slugs and are set up so that the barrels are at the same height as the animal's body. Strings attached to the trigger are set across the trail, so that when the animal comes by, it shoots itself. The skin of the black bear is highly prized, and its hams are considered a great delicacy.

The caribou, known by the settlers and the aboriginals as *deer*,[120] is a large animal of the same family as the stag. Like it, they have cloven

---

119 See Preface, p. 25. (Translator's note.)
120 In English in the original. (Translator's note.).

hoofs, although much wider; their legs are well muscled and slender. The head is crowned with magnificent antlers that, during the growing period, are covered with a fine down of a buff, greyish colour. Their spread is much like an open hand with flattened fingers splayed out, indicating, as with stags, the age of the animal. Because of its light build, it is able to run swiftly and for long distances. I saw one when it was frightened take a standing leap over a brook that was more than 6 metres wide, jumping from one rock to another, like a squirrel going from branch to branch. It then disappeared like a ghost from the view of its admirers, climbing the steepest mountains.

The female is smaller than the male, but it is no less agile. Caribou live on local grasses, moss, and leaves, especially birch leaves, of which they are very fond. They like being in plains where there are ponds, next to large thickets where they can take refuge at the slightest sound. Once there, they do not come out again in a hurry, and can sleep in peace, without fear of being followed. In fact, there is nothing more difficult than to make one's way through intertwined fir trees, and the noise of the branches being disturbed warns them from afar to be on their guard.

Caribou are hunted with a rifle.

There is nothing simpler than to find the places frequented by caribou. The moss that forms a carpet over the plains bears the mark of their hoofs and outlines it for you as if they had walked over snow. The hunter has all the clues he needs in fresh droppings and trodden earth around the ponds where they go to drink and bathe, a scene resembling a rural water hole used by a herd of cattle. He is certain to find these lovely animals as long as he makes no noise. It is therefore quite clear that one should never shoot game when one is on the track of caribou.

They have a very fine sense of smell. Coming out of the thickets to start grazing, they bend their nose down over their front feet, where there is a small indentation filled with a soft, oily substance rather like earwax. When they have thoroughly smelled it, they sniff in all directions, and with their antlers and their ears pointing upright, they listen carefully, lifting their thighs and licking their flanks. Then, after making all these little movements, they calmly begin to eat. This is the moment when the hunter, approaching the plain from downwind, finally comes within range of them. A caribou is rarely alone. In areas where they are numerous, one sometimes sees 12, 15, or even more grazing together. Armed with a large-bore double-barrelled rifle loaded with shot covered by a single ball, the hunter fires from as close as possible, either at the point where the shoulder comes to an end or in the head. This heavy shot spreads out a great deal, and hits the animal simultaneously in ten different, life-threatening places, for its skin is no more difficult to penetrate than a dog's. Ordinary lead shot, carefully aimed into the legs from 40 or 50 paces, makes it unable to move by instantly paralyzing it.

The animal may roll over and get up again, in which case, you fire a second shot, which often finishes it off. Then you run to it and bleed it.

If the animal is only wounded, before showing yourself and following it, you reload your gun, while at the same time noting the direction it is taking. You follow the trail of blood, and if you proceed carefully, you will find it dead or close to death. In this latter case, you should make a point of firing into the head so as not to have to run any further.

If you lose the trail beside a pond, you should look closely at the surface of the water and beneath it. You are almost certain to see the animal there, for the wounded caribou is especially prone to going into water, which, no doubt, makes its suffering more bearable. If you see it showing some signs of life in this situation, you should lie low and wait for it to die before going to retrieve it.

When you are hunting, you often see a caribou lying motionless. You can conclude from this that it has finished feeding. It goes down to the water, bathes, returns to the bank, shakes itself, licks itself, rolls over, and lies down on its side, with its four legs stretched out. All it moves in this position are its ears and its short tail, in response to the contraction of the skin when it is bitten by small insects. Taking advantage of this moment of inactivity, you shoot it at point-blank range.

On the hottest days of summer, it is devoured by mosquitoes. It gets rid of them by throwing itself in the water, and, when it comes out, by making for the top of a bald mountain[121] where the brisk air has driven all these insects away.

If one has the good fortune to kill the sentry of the herd, the senior male, constantly on the lookout and watching over the fate of his friends and relatives, the entire herd, for reasons known only to itself, rallies around the body, and tries to set it on its feet again by kicking it. This is the customary funeral ceremony for these intriguing animals, and it provides the hunter with the opportunity to kill several of them with his second shot.

There are other ways of conducting the same hunt.

When coming down from the mountains, out of their impenetrable lairs, caribou always follow the same paths. Once you have identified these trails as being well used, you should provide yourself with good, new ropes of best-quality hemp. In the path of the animals, you set a strong snare with a running knot half a metre off the ground and about one metre in circumference. When it is in a thicket, the animal walks with its antlers leaning back on its shoulders and its nose in the air. The snare is held in place by little pieces of wool that are easily broken; so the caribou is strangled, or held for the hunter's pleasure. Before setting this foolproof device, you must first rub it hard with grass and aromatic plants to get rid of any foreign odour.

One can also take these large ruminants with a heavy trap, or even with the same deadly contraption that is used for the destruction of the black bear.

---

121   In Newfoundland this term is given to a heap of rocks with no trees. (Author's note.)

The skin is little valued by the savages or by the settlers, but the meat is very succulent, like beef. It makes excellent soups and is a culinary delight.

A fillet of caribou, cooked to medium-done on a spit, is one of the most delicious dishes that a gourmet's palate can savour.

Having talked to you about caribou, I must tell you a few things about the wolf, a powerful presence that inhabits the forests of Newfoundland.[122] This implacable enemy of the caribou feeds on the ruminant's flesh to satisfy its gluttony. The male caribou is so aware of it that in winter it drives the doe in front of it to the areas that are most remote from the wolves' lairs. It does this because it knows that, in the spring, the female has to give birth to a calf, and that its gestation will hamper its progress and cause it to fall victim to this cruel animal. If it can, the male accompanies the doe over the ice to islands close to shore, swimming back after the pack-ice has gone, along with his family, especially when these islands do not offer them a safe refuge or sufficient food.

Not all caribou leave the forest. Herds of them can be seen there in winter as in summer, and always with a sentry in the lead. Wolves also gather in very large packs, and if they see a herd of caribou, they surround the plain and wait in ambush at the places they judge to be the best escape routes.

When their comrades are in position, several of them run off to drive the poor herbivores into the mouths of the waiting wolves, and they all share in the plunder.

The settlers and Eskimos are very wary of these wolves, whom they consider to be the most dreaded residents of the coast of Newfoundland, especially when they are in a pack.

They kill them with guns, or take them in traps, attracting them with the odour of seal carcasses or other animals.

---

122 Carpon uses the noun "loup-cervier" (lynx) but thereafter refers to "loups" (wolves); the two terms were commonly confused. The wolf has been extinct on the island of Newfoundland since 1930. (Translator's note.)

During my last trip, one of these ferocious quadrupeds came to the cabin of a savage at night and tore open the bellies of four of his dogs. The next day, this latter-day Man Friday surrounded the corpses of his poor, half-devoured dogs with traps, and the following night, the wolf paid for the carnage of the previous one with his life. These animals look as fierce as hyenas and are big and prodigiously strong.

The skin, pale with grey patches, is a magnificent fur. Usually it is preserved with the head, tail, and feet attached, for use as a bedside mat or as a carpet in reception rooms.

Let us leave this carnivore with its fierce habits and speak instead of the gentle, shy beaver and its marvellous works.

Of all known animals on the surface of the globe, the beaver is certainly one of those that arouse the greatest admiration for its highly developed instinct.

About the size of an average basset hound, this animal is of a brownish colour. It has an extremely dense coat that is pale russet at its base; its ears are slightly protruding, its head is slightly elongated, and the incisors of the upper jaw are arched and sharpened like a carpenter's chisel. They are set in sockets so deep that the end point of their curvature is almost at a level with the top of the larynx. The eyes are of a lovely oval shape and are bright and sharp.

Their short, webbed feet are black and armed with claws. Above the anus is a flattened tail covered with fixed scales; its shape is like that of a mason's trowel. From this tail a thick oil with a sickening odour is exuded. Between the anus and the reproductive organs, one can see ovoid vesicles that contain a greasy, creamy matter with a strong odour: this is *castoreum*, a substance widely used in medicine. It has to be collected with the greatest care, since the price is quite high.

The beaver sets up house in the lakes and ponds that are furthest from the sea, and especially from settlements, for it delights in isolation.

When you intend to hunt it, once you have reached the interior of the forest where you can see ponds, you should check to see whether there are any alder or birch in the area. The absence of these trees is an indication that you should look elsewhere. When you see lakes or ponds with shorelines covered with this kind of vegetation, if there is a beaver family there, you will soon find some of these trees cut down, stripped, peeled, and cut into pieces as cleanly as if it had been done by a carpenter's axe. I have often greatly marvelled at this work.

The reason why one rarely finds beaver in places where the two species I mentioned do not grow is that they depend almost entirely on these trees to build their dams and lodges. It appears that they dislike biting into other trees such as pine, fir, spruce, and larch, which contain a very large quantity of turpentine.

Beavers always use the lengths of wood that they cut for a variety of purposes, but it quite often happens that some tree trunks are too heavy for them to drag along. If they do not manage to do this, it is not for want of trying. Since they live in a closely knit family, they work ceaselessly side by side. If they need a strong piece of wood to complete some building job, once it is cut down, they seize it with their teeth by the trimmed branches and pull backward with all their might to get it into the water. One can easily appreciate the difficulty experienced by these industrious animals from the way in which the ground is disturbed by the deep imprint of their paws and the scratches left by heavy branches. When they want to drag into the water a load that is too great for their physical capacity, do not think for a moment that their instinct tells them to give up. Come back a few days later and you will see these massive trunks cut into several logs and arranged as if by the hand of a craftsman.

This is how beavers go about building their lodges.

After choosing a likely spot, they get to work, cutting trunks and branches of birch and alder, shaping the ends in a point, and setting them in the pond a short distance from the edge.

The bark on the upper part of these chunks of wood bears deep marks from their teeth: this is because one of the animals, swimming along, holds its stake in an upright position by gripping the upper end, while one or more of these skilful workers pile up stones to hold it in place at the base. After setting up a large number of identical supports in this manner, they place trunks and branches of trees horizontally and in a random pattern to form a solid, circular floor, that they cover with earth. This they beat well with their trowel-like tails, and, in the floor, they create an opening to communicate directly with the water. Then all around this surface, at its edge, they set and reinforce in the same way pieces of wood about 3 metres long, gathered together in a bundle at the top, just like the top of a dovecote or an oven in the countryside at home. The top has quite a large rounded surface. They cover the whole thing with earth that is beaten and well oiled so that they can go and rest on it later. With the aid of their trowel-like tails, which make it as hard as real cement and completely impervious, they leave no contact with the outside air, and in winter their sleeping quarters must be snug and warm.

The size of their lodges varies, I believe, according to the number of inhabitants. I have seen some that are 3 or 4 metres in diameter at the base, others that are hardly 2, but they are all built in the same shape and with the same materials.

The height of their waterside homes is not always the same on account of the varying degree of pitch that they give to the roof. If you have time, it is quite easy to remove the top part to explore the interior.

Sometimes the lodge is 2 or 3 metres from the shore of a lake or pond. In that case they make a linking bridge built like the floor of the lodge, on solid piles, in such a way as to give them easy access to it from the surface of the water. They also use it to reach the roof of their lodges to warm themselves and sleep in the sun.

I have seen some dive into the water at the slightest noise, to go inside their lodge or take refuge in underground caverns communicating with the neighbouring forest, always in an area that is almost impossible to reach. We have to assume that they go first to their lodge, which I believe is for them what the burrow is for the fox, the badger, or the rabbit. It is impossible to reach them without an extensive demolition operation, and at the slightest noise they can slip far away from their enemies.

Their living quarters are always dry, and always at the same elevation above the level of the water.

When beavers see the water rising at the time of the spring thaw, they go to the stream that runs out of their pond to move rocks and earth that obstruct the current. They carry out this work so as to keep their home free of flooding. If, on the other hand, it happens that the water level drops appreciably, the industrious family is soon to be found at the place where the stream was cleared, to undertake an entirely different operation. There has already been too much runoff, and they are afraid of the water dropping even lower; they waste no time deciding what to do. Beavers of all ages and both sexes all busy themselves, each according to their ability, building strong dams to obtain the desired level.

In that case they make a hedge of stakes of the same height, close to one another, held straight and firm by stones and clumps of turf, and threaded together with branches in various directions in the same way as in their lodges; this dyke is exactly like the frames that masons use for their wattle.[123]

Now let us inspect the interior of the beaver lodge.

One of my compatriots, a lieutenant commander, who had never seen beavers or had a chance to marvel at their astonishing wisdom, begged me to give him an opportunity to see this wonder of nature. I led him to one of the isolated places where I knew there was a family of these intriguing animals, a family that I had, alas, thoroughly devastated. My intention was to take the rest with traps, but things

---

[123] Carpon is referring to the centuries-old method of construction known as wattle and daub, where walls were built from a frame of interwoven sticks or strips of wood (the wattle) to which is a applied a layer of clay or similar material (the daub) that hardened as it dried. (Translator's note.)

worked out differently. My companion on the excursion asked to be shown the interior of the structure; so after we had each drunk a small glass of brandy as we perched on top of the lodge, we proceeded to demolish it, which must immediately have resulted in the expulsion of the beavers. When one section of the wall had been knocked down, we found perfectly erected compartments, alcoves full of moss, fine grass and peelings of birch bark. We observed that this was the dormitory, the place destined to receive the offspring. In one of the corners there was another compartment. It was an area with pointed rods set horizontally into the roof, forming a square that was approximately regular; at the back there was a little moss mixed with a few blades of grass, but less symmetrically arranged than in the other area. In the centre could be seen quite a large open area that could be described as the dining room. There were a lot of remains of fish bones and fresh scales from trout, a fish that is abundant in these ponds. We thought, quite correctly, that these animals have a great sense of cleanliness and throw into the water via the emergency exit all the refuse that is liable to spoil. We doubtless visited them as they had just finished their meal, which did not give them time to sweep the room, obliged as they were to beat a hasty, unceremonious retreat.

Runaway or fugitive beavers can be found along the streams; they are an easy target if you happen to come across them. The settlers and Eskimos assured me that these wandering beavers are driven out of their family because of laziness or inability to work. This is after being given a severe physical punishment, easily visible by the scars from the bites that their skin usually bears.

When it swims, the beaver has its whole body in the water. Only the tip of the nose is visible and this appears to be no larger than half a mouse. This single point floating on the surface forms a wake like that of a hornet flapping its wings in an attempt to get back to land after having fallen in the water.

Born destroyers of all that surrounds us, we should exhaust nature if it were not inexhaustible.[124] And you too, beast with such clever instincts, you who were an architect before man himself, you will fall victim to this terrible law:

Venit summa dies et ineluctabile tempus.[125]

On this subject, I would like to share with you a thought that has often crossed my mind, and that I would not like to keep to myself. Would the hide of this animal provide compensation for the expenses required to keep it in captivity? And, if that were the case, could not affluent property owners near suitable bodies of water try it out? The beaver, once very common in Canada, has now become extremely rare. The attitude toward these industrious creatures has been similar to that of the savage,[126] who cuts down the tree to reach the fruit. In the polar regions, the wretched Eskimo hunts reindeer, destroys it, and languishes on the brink of starvation, whereas the Lapp raises the same animal in herds, and, comparatively speaking, lives in luxury of a sort.

Being quite timid by nature, beavers are terrified of the explosion of gunpowder; if one fires a single shot in their peaceful domain, they consider themselves irrevocably doomed. If one of them is wounded or killed, they all take flight and are never seen there again. It is simple to take them in another way. Where they have cut down wood, you set traps that are held in place by a strong iron chain, carefully covered over with moss. They never fail to get themselves caught, but you have to keep a close watch on them, for they do not take long to bite through their foot to regain their freedom.

The best and most foolproof method is to displace a few branches or stones at their dyke or dam, which they are constantly checking; this will make the water run out. You can then set a trap there, on the end of which you fix a heavy rock, the slightest movement of which springs the

---

124 In italics in the original. (Translator's note.)
125 Virgil, *Aeneid* (2.324): "The supreme day has come and the inevitable hour." (Translator's note.)
126 See Preface, page 25. (Translator's note.)

trap shut. You cover it with small branches that are caught by the dam, so that the animal does not see anything prepared. When this trap is set over a certain depth of water, it is dragged into the water by its chain with the animal, who does not have the strength to bring it back up to the surface, and is discovered drowned.

In this way the entire family can be taken, whereas, in shooting them from a hide, one kills only one or two, while the rest will escape.

I am talking of a hunt that I have carried out frequently in the summer season, under the guidance of very experienced locals. Here is how they go about it in winter. Newfoundland dogs are accustomed to hunting certain animals in their country, just as ours hunt those indigenous to Europe.

Except on the mountains, where gusts of wind sweep it away, the snow lies 7 or 8 metres deep on the flat areas of the island. It forms great drifts between the hills, and everything is buried under these alabaster-like layers, except the tops of the highest trees.

On all sides the prospect is the same. The beaver lodges can no longer be seen; only the dogs' sense of smell is able to detect them. These faithful companions, who lead their masters back home via the shortest possible route after far-reaching excursions, go all around the ponds, stop in front of the beaver lodges, and bark until the hunter arrives.

When the dogs have found the spot, the master looks into the woods to see if the tree nearest to it is blazed. This would indicate prior ownership claimed by an earlier hunter, which constitutes an inviolable right among the inhabitants. If the tree is not marked, the hunter climbs up on to the lodge, removes the snow from the top, makes a hole in the roof, taking care not to let anything dirty fall inside the structure. He looks carefully to see where the exit is, makes a hole outside in the snow and ice, and sets a trap there, with the spring turned toward the lodge, and the jaws of the trap at water's level. By keeping a close watch, he can catch all these amphibians, once he has carefully covered over the hole at the top.

To find out how many beavers there are inside their communal house, the hunter takes off the snowshoes that prevent him from sinking into the snow, gives the lodge a good kick, and listens. The beavers leap into the water one after the other, so it is easy to count them. The skin of the beaver sells for 1 guinea per 500 grams, and the inhabitants of these parts consider its meat to be a delicacy. However, I have never enjoyed it whatever sauce it was served in, on account of its taste of fish and wildfowl.

Not all of the animals are as interesting as the beaver, but this is no reason to look down on them.

The Newfoundland otter is the same colour and shape as the French one, but it is much larger and has longer, thicker fur. As in our country, it is always found close to water, and especially to streams and ponds full of trout and eel, which it considers to be tasty morsels.

To catch an otter, you send your hound into the forest. He will sniff it out as he runs along the ground, if there are telltale signs of the animal's prints in the sand or mud. At the first sound from the dog, position yourself by the mouth of the stream, which is never very deep. You will see the otter coming down to throw itself into the sea, and it will be easy for you to kill it there. It is also easy to see, by its prints, the paths that it uses most frequently. So you set traps in the water as for beaver, and you will catch them there if you take care to cover the chain and the trap properly, so as not to arouse the animal's suspicions. In full moonlight, where a stream runs into the sea, at the head of an uninhabited bay, take cover in the bushes or climb into a tree. There you can often expect to kill several, if you fire accurately with a good weapon loaded with shot or double-zero lead. The skin sells for 36 francs locally.

For this hunt, as for all others, the correct choice of dogs is of great importance.

A hound is much better for hunting in both flat country and in the mountains, but it requires the following qualities. It needs to be obedient and to have strong legs. It has to be able to go into the water and retrieve well, to point for both furry and feathered game, and especially to attack on command. Without this latter quality it is not much use. If it is tenacious enough to point all day long for game that does not move, it is likely to have ample opportunity to test its patience in a country where hares and partridge are not at all shy. But if the dog starts to point in a thicket of pine trees, where you cannot see it, you risk losing it. You will be obliged to return home without it, and your hunt will be fruitless.

Rather than a setter that does not stay pointing on command, it would be much better to have a hound, which is good at flushing out game without making you wait for it. If your dog loses its way, take care not to whistle or fire shots with your rifle; the echo of these sounds reverberating around the mountains will often cause it to go off in the opposite direction, and if you do the same again, it will become more lost than ever, and you will lose it. It is much more sensible to stay quiet in the spot where it left you; it will find you by following the scent.

For reasons that escape me, once they arrive in Newfoundland, all dogs acquire the local habits: pugs, lapdogs, bassets, etc. go into the water and retrieve, and I deduce from this that, if they are in any way disposed to hunting, they are all capable of coming through the season to the satisfaction of their masters.

I shall now address myself to Newfoundland dogs: it would be a serious omission not to say a few more words about you, who are so famous, and whom we visit every year. Again I compliment you on your fidelity, and on your amazing instinct, but I have many complaints to make to you regarding certain matters that smack of barbarity. Sometimes the truth gives offence. However, please do not take umbrage to the point of biting me if I return to your country, for I hereby inform you that if you indulge in such excessive behaviour, the final punishment will be immediately meted out to you as a penalty for your brutality.

The reason why I brought dogs from my country across the ocean in order to partake of the pleasure of hunting in yours, was because, to my eyes, you have never shone in this type of activity. Is it because your sense of smell is not sufficiently acute to locate game, or because you do not have enough practice?

In my view, it is the latter that is the sole reason for your lack of success. From what I have seen of several members of your race, with a build such as yours, you are capable of giving useful support to the efforts of a hunter. For what better can one ask of a dog than to point at all kinds of game, to go into water, to retrieve, to hunt rabbit and hare, and to strangle fox and badger if the need arises? Many of you acquit yourselves admirably of these various tasks in Newfoundland. Your masters and mistresses simply require that you accompany them, at heel, during their excursions. Whether they are on foot or on a sled, you are in a position to defend them from their enemies, who are limited to a few fierce animals, and it is no mean feat to deal with bear and wolves when they are starving with hunger. You retrieve admirably game that has been killed, either on land or in water. For this latter element nature has given you an unusual advantage. Your paws are provided with membranes that extend to the end of your claws, and give you the ability to swim and dive like amphibians. This allows you, when hungry, to snap up the fish that you fancy just as they do. When you have none of these creatures from the deep to chew on around the bay, you gang together like cutpurses, and head off, rejecting all hope of food that will never be forthcoming. You make for the plains, where there are large, red field mice in plenty, and decimate these animals at will, depending on your appetite. During the snows, thanks to the kindness of your masters, you live on salt or dried fish, carcasses of seal or polar bear, and the spoils from the caribou hunt. You richly deserve to have a good share in these when they are cut up, for I noted earlier that, when everything is covered with snow, you are harnessed like horses to sleds on which your masters sit, armed from head to toe. They point you where they wish, and you carry out their orders without complaint. When they set you on the track of a herd of caribou, if the footprints are fresh, you can tell either by the scent or by looking at them that a good meal is waiting for you if you guide your hunters well and let them shoot one or more of these animals. Then, instinctively and driven by need, you always do what you alone can to satisfy the hunger that often spurs you on.

In the settlements you alone fulfill all of the duties that are shared in Europe among many domestic animals. You give essential service to your masters, for they have only you as their sole means of transportation. When the sea is frozen, you haul them where they wish, from one harbour to another, faster than a stagecoach on our roads. You do all the hauling of their wood for heating and building, etc. These are certainly good reasons to command our respect.

Alongside such sterling qualities, you have many faults that scarcely do you honour. There is a proverb that says that foxes do not eat their own. But in your home country, you Newfoundland dogs sometimes eat yours.

If one of your kind comes over to France and, on its return, goes to pay you a visit, it is immediately devoured. You have also been known to behave this way among neighbours. So it is hardly surprising that, when you are hungry, other dogs from France suffer the same fate if you find them within striking distance. These facts are shameful, and you cannot dispute their accuracy. Several times I have had the misfortune to see you play this disgraceful fashion.

I remember one day when a captain going by one of your settlements had taken the wise precaution of putting a very pretty dog under his arm. When he reached the seashore, he thought there was no danger and put the little animal that he was so fond of on the ground. He thought that his dear Colibri was no longer threatened by your voracity. But suddenly, several of you, leaping out of the depths of the bushes, where he had no idea that you were lying in wait, pounced on the poor little dog, tore it to pieces, and swallowed it practically without chewing.

So there are no useful animals without faults, not even you, Newfoundland dogs, who have the reputation of having a gentle, and, I was going to add, hospitable disposition. But I see that it is in your stomach, when you are hungry, that you give hospitality to foreigners and even to those of your race. At moments like these, you are hardly models of gentleness, are you?

In France, you are not so cruel; I do not believe that you can be reproached for such atrocities. This is no doubt because, in that country, unlike in your own, you are not fed on slaughter. This must necessarily improve your rather primitive disposition and make you less thirsty for blood.

CHAPTER 8

The muskrat—How to hunt it—The Newfoundland fox, and how to hunt it—The French fox and the Newfoundland fox, a fable

Like beavers and otters, muskrats live by streams and ponds; they eat fish and plants, especially the stems of the water lily.

Once the hunter has found suitable places for this hunt, which he does by circling the ponds, he is almost certain to take all the muskrats there, for they are much less timid than other amphibians.

If one sees broken or cut grass by the edge of the water, or worn and well-used paths under the banks,[127] or fresh droppings on the pebbles and small rocks at the surface of the water, these signs mean guaranteed success.

In the morning at first light, or in the evening, at sunset, you can kill these animals from cover by placing yourself in the areas that they frequent most often.

The most lethal method is traps; they are set along the paths used by the rats. You put a few small branches on each side, leaving a gap that is just the size of the device. You dig a small hole, to fit the shape of the trap, which you place inside it. You cover it with a little grass. This method always meets with complete success.

---

127 Carpon uses the word *banques*; he explains that this is derived from the English *banks*, adding that it describes the overhanging lip of the edge of a waterway. (Translator's note.)

You must, however, take care to attach these traps with metal chains, for the victim, or one of its friends, could cut through ropes, and you would risk losing everything. If you do not set the trap on their trail, you can make do by grilling a little bacon rind, or meat from a bird, and fixing it on the plate. This method is foolproof. Wherever you place the trap, they are attracted by the smell. Even when you set traps on their trails, never neglect this trick if you have a chance to use it. It is by far the best method, and has always worked for me. The skin of a muskrat sells in Newfoundland for 2 francs 50 centimes (2 English shillings), and no matter what treatment it is given, it retains its smell of musk indefinitely.

The most common amphibians, such as seals, otters, beavers, and muskrats are the only animals whose skins are good during the summer season that we spend in Newfoundland. This is why we say that there is only one day in the year when their skins are no good: the day when we do not take any.

The Newfoundland fox, which is quite common in the forests of this island, has the same appearance and instincts as the one found in France, except that it has a much thicker coat. Mother Nature, in her provident wisdom, knowing that in such climes it would not be at all easy to survive lightly clad, was able to provide for the situation by dressing them very warmly. So these creatures have a magnificent coat, highly valued in winter and worthless in summer because of the moulting of the fur. Around mid-September, the skins start to be good. During these last two weeks of the season on the coast, it is sometimes possible to come across them, and I will pass on to those interested my most successful tactics for doing this.

With a good hound, you make for the largest thickets, heading for the upper side, following the mountain ridge where there are no woods. The dog will look for the trail of the fox in the plain and among the rocks, where it has wandered at night to catch partridge and large field mice, which constitute its main food supply. Seeing the dog penetrate the denser part of the woods, you station yourself in the clearings, where there are small strips of open ground of varying length that connect up with other thickets. It is nearly always here that the animal passes, looking for a way to remain hidden while on the run. Whether the hunter sees or hears it, at the slightest noise he has to raise his gun, and fire as soon as he has a chance. As you can imagine, when you have only a small window in which to spot a fox that is liable to be moving at speed, the time lost in putting a rifle to your shoulder is enough for the animal to escape to freedom.

If it goes to ground, the dog scratching at the hole will leave you in no doubt as to where the den is. You must look carefully to see if there are several holes; you plug them hard, and set a trap inside the entrance hole, that you then also three-quarters plug. The fox, seeing a little daylight, prefers to come to that one, and finds itself caught in the trap set in the half-light. If you have no traps, a sulphur wick, placed upwind after all has been quiet for a while, often makes it come out and gives you a chance to kill it. When you are sure of their lairs, if there are several hunters, you take up your position there and kill them a few moments after they have been flushed out by the dog: for they do not allow themselves to be hunted for long before going to ground. In winter, when they are starving, they can be caught with bait by surrounding a seal carcass with traps. But before the snow comes, they can be taken easily by setting traps along their most travelled tracks. You must take care to put on either side of the trap a small branch which forces them to take a little jump at the very spot where their foot is to be caught.

One of the very best methods is lying in wait in moonlight.

You climb into a fir tree, beside the sea, in places where you know that geese and wild duck come to sleep. These birds always alight first in the middle of a bay and come to the shore to settle in the grasses when darkness falls.

Foxes come there to surprise them, and you can easily shoot these thieves without a dog if you are quiet. Since you can often kill several one after the other, it is a good idea to let the first one that you shoot lie where it falls and not leave your hiding place.

In Newfoundland these animals are found in many different colours: some are white, golden, or red, others are black, blue, silvery, or of mixed colours. The white, golden, and red are the least sought after. In the past, the blue and black commanded an enormous price, but since these skins have been imitated by dyeing, they have greatly dropped in value. Since the shades of the silver fox cannot be effectively recreated by this process, its fur costs from 60 to 75 francs locally.[128]

FABLE
The French Fox and the Newfoundland Fox

>A fox, watching over some rabbit holes,
>Turning round, saw, sniffing in a garden,
>A superb animal of unknown kind,
>Whose rare beauty fascinated his eyes.
>Being learned, he began to reflect ...
>"Never," he said, "in the many regions
>"That I have explored since my tender youth,
>Have I seen anywhere a beast like this:
>It's not a badger, a wolf, cat or dog!
>How can I find out for sure what it is?
>From the wood that overlooks the river,
>I can leave the burrow quite easily
>And satisfy my curiosity.

---

128 Newfoundland has red and silver foxes. The colouring of both is variable, which accounts for the various shades mentioned by Carpon. They also interbreed. (Translator's note.)

Silver fox. Photo: M. Wilkshire.

I have a good nose, so with no danger
I'll go and try to find out right away."
Giving up his watch, he came to the mark
Beside the trail; and from there he could see
All that he wanted so keenly to know.
He was a sly one, philosophical,
His speeches were filled with good, sound logic;
So, being one for mature reflection,
He noted well the stranger's description:
"It has a slender build and pointed ears
With an elegant nose and bearded jaws;
It has a huge tail with long, fluffy hair;
Its eyes, like my own, are full of sparkle:
It too is a fox, there is not a doubt;
I shall greet it." So he starts on his way,
Draws near, bows, says "My Lord, with great respect
I have the honour to be your servant."
The stranger replies most politely, says
He is pleased to be in his company
And to converse with him for a moment.
"You see this land? I am bored to death here;
But not because I wish to live no more,
Rather because I miss my own country;
Last year, when abroad, my master brought me
Back to your French soil from the Ha Ha rocks."[129]
"I can clearly see from your appearance
That you, sir, are a fox of quality.
Our brothers here are not silver-coloured;
I compliment you, you are most handsome."
"The creator of nature made us thus

---

[129] A large bay on the coast of Newfoundland, near the Gulf of St. Lawrence. (Author's note.)

To brave the cold of our icy country;
But I was not born to live in your climes,
Where after a few steps I start to pant:
For, you see, today the ground is frozen,
And my whole body is steaming with heat!
You see, I bear the burden of great warmth;
While you shiver and shrink inside your skin,
For me, staying here is a dreadful trial.
Oh! To see Newfoundland's forests again! ..."
"Empty wishes, my American friend;
Never will you see your country again;
But I am pleased to make your acquaintance."
"I shall long remember your kind welcome."
"For those of our race who live in these parts
It is written: 'Honour to foreigners!'
This maxim is in no way new to us;
And I shall give you the proof straight away,
If you will honour me with your presence
In our dark lair, our welcoming refuge."
"I should like to, but I think it is time
To go back to my comfortable home."
"But you would be the lowest of the low
If you had not at least a few minutes
You could spend freely on fine hunting days.
Do you hunt for rabbit, partridge, woodcock?"
"I'm afraid not; mice, rats, moles, and field mice
Are the only creatures I can mix with."
"Small fry—quite good, when there is nothing else;
But we do better, brother, you will see;
To show you I mean to make you my friend,
I seal a bond with you here on this day;

We appoint you the chief of this household
Where my family and I live in riches."

And the signal from father to foxes
Has hardly been given when from all sides
The new friend is given a solemn greeting,
With the young presenting the accolade,
Astonished at the sight of the brightness
Gleaming on every hair of the creature.
"You cannot stop admiring his tunic?
He has just come from North America,
My children; and if he needs anything,
Make sure that he has every attention."
"We certainly will!" cried the wily race.
"He will have the finest from our kitchen."
All leap to his neck in a warm embrace.
"Well, you told me 'Honour to foreigners!'"
"What kindness of heart! And what gallantry!"
"With you, I am feeling happy again."
"Is that not my son just over the hill?
Look, my children: yes, it's he, it's Crafty,
Laden with game, I told you he would be.
Just in time, I am dying of hunger."
Crafty lays his rabbits beside the den,
And goes to tell his father of his trip.
But, at the first look, he stops in mid-flight,
To pay the foreigner his compliments,
Extended with grace, respecting manners,
A talent he has possessed since his youth.
Their guest answers this welcome joyfully,
Finishing with: "Where could things be better?"

The father says: "We shall begin this feast,
Before setting out on a new conquest;
Since we have the honour to have you here,
Would you please be seated beside me, sir?"

The foreigner, seeing the copious fare,
Is not the last to get down to business.
The master of the house splits a rabbit
And puts half right under his neighbour's nose;
All are served just the same; in a moment
Our guest has eaten a satisfying meal.
They rise, praising the dishes' quality,
Complimenting Crafty on his success.
The replete throng announce an amusement
To our American; being polite,
He cannot refuse. They go to the woods
Where hares and rabbits are lying asleep.
Crafty prepares his men for the battle,
All quite ready to stock up on their food.
The American hides in a furrow,
Crafty looks for rabbits, and drives out two
Who are lifeless in two snaps of the teeth.
The other hunters do their job as well,
So that in a while there are twelve dead ones.
The troops gather; in the mouths of the strong
Hang rabbits and hare that they take back home,
Where this time they enjoy a meal so good
That our adventurer no longer thinks
Of either his master or Ha Ha rocks.
"What," says one of them, "if we made a change?
Rabbit and then more rabbit is boring;

We need more succulent dishes to eat;
We will find some to tickle your palate,
Right under the nose of your master's dogs.
We here should look on him as a traitor;
As his foreign guest you should have had some.
We shall punish him, just leave it to us."
"Friends, companions, I thank you sincerely;
But do not forget me; I am with you."
So it was. And that night, when all was calm,
Our Newfoundlander went into the pen,
Wreaking dreadful carnage among the ducks,
Tearing turkeys and capons from their cage,
Cutting their necks, taking them to his friends,
Who took them straight off to hide in the woods.
"That's not all yet; let's come back tomorrow,
Not one will escape, none is swift enough."
When the sun rose, the grieving barnyard
Formed a small committee at the doorway.
Amazed, they looked and saw by the number
How many good birds had been carried off.
"Who is the thief? We shall find out tonight."

Without saying a word, they take cover.
Night falls; the foxes with ravenous mouths
Come back once again to look for the fowl.
While praising the brave prowler's cleverness,
They say to each other, "He's a filcher,
We can let him come out and show himself;
He will pay for his rashness with his life."
They wait for him, and as soon as he comes
They take aim, and four shots are fired at him.

He is hit and falls over; he expires;
His handsome coat becomes a hand-warmer.

If you are from Newfoundland or elsewhere,
You can be deceived by those you call friends;
Remember honour is worth more than life,
Never associate with bad company.

CHAPTER 9

More on hunting—The hare and how to hunt it—Ptarmigan and how to hunt it—Excursions and hunting for curlew—The Canada goose—How to hunt it—Similar information on ducks—Advice to hunters

The Newfoundland hare is similar in appearance to the one found in France; it also has the same habits. But it differs in its size, which is much larger, and in the shade and length of its fur. In spring it is an ash colour; in winter it is as white as snow. This metamorphosis is a great help to it in escaping from the teeth of foxes and the claws of hawks and eagles, which are common in these parts. It would be difficult, if not impossible, to hunt for this animal in Newfoundland in the same way that we do in France. A hare is flushed out by dogs in a forest of fir trees; it always runs away downwind, so as to be able to hear the voices of its enemy clearly. When there is a strong breeze, you do not know where the chase is taking place, and even if you knew, it would sometimes take you a day to get there. You would still be no further forward, for if you are unfortunate enough to get into dense woods, it takes forever to get out of them again. Since one cannot count on the animal doubling back, this hunt is carried out successfully only on relatively small islands with little tree cover. Hare go there in winter over the ice, and cannot get back when it moves away from the shore; then, if assisted by a good dog, the hunter is sure to kill every last one of them, since they cannot escape.

On the mainland you take advantage of a fine day for this hunt, when the hare is no longer deep in the woods but sunning itself in flat areas and among the small bushes scattered over the rocks and hills. By quietly following a docile dog, you are led to a form, where you kill the animal or shoot it as it is running away.

These quadrupeds are not shy; I have seen them appear under my feet and stop to lick themselves while looking up at me. This sense of security resulted in their sudden downfall!

In this country, as in ours, you can kill them from cover morning and night, when you know where they go to feed.

Their meat is excellent, and tastes like that of our own hare, who feed on wild thyme on the barrens.

When it looks as if it will be a fine day, the ptarmigan, the Newfoundland partridge, utters its cry from the first light of day, on mountaintops and in the plains, where it goes for its first meal. It is to be found especially in areas well provided with wild berries such as those that grow on crowberry plants, raspberry canes, currant bushes, and on a small shrub that is commonly called by the French *plate-bière* and by the English *bakeapple*, that is to say apples baked in the oven; in fact, the similarity of taste is remarkable.

Then our fine bird retreats into the neighbouring thickets, preferably where there are birch, for it is extremely fond of the young leaves of this tree. When the weather is fine, it starts out again on its travels around 9 or 10 a.m., and does not take cover in the shade until noon. Around 3 p.m. it once more comes out of the thicket, and does not return there again that day, unless it is obliged to by the strength of the wind or rain, or is pursued by some enemy.

No matter where it is, a good dog will soon find it for you. If you do not have a pointer, you hold a hound on a chain, slip a leather thong through the ring of this lead and tie it to your belt to allow for freedom of movement. You walk through areas that are protected from the wind;

your dog leads you to the game, and soon you see it running under the hound's nose. If the dog barks or thrashes about in an effort to run after it, you give it two or three lashes of the whip, calling out "Quiet!" This does not cause the ptarmigan to run away: they simply raise their heads even higher. You drive all of them in front of you, to group them together and kill as many as possible with your first shot. I have killed 13 with the first shot, three with the second, reloaded my rifle, and, without changing my spot, meted out the same treatment to the three that were left. This is what you should do, not retrieving them until you cannot see any more, but making sure that you begin by firing at the cock and hen. They are the leaders, and could take the rest of their fine family with them into dense thickets, from where they might not emerge for a long time.

With a setter, or any other breed tied on as I just explained, it is possible to use a net to take these magnificent birds that you see nesting under small bushes; you feed them in cages covered with canvas so that they do not injure their heads; the best food you can give them, if you do not have any small local berries, is buckwheat.

The Newfoundland ptarmigan is delicious in the season when these fruits are available; they are its main food supply, along with wild apples, currants, and raspberries.

The meat of this bird is considered by some naturalists as being potentially toxic at certain times of the year.

I have eaten a great many of them, from June through to October; neither I nor my friends have ever experienced the slightest indisposition from doing so. In winter, the settlers love them, and all they get from consuming their meat is good health and the pleasure of eating it. So, in what area and at what time of the year is ptarmigan poisonous? What is the cause of it? Without wishing to be accused of undue curiosity, I should like to have precise information on this point, not fairy tales. One thing that is quite certain is that when the French ships arrive on the

Newfoundland coast, this variety of partridge is not, by a long way, as good as it is in the fruit season. All it has to live on are a few grasses, and fir, spruce, and birch buds; its meat has a slight flavour of turpentine at that time of year, but it is not unpleasant or harmful.

Like the local hare, it adapts perfectly to the French climate; both of them, as in their native country, undergo a metamorphosis in winter by becoming as white as snow.[130]

The curlew, which arrives in Newfoundland between the 10th and 20th of August, leaving around the end of September, comes, they say, from the Cordilleras.

A few days before its arrival, from first light on, you hear little cries that seem to be saying *ti ti ti*: these are the whistling curlew, which fly around the harbours and mountains to announce the imminent return of their comrades; a few days after this vanguard, you see countless numbers of them flying around in every direction, particularly in areas where there is as much of the crowberry,[131] their favourite food, as they can eat. This plant grows on mountains where there is no shade;[132] it is much like moss, and produces a small fruit that is black and round, the size of a pea.

When the curlew have eaten, they cannot move without stumbling and bumping into each other, squawking continuously, like chatterboxes. This is because they are in a state of inebriation: the crowberry contains many alcoholic elements, which keep these birds in a state of drunkenness, especially in the first days after their arrival, because they are so little used to eating it.

Once they have fed themselves on the plains, or on the mountaintops, the curlew go to the seashore to let their stomachs settle; there they swallow fine, white gravel, which immediately makes them hungry again.

---

130 Carpon sounds as if he is speaking from personal experience after taking some of these animals back to France with him. (Translator's note.)

131 We have to presume that this plant grows as well under the bright sunlight of Italy as in the icy climate of Newfoundland, for it was not unknown to the Latin poet when he wrote: *Vaccinia nigra leguntur* (Virgil). (Author's note)
      This is a quotation from Virgil's *Eclogue II*: "the black whortleberry is gathered." (Translator's note.)

132 In Newfoundland these hills are known as *bare mountains*. (Author's note.)

After the curlew have gorged themselves for a few days on the crowberry, popularly known as *curlew berry*, they become so fat that they can hardly fly; if they fall on a rock when they are shot, they split open, and when it is hot their fat drips through the gamebag.

If you walk over the hills you can kill a large number of them by imitating their cry; they land a short distance away when you have called them properly, and since they are not at all timid, you move close to them so that you can shoot them easily. Anyone who does not want to go to the trouble of walking long distances often has better success by taking cover in places where they land at high tide. You can come back loaded with them after waiting for only short periods.

When you empty your seines, you spread these huge nets out to dry on places where there are a lot of crowberries, and, with the help of a few lengths of wood, you raise them 50 centimetres from the ground so that the birds can easily pass underneath; they become caught in the mesh, like quails under a draw net.

Gastronomically, the curlew is one of the best bipeds that nature has to offer, so hunting it is an attractive proposition for navigators on the coast of Newfoundland.

The areas that are richest in game of this species are: Bell Island near Groais, Great Islets, Goose Cove, Fichot, Croque Harbour, Great Brehat, White Cape, North Bay, and the huge and magnificent bay of Quirpon or Carpunt.

The Canada goose, incorrectly referred to as a bustard,[133] is a bird of greyish colour, with a black head and a long, arched neck; it is somewhere between the French swan and goose. The normal weight of this web-footed bird is 7 to 8 kilograms when it is fully grown, and a great number of them come to Newfoundland to nest in the spring; they return with their offspring when winter is drawing near.

In the fruit season, geese are found on the plains in large groups;

---

133 The word Carpon uses is *outarde*, commonly used to describe the Canada goose but also means bustard. (Translator's note.)

this is the moment when their meat is at its most succulent. To carry out this hunt successfully, it is best to have several people. You guess the approximate direction they are likely to take once they fly up from the area where they are feeding.

Hunters place themselves in the hollows between the hills and hide themselves with care. Others do their best to approach the geese, driving them toward the places where the others are lying in ambush. Inevitably, they manage to kill some in one way or another. Sometimes it happens, both in flat areas and on ponds, that you come across some that have barely reached maturity. In that case, a successful hunt is guaranteed and, in a few minutes, they are all yours.

After flying all day long over plains and ponds deep in the woods, the Canada goose is instinctively inclined to go and take refuge at the head of bays, where small grassy areas are crossed by streams of fresh, clear water, running down from the mountains and into the sea. This is no doubt to escape the teeth of the fox and the claws of the eagle.

At nightfall, the geese warn you of their arrival with their loud, rhythmic cries, like that of the swan, and you can shoot them in flight with large lead balls and shot.

After circling around several times, they land in the middle of the bay. Take cover in the bushes and wait for them where you have noticed that the grass is flattened and covered with their droppings. They come ashore at nightfall, and once they are on land, you shoot as soon as they gather together, so as to kill as many as possible. If they come too late and you are unable to see the sight on your weapon, be prepared for this problem by putting a piece of white cloth or paper on the barrel, and you will be able to shoot just as well as in full daylight.

Many hunters are not anxious to spend a night at the head of a bay, but this is no reason for them to miss this excellent game. They should take a supply of a few handfuls of wild fruit, especially crowberry. They can set snares, traps, and triggered snares, popularly known as *jumping-snares*,[134] and, with the bait they have brought, they can attract these birds to their devices.

The stakes to attach them have to be firmly fixed, for the bird is extremely strong. As a precaution, you have to tie the stake with a strong line to a heavy stone; otherwise, you would risk wasting your time and energy.

Another important precaution is the frequent checking of the lines you have set to prevent the game being eaten by carnivores.

The meat of the Canada goose is excellent however it is prepared. Anyone who can lay his hands on one is fortunate!

Let us move on to duck-hunting.

From the tops of the mountains you will see a great many ponds, and even though you cannot see any game, you should still approach these ponds, selecting those surrounded by tall grass and situated in the middle of plains.

Ducks and other waterfowl, after paddling around on the water, go to these marshes to rest. By walking among them a short distance from the edge of the water you flush out the game and kill it easily, especially in August, when these birds do not have enough strength in their wings to undertake a long flight. You take cover while your dog swims after them, and he will bring them back into your range.

If need be, you can take them with snares, and with hooks baited with earthworms or small fish. But for anyone who knows how to use it, the gun is the quickest method.

These birds are much like those in France, and their meat has the same taste.

Teal and wigeon are also found in the same areas, and they are taken in the same way.

These marshy plains provide cover for many snipe, of exactly the same species as in France. They are, however, much less timid, which

---

[134] The term Carpon uses is *sauterolles*. (Translator's note.)

means that the hunter can take them very swiftly. I have never seen any large woodcock in Newfoundland, nor have other sportsmen who, like myself, have been on long excursions deep into the forests.

Hunting of any kind is enjoyable only insofar as it can be carried on without fear or danger. It has a particular attraction here, because of the abundance of game and the ease of taking it, provided one has a little practice and skill. However, it would lose much of its pleasure if the hunter were preoccupied by worry. To avoid this drawback, let us put caution first and foremost. Permit me, then, to offer two pieces of advice before leaving this subject.

When you go hunting in Newfoundland, it is never wise to go alone. You hardly have to leave the shore before finding yourself in total isolation. If you were injured, what would become of you? You would be condemned to die of hunger and be eaten by wild animals, if the searches undertaken to find you were unsuccessful.

Another sound piece of advice.

When you reach the harbour where you are to spend the summer, before setting off on a trip, go to the top of the surrounding mountains. Set a pole there, and prevent it from falling over with a pile of rough stones. From there, look around for the most likely areas for finding game. Set a similar indicator on all of the highest points in these remote locations, so that, having travelled great distances, you can find your way back as the crow flies to your Robinson Crusoe-style abode, where you can happily set down the fruits of your travels.

CHAPTER 10

Various kinds of fishing—Fishing for small cod—Toad-fish—Flatfish and how to catch them—Abundance of crustaceans and how to catch them—Catfish—Trout and how to catch them—Salmon and how to catch them—An eminent man among Newfoundland Redskins—Culinary art of the aboriginals—Reluctance to winter in Newfoundland—Farewell to these parts—Crossing back to France—Fishing for porpoise—Tuna and how to catch it—Arrival in France

I would like to think that my three preceding chapters have been of interest to anyone who enjoys going into the country with a rifle over his shoulder and a gamebag slung on his back. The latter, at least, does not stay empty in Newfoundland, as it often does in some parts of France, where it is not unusual for a city-dweller to return home in the evening crestfallen and exhausted, reduced to filling his bag at the local store, if he is worried about an unflattering reception from his loving wife.

If hunting is pleasurable and highly profitable in these parts of North America, fishing is no less so. Let us say a few words about fishing, first for small cod.

These fine fish should not be dismissed by anyone interested in angling as a recreational activity. Toward the end of the main fishery, it is a pleasure to see them arriving in thousands when the tide is ebbing and flowing beneath the wash houses and stages where, the following year, they in turn may well be salted, for they quickly reach the stage in their growth where they are marketable. If you should take it into your head not to give them time to grow, your line is hardly cast before this famished throng appears at the surface of the water, casting their greedy eyes on the bait that is offered, and the first on the scene quickly swallows it. The liver and eyes of one of these gluttons are a guaranteed lure to entice all of its friends to fall into the trap, and you can reel them in as long as you wish. The meat of these young fish is delicious when it is fresh; some is dried to be taken back to Europe.

Together with these pretty little fish, there are some extremely ugly ones; among others, there is one that has a head rather like that of a toad, which has caused these denizens of the deep to be called *toad-fish*. Their voraciousness is unequalled, in spite of their small size, which is hardly any greater than the mullet along our coasts. The mouth, esophagus, and stomach have powers of dilation so great that they give these fish the ability to swallow something almost as large as themselves.

From the base of the nape to the beginning of the pointed tail, the silky, smooth skin of this fish has shades of green, yellow, red, and violet, like that of the salamanders that are often found in the evening after a rainstorm, in muddy spots, and around old walls. This similarity in shape and appearance with reptiles, especially with the most repulsive, instills in some people an insurmountable aversion to consuming the flesh of these ugly animals. Others, far from feeling sick, consider them a delicacy and claim that their taste is exquisite. There is no need to fish them with a line; you simply spear them with hooks that are attached to both sides of the end of a pole. You dispatch them in this way when they lie motionless on their stomachs on the sand. This is their usual position, for their constitution prevents them from indulging in the nimble movements of fish of other species.

Since they are not agile swimmers, they resort to lying in wait, a practice from which they make an admirable living. From time to time I would amuse myself watching them swallow small cod that I allowed to wriggle on the end of my line so that I could lift both the victor and the vanquished out of the water. I also enjoyed watching the instinctive way in which they would hide under seaweed with their nose against a piece of bait that they were very careful not to touch. All the small cod that came to feast on it promptly entered the funnel-like mouth of this wily toad. This sight reminded me of the tricks of our friend the fox, who has just been fed; in order to obtain a few treats while in captivity, he makes a trail of the remains of his meal outside his house, and then burrows under the straw so that the gullible chickens can be convinced that he is either away or dead. But the fatal moment arrives when the so-called corpse leaps through his covering in a single bound, falling on these poor hens and crunching them up for dessert.

Among the inhabitants of the deep, about whom, friendly reader, I have a few things to tell you, one can see gleaming on a handsome bed of fine sand the flatfish with its sparkling eyes. Its skin, spotted like the plaice, has infinitely varied colours that are further enhanced by bright sunlight. It is sought after by gourmets because of its excellent quality. An hour before the meal, in certain harbours such as Griquet, Northern Bay, Quirpon, etc., you catch as many as you want, and the cook serves them up to you prepared however you want.

They are caught in the same way as the toad-fish.

This variety of plaice is much better at the beginning of the main fishery than at the end, because during this latter period they feed on rotten offal.

The crab, lobster, mussels, and other shellfish that live around stages are also less desirable because of this. If you wish to eat good ones, you have to go and fish them in bays where cod is not split. They are caught with a small net known as a dip net, shaped like a cap, or with the famous implement used for toad-fish, but it is preferable to use the former if you intend to keep them, for they die and decompose very quickly once their shell has been pierced. Another implement, commonly known as a gaff, is also most useful for this fishery. It consists of a very solid hook firmly attached to the end of a piece of wood. When the tide is on the ebb, go down to the rocks covered in seaweed. If you see a hole with a small mound of sand, like a molehill, at the entry, push your hook inside it, and you will pull out at least one lobster, unless the resident has been flushed out by a very clever fish known as the catfish.

When you put anything in contact with this fish, it pounces on it, whether it be wood or metal, bites it as if it were a wild dog, thrashing its head and tail and uttering harsh cries, perhaps showing the despair it feels at having reached the last moment of its life. Since they are good for nothing except doing harm, these vicious creatures are pitilessly cut to pieces.

In a small boat with a shallow draft, go out looking for lobsters among the seaweed, scattered rocks, or any area where marine plants provide some shelter and shade. Along the edges of this submarine undergrowth, there are bare, sandy areas to which you should pay particular attention, if you wish to take huge catches of magnificent lobsters, for this is their preferred habitat. Sacred Bay and Pistolet Bay, as well as others next to the Gulf of St. Lawrence, are full of them. It is easy to fill a boat with them in a few minutes, if you pay careful attention to the sandy molehills where these gentlemen install themselves. They can easily be seen in calm weather, even in places where the depth of water is too great for you to bring them up.[135]

The reason, incidentally, for these small mounds is that this creature likes to rest undisturbed. To do so, it makes a hole of some depth, a task that it cannot accomplish without piling up sand. It lies down in this cavity, which serves as a bed, just like a hare in its form, with its nose resting on its two large claws, both of which rest on the sand that forms the mound. If you want to catch it with a dip net, you place the net behind its tail with one hand, and with the other you push it into it with a stick that you pass repeatedly over its antennae. This tickling is

---

[135] In Newfoundland, the movement of the rising and falling of the tide is scarcely noticeable, except in a few unusual circumstances; it is doubtless due to the fact that they are so little disturbed that one can attribute the clarity of the waters in these parts; at first light, on a calm and clear day, it is not unusual to be able to see whatever objects are lying on the sand at a depth of 7 or 8 fathoms. (Author's note.)

guaranteed to make it start moving backward. But if you wish to eat it straight away, then, to get the job done more quickly, you pierce its shell with the same lethal implement as before.

Crab is fished in the same way, and also with nets shaped like a trap, known in fishing terminology as pots.

However excellent they may be, let us leave these crustaceans in their sandy lairs and return to our fine fish.

Newfoundland trout, like those in Canada, Labrador, and other parts of North America, are of variable size; some are enormous. Except for the colour, they are physically the same as in France, but they are all pink and of the most exquisite flavour. You fish them in small streams or *brihats*,[136] either with a net or a line. The line fishery is the more sporting. Anyone who knows how to fish should take a pole with a reel on which is wound a good line, 12 or 15 fathoms long, and that is free of knots. This should enable you, in areas where there are no roots or overhanging banks, to drown any large fish that you hook. The finest specimens are found by waterfalls close to the sea. The best material for the line is what is known in France as fenugreek or unknown grass.[137] At the end of this line, you attach securely a fathom of silkworm gut or goat hair[138] that you have previously braided; to do that, you leave these small threads of gut to soak for an hour in a little water, then take them out of the water to braid them in pairs, as you would with hemp, taking care to put them in ash from time to time. This enables you to roll your leaders as much as you wish because it makes them less slippery to your fingers.

After this initial operation, you tie them end to end with a double knot. At the tip you tie a red fly with a yellow and gold body.

---

136 This is the name commonly given to streams in Newfoundland. Can this expression be a corruption, via the Norman patois, of *bruits hauts* (loud noises)? In fact, there is one stream that rolls from one fall into another, making a noise that can be heard from 12 kilometres away; among others I can cite the one that runs into the head of Chimney Bay. (Author's note)

137 The term Carpon uses is *herbe grecque ou inconnue*. Herbe grecque (fenugreek) is a kind of moss found on rocks along the seashore in Mediterannean countries and is reputed to have medicinal properties. It also appears to have been used for braiding into lines. (Translator's note)

138 The term Carpon uses is *poil de Messine*. This is the hair of goats from southern Europe, generally considered too coarse for the manufacture of material, but used for making felt and for caulking. (Translator's note)

Although this fish is attracted to all colours, it is nonetheless true that out of three distinctively coloured flies, the one that I have just described is always the first to be taken, when three have been tied on the same gut. Incidentally, this method should not be used, and here is the reason why.

In the waters where you fish, it may happen that all of the lures are taken at the same time by large trout or salmon, which often pull in opposite directions and escape, each one with a piece of your line. This has happened to me, and I shall not be caught out again.

The day after we landed, in 1847, I went on an outing to the head of the South-West Bay at Griquet. I made the trip in a boat, with two of our officers who were in charge of 20 men sent to cut wood for construction.

At the head of the bay I saw a fairly narrow stream that you could step across in several places without getting wet, running swiftly over a bed of pebbles. Here and there, there were small pools of, at most, 0.5 metres in depth.

I looked closely but, seeing nothing, as it was bitterly cold, I went off to do a little hunting to start my blood circulating again.

After killing a few game animals, I came back to rejoin these gentlemen, and in spite of the harshness of the weather, I covered myself in a good fur jacket and put my line, as well as an enormous number of trout, into action. My fly was hardly on the water before a trout was hooked, and in a short space of time and out of a small patch of water I had more than 300 trout, including one weighing 3 kilograms.

To catch a large number of fish in a pond, you need a small boat or a raft that you can steer at will; once you are in the middle, you let it drift and catch as many trout as you wish. In these waters there is nothing but trout, salmon, eels, and a kind of smelt; the latter is taken with worms, whereas eels are caught by bottom fishing with lines baited with small fish or bird meat.

Along the streams or *brihats*, the fir trees are in some places so close to the water that, when the fisherman sees a good spot for fishing, he cannot cast his line without getting it caught up. Then you use another method. You replace the artificial flies with a hook fixed to a piece of double gut, and you put a trout's eye on this hook. With the aid of the reel, you pay out as much line as you want. You cast it between the branches to let it fall into the water, and many a time I have seen the bait taken before it goes under the water, with the trout duly punished for its gluttony.

In Newfoundland these handsome, tasty fish take no account of having escaped capture, and come back into the fray when their injuries are not too serious.

It has happened to me on many an occasion to see a large trout that I was allowing to run with my line, for fear of breaking it, become caught in the stump of a tree, free itself from the hook with a sudden jerk, resulting in the side of the jaw that was hooked being torn. I recaptured my fish an hour later, on a bottom line baited with a little bird meat. In the same way I have taken a great many that returned the artificial flies that they had stolen from me. These are, no doubt, fine and rich catches, but there are some that are even more valuable.

To catch salmon on the surface of the water, the best lure is the mottled butterfly put on very strong Irish hooks, with peacock, woodcock, rooster, and partridge feathers.

With the help of worms and trout's eyes, you can catch this fish on the bottom and in mid-water. In Conche, Cape Rouge, Croque, and other harbours, they set nets in which several hundred salmon are often caught. The area that is richest in fish of this kind is without question the head of Hare Bay. This fishery is a commercial venture, like the cod fishery, and the place, known as a salmon-fishing station, becomes the property of a single outfitter at the time of drawing for berths.[139] They make dams with nets, arranged so that the salmon put their head into

---

139   Every five years, the outfitters who fish on the coast of Newfoundland meet in Saint-Malo and draw lots for the harbours on the island. (Author's note.)
       This was the system put in place to replace the earlier tradition of berths being taken on a first-come, first-served basis. (Translator's note.)

them and stay there hooked by the gills. They are immediately drowned. But you must be careful if you wish to make use of the catch, for if you do not take care to check your nets frequently, eels come and open the bellies of the fish that are caught in this way, and eat their insides.

Seals have an insatiable appetite for salmon. When you see these amphibians arrive from the open sea in large groups, leaping through the water, it is a sure sign that they are pursuing the salmon, who inevitably enter the bay and come and throw themselves into the nets at the mouth of the river. Then you are doubly rewarded, for you shoot the salmon-lovers that come within range, while the others are terrified and go back out to sea, only to repeat the same performance. So the seals play a very important role in the success of the salmon fishery, since they drive these fish to their death, like a hound that clings tenaciously to a hare until its master has put it into his gamebag.

The savages in Pistolet Bay have fish traps consisting of vertical stakes and closely spaced bars, with several openings where they put fyke[140] nets made from hoops of birch, shaped like funnels. And they can honestly say to all these fish: "Come in, my friends, there is no charge, except on the way out." Since there is no depth of water, they kill them with the first blow from a piece of wood shaped like a sabre, and they use them as supplies for the winter.

In Pistolet Bay there is a sufficiently large number of salmon for you to be able to take 100 in a day by hand and with hook and line.

The aboriginal who at present (1847) is living at the head of the bay with his wife and children is called Joseph. He is a most pleasant, hospitable man who renders all possible services to the French and English, who go to him for wood suitable for masts and spars, and for all other jobs connected with fishing, as well as for any other needs. Besides his mother tongue, he speaks English and French; he is endowed with great intelligence, and, as far as I can tell from the conversations

---

140 A fyke net is a cylindrical or cone-shaped fish trap with wooden hoops to keep its shape. (Translator's note.)

that I have had the opportunity to hold with him, he will help all those of his race who have dealings with him to progress toward complete civilization. From his behaviour, I consider him to be a very worthy man, with whom I would live in complete security if his cooking were a little better prepared, but, like all his compatriots, he cooks the way he likes it, and for us French, it is a case of *noli me tangere* (do not touch it).

I shall put those interested in a position to judge.

After a friendly welcome, a civilized savage will cordially serve you a few seal ribs that have been tossed onto the lid of a moderately hot stove. After this brief sizzling, on high feast days they proceed to the rapid boiling of a fox, cut into pieces, in oil from the livers of cod or seal. If these animals are not available, they might offer you a salmon and some trout prepared in the same way. These people have fine taste, do they not?

Indeed, to do justice to such dishes, one needs an appetite and a stomach like the ones of these likeable hosts who burst out laughing when they see us looking distastefully at the fine fare that they themselves devour eagerly, almost in a raw state. As they eat little bread, they all tell you that meat no longer has any nutritional qualities when it is cooked, and that they would die of weakness if they were to eat it. So raw meat is their special food, and their version of an elaborate banquet is one where at the end of the meal you can wash down these tasty dishes with a few glasses of cod-liver oil.

Let me point out, however, that they prepare with great success hot drinks of wild tea that they sweeten with molasses and fortify with rum. They pour you this improvised punch in large cups and fill your pipes with excellent American tobacco.

I have several times received a friendly proposition to remain over the winter in Newfoundland and have been on the point of accepting. However, wiser reflection always steered me away from these fleeting fancies, and in the end I greeted my friends as follows:

> On your hillsides bristling with conifers,
> In mid-winter all you see is treetops:
> I have no wish to stay in all that snow.
> May your snowshoes[141] give you all protection!
> In your country, even in September
> I shiver with cold when far from the fire;
> So until next summer I say goodbye,
> If God keeps me alive until that time,
> And if I feel like coming back again.

So, after a stay of three months among these poor islanders, our thoughts went to our own dear country. The preparations for our return were quickly completed, and on 20 September 1847, we raised anchor and left Griquet Bay under full sail.

Generally, the return from Newfoundland to France is swift. As September approaches, the wind in these parts blows almost constantly from between west and northwest: a good, steady breeze from that direction can bring us back to within sight of our fair France in 12 to 15 days. It is rare, despite the problems that can occur during the journey, to have crossings of more than 25 days. In that season you are not held up by the ice pack, the presence of which along the coast in June can keep you offshore for what seems like an eternity when you are trying to land.

Despite the disappearance of this treacherous progeny of the polar regions,[142] you still see here and there on the return journey some huge pieces that the warmth of summer has been unable to melt. A strict watch day and night allows you to avoid easily the dangers of a collision. In misty weather the proximity of these masses is signalled by the noise of the waves breaking against them. In clear weather you can see the

---

141 Snowshoe: a strip of bent wood, with the two ends brought back into contact with each other, giving this equipment an approximately oval shape. The entire area in the middle is filled with straps of sealskin threaded in every direction; in the middle is a boot to hold the foot. Shod in this manner, one can go anywhere without sinking into the snow. (Author's note.)
142 This ice has sometimes been seen 450 nautical miles from the east coast of Newfoundland. (Author's note.)

shape of them and the white waves of foam that seem to rise up in anger against these icy mounds, just as they do against rocks on a shore. These pieces of floating ice increase the disturbance of the water a hundredfold when the sea is whipped up by the wind. You have to use the greatest caution to avoid these floating hazards, for a collision of this kind would deprive the crew of any chance of survival. With vigilance, however, these dangers can easily be avoided.

So let us cast aside these sombre thoughts and move to something more cheerful.

In this vein, who says that while we are travelling along we cannot indulge in a few reflections on gastronomy? Do not be shocked, friendly reader, if we return to the pleasures of the table; I can assure you that they are music to the ears of those who have been deprived of them. A little feasting, as the good man has said,[143] is indeed a happy prospect for men on board. This is the only distraction in their floating house. Remember that when you are confined to the limited space of the deck of a ship, you cannot, as on land, vary your leisure activities. For this reason, the table has to become the sailor's best-loved pastime, but men's pleasures are always incomplete. Despite the abundance of food, if it is not varied it soon ceases to tickle the palate. This proves the truth of the old proverb: *Mutton, nothing but mutton, is boring and distasteful.*

Having made a considerable dent in the bacon barrel, you say: "How I would love to sink my teeth into a good piece of fresh fish! I would savour every last morsel!" This is sometimes a strong and, incidentally, quite natural craving, but how can it be satisfied? There are no fish markets in the middle of the ocean.

If that is what you want, you have to fish for it. So this is the task that I am going to teach you. You know that before being a master you

---

[143] The expression Carpon uses for feasting is *chère lie*, which is found at the end of Chapter 25 of Rabelais's *Gargantua*, to which he is possibly alluding here. (Translator's note.)

have to be an apprentice, and that you learn by doing. Well, by analogy, it is by fishing that you become a fisherman!

You are not used to sea voyages, and consequently you are not well acquainted with the inhabitants of the deep. You look in ecstasy on schools of porpoise, and you ask your friends what is the name of these large fish and if they are good to eat. You ask about how to catch them. You will soon be satisfied. Hardly have your questions been put before you see nimble practitioners, skilled in the art of handling the harpoon, leap astride the spritsail yard, with the metal part of the instrument strapped to the halyard of a studding sail. They plunge it to the hilt into the body of these porpoises that had the effrontery to leap while moving around the ship, as if to mock the crew. Punished for their boldness, they are forced up on deck by the sailors' gaffs.

Those of you who are curious to show how well you can carry out this exercise will get the gist of it as soon as you have seen it done a couple of times, and experience will soon make you a skilful harpoonist, for, as Sancho says: *Fabricando, fit faber*.[144]

The fleshy parts of this viviparous fish ought to have a place in the culinary repertoire. They are eaten grilled or as steaks, after they have been left for a day or two in a marinade of vinegar, oil, pepper, salt, and chopped onions. If you drain the blood of the porpoise by towing it behind the ship in the fat-pork bag, you can prepare it in the same way as beef braised with carrots; the difference in taste is then so slight that anyone who did not know would not notice it. Sometimes the liver, the heart, and the lungs are also eaten. The rest is good only for rendering down into oil. But for sailors, all of this is not the most profitable sideline.

Let us tell our readers about an activity that is really worth the effort: catching tuna.

---

144 Literally, *working makes the worker*, or *practice makes perfect*. A reference to Sancho Panza in *Don Quixote* by Cervantes, though this was also a well-known Latin proverb. (Translator's note.)

The tuna is a fine-looking fish, round in cross-section, with a skin of a solid dark colour over the back, pale and ash-coloured under the belly. A forked cartilaginous tail forms the end of the backbone, which is made up of segments, also of cartilage, connected to a network of nerves covered with thick, fleshy muscles. On each side of the gills there are long, flexible fins which, in conjunction with great muscular strength, give the creature most unusual agility.

Tuna is abundant in certain parts of the Mediterranean but less common in the ocean. It is most frequently sighted about half way in the crossing from Newfoundland to France, and this is the preferred area for tuna fishing.

As it is possible to hook huge ones,[145] it is wise to use very strong hooks that are well tempered and tin-plated, cod hooks in fact. It is not too much to use a couple tied together with a piece of tarred line, but this gear can often fail. For greater strength it is better to have them both on a single shaft. You then bend this in the middle so that the curve of one of the hooks is parallel to that of the other.

A piece of cork shaped like a small fish has to be covered in white cloth coated with suet. Two hen's feathers stick out on the sides, for you have to imitate the flying fish as closely as possible, the tuna being extremely greedy for it. This artificial bait is attached with brass wire to the centre of the hooks and on their shafts. Another heavy copper wire, 1.5 fathoms in length, is passed through the opening where the ends of the two stems come together, and is wound onto itself over a length of 4 centimetres only.

The other end, intended to receive the line that has already been tied to the stern of the ship, is prepared in the same way, and then is thrown into the sea. The movement of the ship keeps the deceptive bait in continuous motion, and the breaking of a piece of sail thread that holds the line onto a boom, signals that a tuna has been hooked, a

---

145   This fish is also found around Newfoundland; in 1848 a seine master from Granville caught one that weighed 200 kilograms in Belle Isle, located between Labrador and Quirpon. (Author's note.)

method which rarely fails. Then some of the men haul it in hand over hand, so as not to leave it time to struggle in the water, and to force it to keep its mouth open, which brings on the beginnings of asphyxiation; others armed with gaffs hook it and promptly pull it up on deck for you.

In spite of its injuries, once the tuna has been freed of its hooks and set down with its nose in the scuppers, it executes rolls that are as regular as those of the finest master drummer. These rolls come from the incredible speed with which it moves its head and tail.

The meat of this fish is much like veal, both in colour and its taste: it is delicious however prepared. In countries where this fishery is carried on as a commercial venture, a large quantity is marinated.

These are the main incidents that amuse the traveller during the crossing on his way back to France. As I said, this crossing is completed quickly, and nearly always safely. So, after 16 days of calm sailing, we returned to the port of Granville, with our fine cargo of dried cod on 7 October 1847.

In the preceding account I have attempted to interest my compatriots in one of the most important tasks of the merchant navy, which is also the nursery and training school for that of the state. During the course of this work I had to struggle with a problem that the most skillful of writers are sometimes unable to overcome: that of clearly rendering an object through its description. Considering the obstacles that lay along my path, and the honesty of my intentions, I feel sure that the public will forgive the many shortcomings in my work. I hope that I have at least come close to my original goal:

Lectorem delectando pariterque monendo![146]

THE END

---

146 Horace, *Ars poetica* 343f.: "both delighting and instructing the reader." (Translator's note.)

*Account by Baron D.J. Larrey of his voyage
to Newfoundland in 1778*

Mémoires de chirurgie militaire et campagnes
Paris: Smith, 1812, tome 1 pp. 1–48.

Chapter 1: Campaigns and Memoirs

North American Campaign

When I was 13 I left my place of birth (Baudéan, near Bagnères-Adour, in the Hautes Pyrénées department, formerly the province of Bigorre) to go to Toulouse, with the intention of studying the art of healing, under the guidance of my uncle, Mr. (Alexis) Larrey, medical officer and professor at the general hospital of that city, and corresponding associate of the Royal Academy of Surgery of Paris.[147]

After completing my elementary studies at the college of Esquile and the schools of medicine and surgery of Toulouse, I made plans to move away from that city and go to other universities to acquire the knowledge required to practice the profession I had chosen.

I headed for the capital, arriving there in August 1787. A few days

---

[147] Director of the Toulouse Medical School. (Author's note.)

Baron Dominique-Jean Larrey. Stipple engraving by A. Tardieu. Public domain via Wikimedia Commons.

later, the famous Mr. Louis, Permanent Secretary to the Academy, announced a competition for a limited number of places as assistant surgeon in the navy, in the department of Brest. This development gave added impetus to my natural interest in travel; hence, even though it meant setting aside my initial plans, I did not hesitate to put my name forward, and I was fortunate enough to be given one of the positions available. I left immediately for the port of Brest, where I was to be ranked according to the results of a further examination. Since the season was favourable, I made this journey on foot,[148] with another assistant naval health officer.[149]

We were observant to all that aroused our interest and that merited our attention. After going through Mortagne, we stopped

---

148   The distance from Paris to Brest is 590 kilometres. (Translator's note.)
149   Mr. Lescot, a pharmacist in Paris. (Author's note.)

at the austere monastery of La Trappe, where in times gone by the unfortunate went to seek shelter and consolation. We were given hospitality for two days, which we devoted to visiting the interior of the monastery and touring its vast enclosure, including woods, arable land, pastures, and gardens. The principal monument that they showed us was the tomb of the Count of Comminges and his most unfortunate Adélaïde. The memory of these two lovers shut up in the same cloister, doing the same work, undergoing the same privations, endlessly pining for each other, and meeting every day without recognizing each other, could hardly fail to arouse our pity. "These two unfortunate souls," said the priest who was showing us around, "did not recognize each other until the last moments of their life. The death of one followed hard on the other, and they were reunited in the same grave."[150]

We followed the monks of this monastery in their religious exercises and in their various tasks; they cultivated the land and made themselves all that they needed for their clothing and the various necessities of life. On the third day, we left this place of retreat with a feeling of regret at leaving behind a number of young monks whose sad faces and emaciation indicated profound grief.

On our way through Laval, the birthplace of Ambroise Paré, the father of French surgery, we were shown to the house where he had lived. On going inside I was overcome with such a feeling of veneration that I allowed myself a gentle illusion: I felt that I was going to see this great man appear before us, when suddenly the presence of the owners of the house—they were weavers—coming to show us the bedroom that he had occupied, destroyed the power of the image that had taken hold of my imagination.

We continued on our way, and, on passing through Rennes, we

---

[150] This melancholy tale was popularized in a verse drama by François-Thomas-Marie de Baculard d'Arnaud called *Les amans malheureux* (*The Unhappy Lovers*), published in 1764. It would have had special resonance for Larrey since the lands of the Comte de Comminges were adjacent to the area where he was born. (Translator's note.)

were anxious to see the Parliament House. The sight of the torch-lit chamber with black hangings where prisoners were subjected to torture left a terrifying impression. From Rennes we made directly for Brest. I had never seen anything more majestic or more impressive than the fleet anchored in the enormous roadsteads of this port; we could see it from the high ground that overlooks it at a distance of about half a league [c. 2.4 km]. This was the first time that I had seen the sea, with its waves gently stirred by the wind, and it reflected with infinite variation the rays of a beautiful setting sun, offering me a sight that filled me with admiration. I stayed for a few moments in rapture, and would probably have remained there for several hours if we had not heard the gun sounding the retreat. We had to hurry to get inside the city before the gates were closed.

The chief naval health officers, Messrs. Billard, Lapoterie, and Duret, all three famous for their work and their writings, received me with kindness, and set me the second examination, along with the other surgeons who had come from Paris. I was appointed medical officer in the Royal Navy, at the age of 21 and, contrary to the custom, without ever having been to sea.

However, the Dutch, in support of whom the ships has been outfitted, had made peace with England, and since they were the reason the ships had been fitted out, the order was received from the minister to lay them all up, with the exception of those that were to go to the colonies to ensure respect for the French flag and to protect trade.[151] For the same reason, practically all the naval assistant medical officers were laid off, and I was one of the small number that the General Inspector and the Health Board chose to retain.

Soon after, I was sent on board the frigate or corvette *Vigilante*, as medical officer; it was under the command of Captain Chevalier

---

151 After a very troubled period in the 1780s, when the Netherlands had been a satellite of France, the Dutch entered into an alliance with Great Britain and Prussia. This was signed on 15 April 1788, just before Larrey's ship sailed for Newfoundland. (Translator's note.)

Saques de Tourès. While waiting for our departure, I spent the winter giving young students a number of anatomy and surgery lessons. I visited the penal institution where the convicts were kept, the arsenals, the stores, and the shipyards; I devoted myself to the study of navigation and everything concerning the functions that I was to carry out on board.

Among the convicts detained in the penal colony I was shown a man of 67 with the name of Louis Bourbon. He was kept in isolation in a small room, and treated with particular care. This old man was a very rare case: he could see things only in the shadow of darkness, and in daylight he was completely blind. Thirty-three years without any break in an underground dungeon had changed the functions of the organ of sight. The conversation of this unfortunate man was of great interest; with his resignation and the cheerfulness of his personality, he painted a fascinating portrait of his misfortunes. I have never heard anyone draw out of the flute sounds that were more harmonious, more filled with emotion, or more perfect. This instrument was the one thing that consoled him; his constant habit of playing it had caused his elbow, by pressure on his chest, to make a depression on the ribs in that particular spot, which we noticed some time afterward, when he died. We also observed a second and equally rare anatomical phenomenon when we opened the body of another convict, in whom we were astonished to find all of the viscera transposed.[152] Inside his chest, the heart was inclined toward the right; in the abdomen, the liver was to the left, the spleen on the right. The small extremity of the stomach was also on the left, and the intestines had undergone a corresponding transposition. This subject is preserved in the anatomy display of the naval school. A number of autopsies and several experiments that I conducted with Professor Duret provided us with other observations of equal interest that I shall have occasion to make known.

---

152 Several authors, particularly the immortal Bichat, report similar examples. (Author's note.)

The industry of the convicts is remarkable and provides proof of what perseverance in one's work can achieve. Being deprived of any kind of sharp or piercing implements, as well as all tools of any size such as mallets, hammers, or pincers, using nothing more than nails, pieces of files, etc., they succeed in making small ships of astonishing perfection, decorated with ivory, ebony, or mother-of-pearl; the rigging is put together with complete precision, and can be adjusted as desired. They make all kinds of jewellery, drawings, and mechanical instruments. They had even managed to copy banknotes and to make considerable sums of money from this counterfeit currency.

In April 1788, the order was given to prepare the *Vigilante* to sail on the first favourable winds; as medical officer, I was responsible for the supply of medications, dressings, and surgical instruments. I was also responsible for examining the supply of light food intended for the sick during the crossing and for having it properly stored and secured. I completed these tasks with great care, for I firmly believe that the medical officer of a ship has to pay great attention to them. We were on board a few days before raising the anchor. I spent them studying the ship, especially the rigging, various manoeuvres, the stowing, and the quantity and quality of the provisions taken on board for a voyage of this duration. I also learned about the working conditions of the sailor, the nature of the duties he has to carry out, their length, and the rest period that follows them.

Knowing that our ship was to go to North America, and specifically to the island of Newfoundland, to protect the cod fishery, I gathered from Dr. Lapoterie and several officers who had sailed in those parts all the information that they were able to give me on the nature of the climate and its effect on the health of Europeans, on the character of the residents of Newfoundland, the island of Newfoundland, and what that country produces. I collected information on the difficulty of the crossing, on the nature of the seas and the climates through which we had to pass to arrive at our destination. I armed myself with the works most likely to enlighten me and guide my conduct both on board the ship and on arrival in Newfoundland. I had an assistant medical officer and a student, both of whom were very knowledgeable and extremely eager. From the vast knowledge of the captain and the second mate, Chevalier Dutrevoux, who gave me their confidence and their friendship, I drew invaluable information on the study of navigation, natural history, and the geography of western countries. I did all that I could to profit from the lessons that I was receiving from the officers and the boatswains, for I was extremely anxious not to miss any opportunity to educate myself. And I was bursting with impatience to be launched on the vast ocean.

The winds were favourable, and the signal to leave was given. We sailed on 3 May at 3 p.m. The sky was clear, and the sun, in its second degree of declination, appeared to be preceding us on the path that we were to follow. The readying of the ship and the raising of the anchor are difficult manoeuvres and certainly most interesting for anyone who has never sailed. I shall pass quickly over the details of our navigation that are the same for all ships at sea. I shall dwell only on the unusual events that happened to us, and on observations on physiology, hygiene, or pathology that may be of some interest. Being kindly treated by the wind, we passed through the channel leading into the roads and rounded the two headlands formed by its shores in less than three hours. The land was receding, and soon it disappeared from our sight. The sun seemed to have been swallowed up at the opposite side of this watery plain. Light gave way to darkness, and for the first time I found myself on the open sea. This sudden transition and isolation made a most powerful impression on all of my senses. The prospect of an unfortunate end came to mind, and the saddest of thoughts quickly took the place of the excitement I had felt at the hope of seeing a new country and so many different things in the course of a long voyage. I was unable to hold back my tears, and I greatly missed the land that I had just left behind me.[153] It would be difficult to express all that I felt in those first moments. I spent all night on deck, as I have often done since, in order to follow the movement of the ship, the manoeuvres of the pilot, and the work of the officer of the watch.

We had good winds until the night of 5 May. I had not yet experienced seasickness, and I was content. Suddenly a dreadful storm descended on our ship; a few sails were torn, and some yards broken. The rigging was lashed by the wind and made an awful whistling noise. The sea became rough; the waves swelled quickly, rising up like mountains on both sides, and were soon breaking over the deck. On several occasions it was as if we had been submerged, and were in imminent danger. We quickly folded the sails, brought down the yards, and housed the masts. The frigate hove to, and we stayed there for 24 hours. Meanwhile the storm abated, the waves calmed, and favourable winds put us back on our course. I had been very much affected by seasickness during this bad weather. I had heard a great deal about this illness that is not described anywhere, and of which I had no experience. Those who have never felt it consider it to be a temporary and short-lived indisposition, but woe betide those whose constitution makes them susceptible to the causes that produce it! To my mind, it is the most inconvenient and the most unpleasant complaint with which anyone who goes to sea can be afflicted.

This sickness is felt to a greater or lesser degree by those who go to sea for the first time. However, there are people who are hardly bothered by it at all, or who, after their initial discomfort, are then able to face all storms without experiencing any indisposition. But there are others who, after several voyages, are constantly sick in rough weather and are unable to ward off this complaint. I shall attempt

---

153 I was particularly upset at leaving a loving mother, who had been a widow for a long while, and who I knew would be greatly upset on learning that I had sailed. (Author's note.)

to shed some light on the reasons for this difference by discussing what produces seasickness; the symptoms are generally known, but we need to understand what brings them about.[154]

As long as the ship remains balanced, and its progress is steady and regular, however fast it is going, the sailor feels no indisposition. But if headwinds impede the vessel's progress, or if, as a result of a strong gale, it is being tossed around by the waves, the seafarer is affected by the two chief movements to which the ship is subjected. The first of these is known as *rolling*, where the ship is moved from starboard to port with varying degrees of force. The second movement is known as *pitching*. It consists of the rising and falling of the bow and stern respectively. In the first case, anyone without experience is convinced that the ship is about to capsize. In the second, he is afraid of it going straight down to the bottom. Initially the mind is disoriented by these erratic movements; added to this mental cause, which is absent in experienced sailors, there is also a physical one. These unnatural movements create shocks which are concentrated in the brain, the most susceptible part of the body, due to its mass, its softness, and its lack of elasticity. After they have experienced this disturbance, the molecules of this organ settle back upon themselves, and it is this that produces all of the symptoms that characterize seasickness. The greater the mass of the brain, and the softer the consistency, the more it is susceptible to the effects of these causes, and this is why young people and those who have a large brain are most subject to seasickness. People of advanced years, whose brain has shrunk in size and is also of a firmer consistency than in younger subjects, are less liable to suffer from this sickness. The inhabitants of seacoasts and cold climates, in whom the brain mass is generally less developed than in those who live in warm countries and inland, adapt much better

---

154 As noted in Carpon's chapter 2, his remarks on seasickness were borrowed from Larrey's observations here.

to the vicissitudes of navigation, that is to say, they are less subject to seasickness.[155]

The first effect of this shock to the brain is the sadness and panic-stricken terror that overcome the individual. His face becomes pale, his eyes fill with tears; he is unable to face any food; he remains silent, seeks out solitude and rest. He staggers as if drunk, suffers from giddiness and ringing in the ears and an unpleasant heaviness in the head. Nausea sets in, and then vomiting soon afterwards, which becomes frequent, painful, and continues almost without respite until the cause comes to an end. This vomiting is the chief symptom of the sickness, and is sometimes accompanied by the passing of blood and by convulsive movements. These are probably brought about by sympathetic irritation or by the disturbance that occurs in the two pneumo-gastric nerve cords (8th pair), on which the effects of the disturbance to the brain appear to be concentrated. Since these effects are concentrated entirely in the stomach, it is this viscus that is first to feel this morbid condition, whence it is communicated sympathetically to all of the organs of the chest and the lower abdomen. This produces feelings of faintness, suffocation, the suppression of alvine secretions, and persistent constipation of variable duration. The patient's strength is appreciably reduced to the point of exhaustion. His legs no longer support the weight of the body; when he attempts to walk, he loses his balance and falls over like someone who is inebriated. He hides in the first corner he finds and stays there without moving until vomiting forces him to change his position. The patient stops eating, since he cannot keep down any kind of food; he begins to lose weight at an increasing rate; his intellectual faculties suffer, as do all other organs of animate life.

---

155 I am unable to determine accurately the reason for this difference. But experience teaches us that all animate creatures, as well as plants, are subject to the effects of winds or gases from the sea, especially on coasts with a northerly exposure, and are generally stunted in their development, either in whole or in part, and remain in a state of relative compactness and reduced size. (Author's note.)

This deterioration often reaches the point where, far from fearing death, as in the early stages of the sickness, most people wish for it, and some even attempt suicide. Cases of this have been known.

This sickness would no doubt have an unfortunate conclusion if it were to last a long time. But it is rare for the causes that produce it to be present with the same intensity for more than seven, eight, or nine days. The more violent the storm, the more quickly it passes, and the problem comes to an end at the same time as the bad weather. The return of favourable winds or the trade winds brings seasickness to an end as if by magic and restores the patient to the full possession of his faculties. His strength quickly returns, and he has soon forgotten his torture. But at the first unfavourable winds, especially if they are powerful, the same problems recur, and in some follow the same course as before, while in others they are very different. And there are those who never suffer from any recurrence. The organs gradually become accustomed to these shocks or disturbances, and in the end carry out their functions without any problem or upset. There are also those for whom the problems are just as serious on the second or third voyage as on the first. It is difficult to explain all of these differences: in all cases, it is the brain that is most affected. The proof of this is to be found in the relief that is obtained by putting oneself in a hanging frame, and by covering one's head with a tight bandage. As long as one remains in this position, seasickness is calmed, but it comes back as soon as one leaves one's hammock and comes in contact with the ship again.[156]

Although this sickness is most unpleasant, it is rare to see those affected die, unless there are other complications, but it can continue for a long time and lead to marasmus.

There are very few known ways of preventing this illness; none has proven to be effective in curing it. It is essential for the cause to cease

---

156 It has been known for people travelling in carriages with a poor suspension, especially with their back to the direction of travel, to be troubled by this sickness. Camels in Egypt produce the same effect in those who mount them for the first time. (Author's note.)

for it to come to an end. However, it will be less powerful and of shorter duration if, prior to the period when it is liable to occur, one includes in one's personal hygiene strong lotions of water mixed with vinegar, applied to the entire body, great sobriety, vegetable acids mixed into one's food and drink, and the use of a pipe, in moderation. One needs to avoid exposure to cold and damp air at night and to stay as little as possible below decks and in places inside the ship where one breathes foul and noxious air, which in itself predisposes one to vomiting. One should follow the example of experienced sailors, who, during their hours off duty, walk around on deck, where the air is purer, and where one's eyes become accustomed to the movements of the ship and the waves.

When seasickness sets in, one should eat very little and take only food that is easy to digest, that can absorb the gastric juices, very copious in these conditions, and can fortify the stomach, such as crusts of bread and biscuit, soaked in coffee or good wine, or in oxycrate or lemonade, for those who do not like coffee or wine. Tea and a light lunch are just as beneficial. But one should avoid fat and sugary foods, salads, soups, and vegetables of all kinds. One should allow oneself no more than a small quantity of roast meat and rice prepared in the Turkish manner. One must keep warm, take exercise, relax with music or by any similar means; in this way the effects of seasickness can be calmed and the unfortunate consequences prevented.[157]

After a few days of pleasant sailing we ran into a storm that was much stronger than the first, and of much longer duration, which took us 200 leagues [c. 1,100 km] from the Grand Bank[158] of Newfoundland, sufficiently close to the Azores for us to be able to see the coast. We stayed hove to for three days at the mercy of the waves.

However, we finally went back on course for the Grand Bank of

---

157 Dr. Kéraudren, Chief Medical Inspector for the navy, whom I had occasion to consult on this subject, also thinks that with this condition it is the brain that is affected first, and that the effects that are felt are determined particularly by the influence of that organ. (Author's note.)
158 Larrey uses "Grand Bank," not the plural. (Translator's note.)

Newfoundland, where we had intended to stop to fish some green cod. A few leagues from the Bank we were surprised by a flat calm, which delayed our progress yet again. These moments were for me the happiest; I felt well, and I enjoyed the beautiful sight that nature offered us at every moment. On partly clear days, the sunset was always remarkable for the infinite variety of reflections and the way the light was broken up. This is also a time when fish appear on the surface of the water; we could see a lot of cetaceans, such as porpoises of all sizes, sperm whales, whales, and swordfish. In particular I observed with great pleasure a strange battle between two of these creatures. The swordfish suddenly leaps out of the water and falls back into it just as quickly, pointing its saw at an oblique angle at the side of the whale, which immediately dives and somersaults to escape the attacks of its enemy; as it goes down it tries to strike the swordfish with its tail. Then it comes back up to the surface of the sea, spouting water through its blowhole, so as to drive away its adversary, which continues to pursue it just below the surface so that it can carry out another surprise attack. I saw these battles repeated several times without either of the combatants being wounded. A whale of enormous size followed our corvette quite closely, but taking care not to draw too near, no doubt for fear of being crushed. Indeed, there is no comparison between the strength of the tail of that creature and that of the keel of a copper-bottomed warship. This is sure proof of the groundlessness of tales that are told of the dangerous consequences of these cetaceans passing underneath ships.

  The winds suddenly shifted to the southeast, and at last we arrived on the Grand Bank, where we fished for cod with a hand line in 60 fathoms of water. These fish are usually headed and gutted as soon as they come out of the water. I was surprised at the speed with which the man responsible for this removed his hand from the belly of the fish. I pointed this out to him; he answered that the extreme cold that he felt in his hand when he put it inside the guts of the fish obliged him to withdraw it quickly. I tried it for myself, and could feel as he did that they were icy. If I had had a thermometer, I should have been able to determine the approximate temperature at the bottom of these seas, for I believe that it is similar to that of the creatures that inhabit it, varying according to the depth.

We set sail again for Newfoundland, and left behind us on the Grand Bank several Dutch fishermen who appeared to brave any storm and all kinds of foul weather in order to continue their fishing. The cod from this area is known as green cod and is delicious, which is why it is the most sought after. Some distance from the Grand Bank we were surprised by a very thick, cold mist. We could hardly see each other on deck from a distance of 4 paces. At that time the frigate was moving at just 2 knots. For seamen who were used to these parts, this sudden change in temperature indicated that we were close to ice. Because of this fear, the ship was slowed, and the course changed a little. A few hours later, the fog cleared, the winds picked up, and we went back on course again. Immediately we saw two huge mountains of ice toward which we had been moving without knowing it. We avoided them easily by edging north. These pieces of ice were as large as a three- or four-storey house. The part above water was shaped like a cone; the part that was submerged appeared to be equal in volume to the part above water. We soon saw many others, and then we came to a pack of ice that appeared to stretch to Newfoundland. If the fog had been thicker, we would undoubtedly have perished there. We moved along the edge of this hazard for some time so as not to go too far off course. A few of our sailors saw some chicken coops floating in the water, with some dead chickens and a few ducks that were still alive, which they took. We also saw a hat, a few pieces of wood, and a small topgallant yard with its sail. This wreckage led us to assume that a ship had gone down. And so we were doubly careful and quickly moved away from the danger by heading more to the east. The next morning, around 10 a.m., we discovered that we were level with Belle Isle, which we passed quite close to. The men on duty saw signals at the foot of this little island still covered with snow, and advised the officer of the watch; with his spyglass the latter was able to see men on the shore who had been waving their hats for a long while. We let the frigate draw a few degrees closer, and hove to; the main longboat was immediately put into the water, and an officer with enough men for the task was ordered to go and rescue these poor souls.

All of us were speculating on their fate; we were anxious to see them, and yet fearful of what they would tell us. I would have jumped into the longboat if the captain had given me permission. The journey was completed quite quickly, for the winds were fairly strong. The longboat drew alongside us, and the bosun's whistle was heard giving the order to help these poor men board our ship. Immediately, the entire crew was on the starboard side, and the men in the boat were brought up.

I rushed to the survivors; there were 21 of them, out of 23 who had been cast up on this island. They were pale, haggard, bitterly cold, dying from hunger and thirst. I observed that several of them had frostbite in their feet and a few fingers. We quickly took them down to the captain's cabin and the main wardroom, where we had put mattresses and blankets for them to lie on. A few embrocations of cold brandy with camphor, bouillon made from stock cubes, and good wine with sugar revived them and brought them back to life. Then I looked after the local gangrene which affected most of them.

Hardly were they restored when, sensing our eagerness to know the cause of their shipwreck, they asked to be able to tell their story. Here, in essence, is what we were told by Mr. Doré, the leader of this little band, formerly a lieutenant in the Royal Navy and a merchant captain.

He had been in command of a ship with a crew of 80 men, heading for the cod fishery, when, 15 leagues [8.25 km] northwest of Belle Isle and with darkness falling he was surprised by the densest of fogs that made it impossible to see where he was going. He nevertheless maintained his course for several hours. The intense cold felt by the men on duty warned them of the proximity of ice that they could not see because of the fog. A few moments later a violent shock was felt in the ship; it had just struck a huge piece of ice. The alarm was immediately sounded, all of the crew went up on deck, and they tacked to avoid the danger. But they fell from the frying pan into the fire. As the ship was starting to get under way in the other direction, it was suddenly on its beam ends. In spite of the manoeuvres and all the efforts of the crew, its sides burst open, and water flooded inside.

The danger was now inescapable, and they quickly discovered the extent of it, since at that very moment the rising sun cleared the fog. They were caught between the pack ice that we had seen and one of the mountainous blocks of ice referred to earlier. The ship was about to go under! Most of the men were terrified and quickly jumped on to the flat surface of the pack ice that appeared to stretch to land. Captain Doré, being more cautious and experienced, attempted to restrain them, and gave orders to have the boats launched to save the men. Only 22 obeyed; they took the first boat, cut the lashings, and without thinking of provisions, put it into the water, took the compass from the binnacle, climbed aboard, and pushed it off into open water. Fortunately, this boat was equipped with a small sail and two oars. But they had only two flat biscuits for all of them. In less than two minutes, the ship disappeared. The remainder of the crew was already a long way away on the pack ice, and it was only with difficulty that Doré was able to restrain his men from following their crewmates, believing that their chances of being saved were better. Both groups had travelled quite a distance! ... Alas, the men in the boat soon saw the others coming back toward the spot where the ship had gone down, crying desperately for help ... Here the captain's voice grew weaker; he had broken off his tale to let his tears flow; the hollow and leaden eyes of his companions were also full of tears, and there was not one of us who was not greatly moved.

"We saw them all perish on the ice," he added after a few moments of silence. "They were all falling one on top of the other; a few even jumped into the water, and were swallowed up for ever." Their death must have been dreadful, for these banks are covered with polar bears and seals that must have devoured them as they fell.

"It was impossible," continued the captain, "to go and get our crewmates, even though we were anxious to do so. Our boat, which could hardly carry us, was much too small for such a large number. We grieve for all of them, but included among them were my brother, one of my cousins, my boatswain, and the medical officer, my friend. For me especially their death will be a source of never-ending grief.

"We increased our speed as much as we could," he added, "heading for the north-northeast. Twenty-four hours later, we saw the island where you took us on board, and where bad weather and the lack of food forced us to go ashore. In addition, my men were exhausted with fatigue, hunger, and thirst. It was hunger that caused us the most suffering. We had shared out the two flat biscuits and swallowed snow to quench our thirst. When we again experienced the need for food, we hunted in vain for roots on that barren land, and we were in the third day of our suffering, experiencing the agony of death, having already lost two of our number to cold and other privations, when you saw us."

The details of this shipwreck caused us much sorrow, and on the shore, covered with a little sand, we could see the bodies of the two unfortunate men whose terrible death had just been related to us.

Finally, on 26 June, after 54 days of difficult and dangerous sailing, we arrived at the bay of Croque, in Newfoundland, the site of the main cod fisheries, and we stayed there until 31 July.

The next morning, after we had trimmed the frigate and put the boats into the water, we went ashore, the captain indicating the places where the officers' quarters were to be set up. He also ordered the men to help build the cabins. First, I had one built for my patients and for the survivors of the shipwreck who had undergone operations. Then I had mine built next to theirs, with a small garden that I cultivated myself. During our stay there, I frequently visited the European fisheries; I stuffed birds and quadrupeds, went hunting, and quite often went on expeditions inland.

The cod, taken with hand lines, rarely in nets, are first of all split and gutted by people whose sole task this is. Some cut off the head and flatten the fish, others salt and dry it, etc. All of this is done quite quickly; boys are busy collecting the tongues and the cod roe, which are prepared separately.

Even though this island is situated no further north than between latitudes 46° and 52°, the climate of Newfoundland seems very cold and damp. When we arrived, at the end of June, the mountains were still covered with snow. We could see that in some places it was extremely deep and frozen, which leads me to believe that it never melts. Forests of pine, spruce, larch, and birch grow on these mountains. The smallness of the trees is an indication of the harshness of the climate. Wild pear trees a few inches high can also be seen, with a fruit that is no bigger than a pea. All of the plants are generally stunted and smaller than in Europe.

One of the animals to be seen on the island is the polar sea bear, much larger and more ferocious than the common black bear (which is also found in Newfoundland). Sometimes this creature follows fishermen's boats, especially when the boats are small; it overturns them with its front paws when it can get a grip on them, then seizes the fishermen. It often lays waste to the fishing rooms, and the men are then obliged to join together in large numbers to attack it. One day when I had gone hunting inland and become lost, I saw one of these ferocious beasts through the trees, on top of a small hill as I was passing below. Its enormous size and the movements of its head filled me with fear; I could not help giving way to the feeling of terror that overcame me and I took to my heels. It is quite likely, however, that the animal never saw me.

In this country one also sees a kind of large deer known as caribou.

It differs from the common deer only in that it is larger, and during the growing period its antlers are covered with a short, brownish hair. Sometimes these caribou come close to the fishing rooms; one night one of them got into our sheep fold, where we also kept a cow, which became pregnant by this animal. The cow must have given birth to a crossbreed, but circumstances prevented me from verifying this, although the animal was brought back to Brest. It is claimed that in this country there are deer like those in Canada. There are no wolves, but lynx are often seen.[159] I saw a black fox, with a tail that was white at the tip; they say that its fur is very sought after. I much regretted not being able to take any while hunting. Beavers are not uncommon. While destroying one of their lodges, I surprised two of the young, one of which escaped. The construction of their houses is most interesting, and justifies what naturalists have said about them in this respect.

In Newfoundland there is a kind of wild cat that has musk, like the civet. The hare are of the same species as in Europe, but larger; they are grey in summer and white in winter. The edge of their ears remains constantly white. The Europeans who have settled on the island claim that they change colour without changing their coat. They are killed more easily than in Europe because they are less easily frightened.

There are several remarkable varieties of birds in these parts; there is a species of red partridge (ptarmigan, Linnaeus's *Tetra lagopus*) that is very common but differs from the European variety in that it is larger. The eye ring has a fleshy, scarlet ridge. Its bill is red, and the tarsi are covered to the nails with a very thick grey silk or hair. These partridge are red with brown blotches in summer and white in winter. I saw them in both states. It is also claimed that this change in colour takes place without the birds losing their feathers.[160] Blackbirds are also reddish brown in summer and

---

159 There were wolves in Newfoundland at that time, a subspecies of the grey wolf. In 1839 the government instituted a bounty of £5 per head on wolves, and their numbers declined to the point where they became extinct. It is believed that the last one was shot in 1910. (Translator's note.)
160 In fact ptarmigan do moult. (Translator's note.)

white in winter.¹⁶¹ This change probably takes place in the same way as with partridge. These birds are practically tame, and probably remain hidden in holes for a part of the winter, out of the daylight, where they grow pale, or perhaps nature has endowed them with this ability to change colour to enable them to escape the fox. We also saw a variety of whitish grey tit, about the same size as hummingbirds in Senegal.¹⁶² There are very large numbers of them, and they can be taken by hand. The harbours and rivers are full of all kinds of waterfowl.

The Indigenous inhabitants of Newfoundland are of the race of the Labrador Eskimos.¹⁶³ They rarely come to the coast frequented by the fishermen; they trade with them only in places that are generally well inland and via the intermediary of a few Europeans who have been settled in Newfoundland for a long time. While hunting one day with one of our officers, I met two of these savages, who ran over to us. The officer, who knew the country very well, calmed the fears that I felt on first seeing them when I recalled that they were said to be cannibals. They were clothed completely in skins of bear and seal, which are common in those parts. Their dress consisted of a large hat in the form of a helmet, a short and very full coat, a kind of loose-fitting trouser, and ankle boots with soles of thick leather. Over the coat, a long strip of skin served as a belt. They had bows and arrows, the latter having a very sharp head made from a piece of bone.¹⁶⁴

They were carrying smoked meat and a few skins in a kind of haversack. They were not very tall, but otherwise quite well built, muscular, and with dark hair that was flat and fairly short. One of them had a dark beard, not very full; the other was young. Their eyes seemed to me to be small, deep-set, with a sinister look, shaded by

---

161 It is not clear what bird Larrey had in mind here (the word he uses is "merle"). There is no blackbird in Newfoundland that changes colour as he describes. It is possible that he could have in mind the ruddy turnstone, a shorebird that does change its plumage for winter by moulting, like the ptarmigan, though they do not become white all over. There is also the American Robin ("merle d'Amérique"), but this does not become white in winter either. (Translator's note.)
162 Larrey may be referring to the black-capped chickadee, which is indeed a member of the tit family. (Translator's note.)
163 See Preface, p. 25.
164 This description is strikingly similar to the one given by Carpon in Chapter 6 of *Voyage to Newfoundland*.

short, dark, and furrowed eyelids. They had straight noses, flaring out a little toward the tip; their lips were quite full, their teeth yellowish, their complexion tanned and swarthy. We did not understand their language at all, but they led us to understand with signs that they would like to eat and drink. We offered them some brandy, biscuit, and cheese that was left over from our provisions. They grabbed these hungrily, put down their arms, sat down, and appeared to devour this food, yet they saved a little brandy and biscuit. They were more generous than I would have thought, and in exchange gave us some skins prepared as furs. They excel in the art of preparing these skins and sewing them for different purposes. They use fish bones as needles, and strings of gut of varying thickness for thread. They appear to be less cruel than travellers believe. Let me say a few words about their qualities, their customs, and their medicine. When we left them, it was with some regret at not being able to converse with them or visit their huts.

According to the various details that we gathered, we learned that these huts are built in the shape of tents, with the supporting poles firmly lashed together, and are located at the entrance to a cave or at the foot of a rock. They protect the entry with a palisade. They make a fire in the middle of the hut, and treated animal skins spread around the fireplace are used for beds. A large part of their food is made up of salt fish, plants, and what they hunt. To drink, they have a fermented liquor made from spruce buds, and, in the depths of winter, whale oil, which contributes more than a little to their ability to keep themselves warm. They also rub it all over their bodies to strengthen their limbs and maintain their agility. The Eskimos are extremely jealous of their women, whom they do not allow out of their huts, which prevented us from seeing them. Both these Indians and the settlers lay in their supplies for the winter in the fine season, then do not leave their retreat again. As we have already noted, the climate of Newfoundland is extremely cold in winter and damp in the spring, due to the effect along the coast and particularly on the Grand Bank of the thaw and constant fog that settles in during the early months of this latter season.

Initially the men who went to the Newfoundland fishery were afflicted with scurvy, and a large number of the crew also experienced catarrhal infections. We used all appropriate means to prevent these tribulations, but prior to our departure from Europe, not enough care had been taken to protect us from the intense cold of the climate that we were to live through in two different seasons. One should never sail for Arctic seas without the crew having a supply of two types of clothing, one well lined and very warm for winter, and the other light for summer. The change in temperature, the use of vegetables that we had successfully sown and harvested,[165] or local ones, fresh bread, hunting, and fishing allowed me to put an end to these sicknesses quite quickly and successfully. Cods' heads in particular, cooked with these vegetables, provided me with a broth that was as tasty as it was antiscorbutic.

In the month of July the prevailing north-northwest winds brought fine weather and heat. In fact, it became so intense in the valleys and harbours that around the end of that month our thermometer went up to 27° or 28° above zero. When the sun is under the tropics, the nights disappear to the point where, so to speak, the fall of darkness beckons the first light. Many times I came back from a hunt at 11 p.m. or midnight, convinced that it was hardly any more than 7 or 8 p.m.[166]

In spite of the harshness of the frost and the large quantity of snow that remains throughout the winter on this island, to a depth which we estimated at 5 to 6 feet based on what we saw, the numerous forests of Newfoundland are full of birds and insects. In particular one is greatly tormented by a kind of gnat known as a mosquito, whose bite produces

---

165 Larrey says earlier that they arrived in Croque on 26 June, leaving a rather short growing season for vegetables to reach maturity in northern Newfoundland. (Translator's note.)
166 A very similar comment is made by Carpon in Chapter 6, of his *Voyage to Newfoundland*. (Translator's note.)

a swelling in the immediate area and fever, which, it is true, is short-lived. We were all troubled by them. It would, I believe, be a very cruel torture to inflict on any man to tie him naked to the trunk of a tree, with his hands tied behind his back, exposed to the bites of these insects. I have no doubt that he would succumb in less than two hours.

Saltwater lotions, rest, and cooling applications were sufficient to dispel the effects of these bites. Following my advice, we succeeded in preventing them by rubbings of lightly camphorated oil and by the use of a gauze net that we were in the habit of wearing over the face.[167]

In the harbours of Newfoundland, we often saw the dazzling lights that form at night, especially when it is hot, around oars or in the wake of ships. The research that I have carried out leads me to believe that this glow is the result of the presence of a large number of minute phosphorescent animals and decaying animal matter suspended in the water. The places where these phenomena are most frequent are consequently unhealthy if one stays there for any length of time.

We left Croque on 31 July to go and inspect the whole northern part of the island. We anchored in Canada Bay where there is a waterfall 60 feet high. We fished a very large quantity of salmon, the smallest of which weighed 15 pounds. From there we moved to White Bay, where we entered the Arctic Sea, to beyond Orange Bay[168] on the coast of Labrador, between 55° and 56° north.[169] We were to have gone back through the Strait of Belle Isle to visit the Gulf of St. Lawrence. But bad weather and ice forced us to stay in Croque Bay, where we remained for a few more days. Our rooms were in the same state as we had left them. I confess that I left this isolated spot with some regret.

---

167   A paraphrase of this section on mosquitoes is found in Chapter 6 of Carpon's *Voyage to Newfoundland*. (Translator's note.)

168   The name Orange Bay is not in current use in Labrador, and the Gazetteer gives no listing for it in Labrador. However, a map published by Pierre Mortier in Amsterdam in 1700 entitled *Le Canada ou Partie de la Nouvelle France Contenant la Terre de Labrador la Nouvelle France les Isles de Terre Neuve de Nostre Dame &c* shows Orange Bay (in English) on the coast of Labrador with its entrance just above 50° north. Centre for Newfoundland Studies, Memorial University Library, G 3400 1700 M6 Map. Since the drawing of the coastline does not correspond to modern maps, it is not easy to see what the modern equivalent would be. (Translator's note.)

169   56° north would have put them in the far north of Labrador, practically as far as Nain. What they would have been doing there is not clear. (Translator's note.)

From Croque we went to St. John Lateran,[170] an English settlement with a very favourable location in the southeast of Newfoundland. The harbour entrance is protected by a tower bristling with guns. Once the signals of recognition had been exchanged, we were allowed to enter the harbour. As we were passing by the fort, we were greeted with several gunshots, and the governor of St. John's immediately sent a naval officer to help us anchor and trim the ship, which was done in a few minutes. In the harbour we found quite a large number of merchant vessels, one warship, and a few frigates. The city rose in the shape of an amphitheatre to our right; the shore on the opposite side was covered with fishing premises which were all much finer than those of the French and Dutch. Practically all of the houses in the city are built of wood, but they are nonetheless of considerable size and comfortably arranged inside. The captain received an invitation to dine the next day with the governor, and we were invited by the officers of the warship, the *Salisbury*, under the command of Mr. Riou, one of the companions of Captain Cook. Before going there, we went ashore to visit the city and the surrounding area. We were astonished at the beauty of the English women whom we met during the course of our outing; almost all of them are of good height, attractive, with handsome figures, fine hair, pleasantly shaped faces, lovely eyes, and brilliantly white teeth. Some of them had dark hair and eyelids of the same colour that contrasted attractively with their blue eyes.

Captain Riou had had the ship dressed and received us with great honour. In our presence he ordered a demonstration of the crew being piped to general quarters, gun practice, and the boys doing drill; all of these movements were remarkable for their precision and their swiftness. I was pleased to see that this vessel was kept extremely

---

170   Larrey gave the name of the capital of Newfoundland, St. John's, as *Saint-Jean-de-Latran*, after the basilica of St. John Lateran in Rome, named after John the Baptist, like the city of St. John's. It is possible that Larrey added "de Latran" simply to distinguish it from any of the other places in Newfoundland also named St. John or St. John's. But *Saint-Jean-de-Latran* is a highly unusual variant. (Translator's note.)

clean and tidy below decks. We sat down to table at noon; we were still together at midnight.

Nearly all of the English officers spoke enough French for us to be able to follow their conversation. Mr. Riou, who had followed Captain Cook on his last voyage around the world, related several of the adventures of that famous traveller, and the way in which he perished on the island of Hawaii in the Pacific Ocean, after having sighted and explored the Sandwich Islands.[171] At midnight our captain, who had returned on board the frigate, sent us the order to prepare for departure. We took leave of our hosts, and quickly returned to our stations. A few moments later the order to set sail was given. We were about to raise the last anchor when the winds, which had been quite strong, suddenly shifted and increased to hurricane force. We were in danger of being driven ashore or of suffering severe damage on passing below the fort. We quickly dropped the anchors again, reefed the sails, and delayed the departure until daylight. The winds had dropped and had shifted in our favour, so we left the harbour easily, and in a short while we were on the open sea. We headed for St-Pierre and Miquelon, a French colony that we had to inspect. It is to the south-east, at the tip of Newfoundland. On the second day's sailing we were blown off course by the currents and a violent storm that blew up from the land, leaving us more than 200 leagues [c. 1,100 km] from our destination, off the coast of New England. We were hove to for three days. However, favourable winds followed this gale, and brought us back to St-Pierre, where we arrived on 23 September 1788. The harbour and the little town of the same name are quite like St. John's.[172] The ship was anchored in a favourable spot, the boats were put into the water, and the frigate was being trimmed when a very strong wind sprang up from the southeast and continued to increase until 3 a.m. It was one of the most terrible hurricanes that I

---
171   The death of Captain Cook in Hawaii was only nine years prior to the events related here. (Translator's note.)
172   Extracts from Gobineau's *Voyage à Terre-Neuve* were published in *Le Tour du Monde* in 1863 with engravings purporting to show the two communities, but the illustrations were transposed–see pp. 401 and 412. (Translator's note.)

have ever seen. We were forced to use all of the cables and chains to tie the ship to the mooring in the roads. We housed the yards, the top and topgallant masts. In spite of these measures, the frigate drifted several fathoms, and would have run aground on a very steep rock close by if we had not rushed to drop the anchor of mercy. This tremendous resistance halted the forced movement of the ship, but at that very same moment the moorings of the captain's boat were broken by the waves, and the boat was carried out to sea. Eighteen men who were in the longboat, including one of the chief boatswains, wanted to go after the boat and bring it back on board; the longboat itself was carried off by the waves and swept out to sea but it managed to catch up with the boat. Two men had just got into it when the waves drove the two small boats apart again. Then we lost sight of them. Although we were ourselves not free of danger, all of our concern was focused on those poor men, who we thought had gone under. We spent the night in the most terrible anxiety, both for the considerable loss that we had just suffered and for the dangers that still threatened us.

At about 4 a.m., the hurricane came to an end, and the sea was calm at sunrise. We trimmed the ship, put the yards and the masts back in place, and sent the one boat that we had left, the third, to check the shoreline. The men from this boat informed us on their return that half a league [2.75 km] from the harbour and on the uninhabited coast of Newfoundland they found the longboat broken into scattered pieces and two sailors' hats, which they brought back. This news threw us into consternation. We felt certain that these fearless men had perished in the shipwreck and had been devoured by seals and polar bears even as they were expiring, since our men had been unable to find even a single body.

A few hours later, some fishermen from the tip of the island signalled that they were carrying two shipwrecked men in their boat. We went out to meet them, and the two men were seen to be from the crew of the longboat. They were the two men who had gone into the captain's boat. One of them, the second boatswain, was no longer alive; all of the aid that I administered to bring him back to life was in vain. The other was in serious condition and in a state of torpor; I treated him as best I could, and he recovered. According to what this man told us, after the boat had been lashed by the wind for some time, it had broken apart on the rock known as *l'Enfant perdu* (the Lost Child), where these two unfortunate men were cast ashore. The violent blows that they had received and the harsh cold that they suffered during the night had caused the death of the boatswain. The other was feeling very ill himself when the fisherman's boat passed close to the lookout, where he saw them.

We were still anxious about what had happened to the other 16 men who had stayed in the longboat. We were losing hope of seeing them again, when two days later we saw some men on the shore who were signalling to us to go and get them; these were our brave companions who had been brought right up to the shore of the roads by savages.

Having survived the wrecking of their boat on the coast, they had gone inland at night in the hope of finding help and shelter. Some distance from the shore they found some Eskimos who led them to their huts. Once these savages had undressed them, they put them on animal skins, rubbed a warm aromatic liquor all over their body, wrapped them in the skins of animals that had been recently killed, and made them swallow a soothing drink. They dried their clothes and perfumed them; then they took them back to St-Pierre roads. This was how these islanders who are said by travellers to be cannibals behaved. Our men could not have received more effective and kinder treatment than that they were given with so much readiness and humanity.

It would be difficult to express the surprise and joy that the return of these men aroused in us. We held a funeral for the boatswain, who was mourned by all, and we set sail a few hours later to return to France; this was the evening of 27 September.

The winds were favourable for the first six days. But then they turned against us and became so strong that we were again forced to heave to. The waves and currents threw us far off our course; then, still driven by the unfavourable winds, we entered the Channel. It was only with the greatest difficulty, and after several days of navigation, that we came level with Ouessant, but were driven away from it again by headwinds. Our lengthy stay in Newfoundland, the delays that we had experienced on different stages of our journey, and the food that we had given to the men who were shipwrecked on Belle Isle, had all put us in a position of terrible shortage. For several days we had been reduced to 4 ounces of biscuit each, and one bottle of bad water that had to be strained through a cloth to remove the worms. The bad weather that we again encountered forced us to reduce this pittance even further. All we had left was a little brandy and a very thin, pregnant cow. We made fruitless attempts to reach the nearest port, for we were only about 60 leagues [c. 330 km] from the coast of France. We had not met any other vessel that could have assisted us. Just as we had run out of supplies, we saw a Danish ship heading north, and in precisely the opposite direction to us. We let it draw near, made a distress signal, and hailed it to ask for assistance, but it tacked and put out extra sail to get away from us. We fired several gunshots, in vain. This incident took us even further away from our home country, and we were about to be subject to the horrors of famine, when at last the winds changed. We set all of our sails, and in 26 hours we could see the land that I had been so sad to see disappear. When the boy in the crow's nest announced this news, the whole crew let out a cry of joy, and from then on we found renewed strength to carry out the urgent tasks that had already weakened three-quarters of the crew. We passed by Ouessant Island, and we entered the Brest roads, tacking between the shores of the channel. Finally, we anchored at the entrance to the harbour on 31 October 1788.

During these six months of navigation we had lost only the second boatswain who had been cast ashore, as we have noted, with another man, on one of the rocks close to the entry to the St-Pierre roads. But during the voyage I had had to treat approximately 80 people for a variety of illnesses, not including the men wrecked on Belle Isle. At least half of them were affected by scurvy in varying degrees; some had been dangerously ill from it; others had recovered from putrid, nervous, malignant, and eruptive fevers. Among the latter there had been a case of confluent smallpox that appeared extremely serious. The rest had had catarrhal, gastric, rhumatic, syphilitic, and opthalmic conditions. The effective medication that I had on board, the light, refreshing food, healthy broth, full-bodied wine, and fresh bread contributed greatly, with the conscientiousness of my colleagues, to curing these patients. I had amputated the frostbitten toes or feet of several of the shipwrecked men, and I had also successfully carried out a few other delicate operations.

The cleanliness of the ship, the vapours of nitre and sulphur that were frequently sprayed at my request, the changing of the air by means of a bellows and a sleeve, the daily muster ordered at my request, the frequent lotions of vinegar and water that I prescribed for the men, constant activity, except during hours of rest, dancing, nourishing food, and drinks mixed with vinegar and brandy are the means that I used to maintain the health of the crew and to restore those who were convalescing.

On entering the port, the frigate was laid up. I made a request to be released from the service in order to return to Paris. It was granted only with reluctance, and I have to say that at the same time I received the most honourable expressions of satisfaction and regret from the Brest Health Board and from the General Inspector.

A report on the season's activities by Captain Venancourt, commodore of the French naval station in Newfoundland in 1821, to the minister for the navy

Annales maritimes et coloniales, 1821, IIe partie, pp. 953–65.

Information on the island of Newfoundland, its inhabitants, its agriculture, and ways to expand the cod, salmon, herring, and whale fishery in these parts

The considerable advantages, both for the navy and for business, that could be derived from the cod fishery on the shores of the island of Newfoundland, ought to have attracted attention a long time ago. But the Treaty of Utrecht, which granted full ownership of this island to the English, greatly reduced trade; nothing less than the full attention of the government is required if this fishery is not to be completely wiped out.

The most important of these fisheries, for cod, appears to be reserved for the inhabitants of St-Malo, Saint-Brieuc, and Granville, who prosecute it on the Northern Peninsula only; the three other fisheries are completely neglected. The cause is probably the lack of knowledge among French outfitters of the west coast, where these four species of fish are very abundant from the month of May until October. Last year

(1820) English schooners fished there until the end of December, at Codroy and the surrounding area.

The outfitters at our various ocean ports, and especially those of La Rochelle, Bordeaux, etc., because of their location and the products from their region, would be able to carry on these fisheries more successfully than cities that do not have any salt, wine, brandy, or flour; in addition, their labour costs are lower.

Sailors from these shores, especially those of Les Sables d'Olonne, are just as enterprising as the Normans; they simply need to be pointed in the right direction. It is up to the government to encourage timid speculators, and even to underwrite their initial attempts. Their ships should also have on board a few good fishermen from Granville, who would teach them the various methods of fishing, and especially that readiness to work long hours that is needed to take advantage of times when the fish are present; among other things, this requires that the men be well nourished. Before the Revolution a bounty of 100 francs per man was offered to ships prepared to go and fish on the west coast of Newfoundland, and despite these advantages and the even more significant one that that coast presents to them, the inducements offered were to no effect, which shows how difficult it is to overcome the force of habit, and, I am not afraid to say, the timidity of our outfitters!

They would find the fishery on the coast of Newfoundland even more advantageous if they were prepared to work together, so that a company could have an authorization both for the Northern Peninsula and for the west coast. At the beginning of March it would send out the required ships to begin the fishery at the beginning of May, which is the period when cod and herring are present in great abundance from Codroy to the Bay of Islands. It is this part of the coast that produces the earliest fish caught in Newfoundland, which should certainly be reserved for French fishermen, and any foreign fishermen who show up should be quickly turned away.

These two species of fish slowly work their way up the coast toward the north until the end of July, when fish become very plentiful on the Atlantic coast of the Northern Peninsula. Ships from all the various firms would join up, find more than enough to complete their fishery, and in the process overcome the delays that are often caused by the ice pack on the Northern Peninsula, and the years when the abundance of fish rises or falls.

But the cod fishery is not the only one that should occupy our outfitters. Herring and salmon, combined with the cod fishery, would provide them considerable profit. I see no difficulty in adding the whale fishery, for whales abound in Bay St. George in the months of May and June, and then follow the coast northwards.

Some people think that this could harm the cod fishery. From all the information that was given to me by the English fishermen along the coast I can attest that that is not true. They pointed out to me Gaspé Bay on the coast of Canada as an example, and Fortune Bay on the island of Newfoundland, where they regularly take abundant catches of these two species of fish. It should also be remembered that very few cod are caught inside Bay St. George and that the whale fishery is particularly easy since it can be carried out in water that is no more than 60 fathoms at its deepest, and because whales come right into the harbour of St. George's.

Means of preventing foreigners from supplying our colonies and ensuring that those colonies receive necessary supplies at the best possible price

If all that I have just said were to be put into effect, it would result in a considerable increase in the fishery, which naturally ought to draw the eyes of our administration toward our colonies. The Americans have always provided them with the vast majority of the salt cod that they consume, often at a very high price, which speculators have every interest in maintaining. The result is that the colonies experience great shortages, and are forced to open their ports, if they do not want to see their Negroes starve. Then French traders complain loudly, and rightly so, for if at times like that, French interests send supplies to the colonies, it is not profitable. A few cargoes of salt cod and flour sent in great haste by the Americans result in supplies being plentiful for a few months. These sudden changes in price are advantageous only to the Americans and speculators; in short, residents of the colonies always pay very dearly for these vital necessities, and French dealers do not dare to take the risk.

In order to encourage our cod fishery and to ensure that our colonies are supplied (the only way to have them prosper), it is therefore crucial to set invariable rules for rates for the exchange of goods for salt cod, so as to enjoy all the advantages of peace.

The government has of course already done a great deal by providing incentive bounties for the fishery, but it will have only imperfectly achieved its goal if that branch of French industry does not extend to our colonies, both to put a stop to the importation of foreign cod and to open a new market for that fished by the French, and also for the well-being of those same colonies.

To achieve this it should send to the chambers of commerce of Granville, Saint-Brieuc, and St-Malo on the one hand and, on the other, to a representative forum for the colonists, a proposal for the following arrangement, to the advantage of both parties.

1. Make the chambers of commerce aware of the price that the inhabitants would pay for salt cod delivered to the colonies, in well-conditioned, 1,200-pound hogsheads, which, after being bleached, could be used to contain raw sugar.
2. The price of this cod would be set according to the average rate of

recent years (by this I mean the rate at which the merchants buy, not the one at which they sell to residents) and the agreed number of hogsheads.

3. This cod would be paid in colonial produce, the price of which would be set according to the rate over recent years.
4. The contracting parties would enter into an agreement that would set the number of years that their commitment would last, as well as the price for salt cod and colonial produce.
5. In the case of cod or sugar having deteriorated or being of bad quality, it would be refused or sold by arbitration, or replacement supplies would be bought locally, which would be paid for by those who failed to respect their commitments.
6. Since salt cod does not keep for a long time in the colonies, it is absolutely essential for the health of the inhabitants that it arrive fresh three times a year. For example, the first delivery could be made in July, with cod caught on the west coast in May and June, with the second in November, from cod caught on the Atlantic coast of the Northern Peninsula, part of which would be stored either in France or in St-Pierre and Miquelon, and the third delivery would be made in April of the following year.

The government gives a bounty of 20 francs per quintal of fish taken to the colonies; assuming that the price of this fish is 20 francs, the French dealers will make a fine profit, since the cost to them, caught and dried, is about 15 francs.

As for the colonists, having salt cod delivered directly, they will find the reduction in price especially advantageous, since dealers or their agents who provide it to them are often obliged to sell sugar at very low prices to have money available to pay the Americans, who cannot take sugar in payment.

This proposal is especially appropriate since for a long time our colonies have been lacking spare cash, and having been devastated several years in succession by windstorms, it is essential to provide them with provisions in exchange for their products, and at the best price possible, so that they may use their excess revenue to improve their agriculture.

Commissioners appointed by the Chamber of Commerce and the assembly of the residents would reside in the ports of: St-Pierre, Fort Royal, Le Marin, and La Trinité for the island of Martinique; Basse-Terre, Pointe-à-Pitre, Sainte-Anne, Le Moule, and Port Louis for the island of Guadeloupe; and on the islands of Marie-Galante and Saint-Martin. They would receive the salt cod and distribute it to the inhabitants, and take sugar from them in exchange. These commissioners would take a commission of 2.5 per cent for all goods that they receive or deliver.

The government would further demonstrate its benevolence, both for its own trade and for the colonists, by applying to flour what I have outlined for cod.

In a normal year, France harvests far more than it consumes; in addition, the storage facilities in Marseilles attract a huge quantity of grains from the Near East and the Black Sea, which French ships could transport to our colonies. However, again it is the Americans who supply this market. A small bounty for a few years would be sufficient to take this trade away from foreigners. Think of the sacrifices our neighbours make when they are setting up in competition against us!

The only trade that would remain for the foreigners would be cattle, lumber, and salt meat, which could also be put into the hands of our nationals if the government would draw from Cayenne all the resources that that colony is capable of producing, and set up the salting of the meat in France.

*Dangers of navigation in Newfoundland
and ways to overcome them*

Navigation in Newfoundland is without any doubt the harshest and the most dangerous that we have, and hence provides an excellent training ground for sailors. This school is especially advantageous since every ship uses 10 times more people than any other navigation, and this in a country where there is nothing to be feared from climatic conditions, while navigation in the East and West Indies causes almost as many sailors to perish as are trained.

Naval training, maps published in 1784, and a few pieces of information given by officers who did not have the time to verify them are far from precise. And even if they were, how can one recognize the capes and bays marked on them that one sees for the first time, and almost always in foggy weather? Added to these difficulties are the dangers of this coast, particularly the southern part and the straits. Here the men encounter ice, which demands vigilance and precision in manoeuvering that cannot be acquired immediately, especially for a ship that has just been fitted out. In addition, warships require continual attention, given the difficulty of slowing their speed, which often exposes them to the danger of being lost against these enormous blocks of ice that cannot be seen in foggy weather until one is very close. In order to avoid the king's ships being exposed to the innumerable dangers presented by navigation in Newfoundland, of which a good number have already experienced the effects, it would be desirable for these ships not to be sent out from France without a pilot, or at least without an officer who has already experienced other seasons there.

In support of what I am suggesting I could offer numerous facts that are quite well known. It is by accompanying fishing ships on their travels, and turning away from the coast English and American ships, that we will succeed in foiling fraudsters, and allow the French fishery to expand as much as possible, for I have noticed that American ships, fishing by hand lines in the same area as the French, fill their boats with cod, while ours take only a very few. In attempting to discover the reason, I discovered that it lies in the difference in bait. French fishermen use herring and caplin, while the Americans use a shellfish, a kind of clam that they bring with them from home and of which cod are particularly fond. This shellfish is found in small numbers in the barachois at Miquelon and on the coasts of Newfoundland.

For sailors, the cod fishery is a branch of industry that accustoms them to a harsh life, to braving the heaviest weather, and to counting on nothing except their own resources. Hence, they all become quite good carpenters, caulkers, and sailmakers. What an excellent school for our young officers if the government would allow them to take part! Later one might see them in a battle, or involved in a demasting or a shipwreck repairing the damage themselves and urging on the crew by their example, or preventing by their foresight the unfortunate accidents to which the men are continually exposed.

If the government were to reinstate marine artillery crews,[173] it would be quite feasible to take a number of these and put them on board fishing ships; it would have to deduct the bounty allotted according to the number of men provided for the trade.

The outcome of all these measures would be that in a few years the number of our sailors would increase considerably and we would have excellent Newfoundland pilots, included among whom would be many officers. The government, having seen the advantages of such a system in peacetime, would derive even more from it in times of war.

---

173   These belonged to a corps of marine artillery known as "équipages de haut bord," created by Napoleon in a decree of 1 April 1808. (Translator's note.)

Population

The population on the French part of Newfoundland is increasing every year, especially in the area of Bay St. George, where, 40 years ago, there were only two families: one living at the big barachois, and the other at the harbour of St. George's. These two families have produced 18 others in existence at the present time, of which five live at the big barachois and 13 at the harbour of St. George's, which makes for a population of 119 individuals, including a large number of marriageable age, who in turn will doubtless have a large number of children, for the kind of life that they lead, as well as their food, gives them a marked tendency to increase, and this in the healthiest country in the world.

It seems to me that this considerable increase in population in the French part of Newfoundland ought to lead the French government, which up until now has perhaps not been sufficiently made aware of the situation, to be less tolerant, for these families have taken possession of all points along the coast where it is possible to fish salmon, and in addition share the opportunities of the cod fishery with our fishermen. The result is that when our fishermen wish to become involved in this kind of fishery, which is so profitable for them, they will experience great difficulty.

There will of course be claims made to the English government by these inhabitants who are benefiting from our hospitality, and these claims will attract the attention of their government due to the population increase mentioned, the beginnings of an agricultural settlement, and a large number of cattle. It is a real colony, where several English schooners arrive every year, including one from Jersey and the others from Canada, bringing them items made in England, provisions, and everything necessary for building and fitting out their fishing boats. In exchange they take salmon, at the rate of 45 shillings a barrel, and furs. In addition to these schooners, our fishing vessels that come to

St. George's during the fishing season contribute to the activity of this burgeoning colony, which, due to its free port, as well as everything else that I have just noted, cannot fail to increase considerably.

So the English government, hearing the claims of these families, might, in the vagueness of various treaties on the fishery, find grounds for entering a debate and restricting the French exclusively to the cod fishery. I state without any hesitation that continuing our tolerance any longer would only add weight to the claims of the English, and would drive the French away more than ever from the idea of forming fishing settlements there that would make the fishery much more lucrative, and would relieve the government of the bounties that it is obliged to pay in order not to let this branch of industry collapse.

Savages

In Codroy and in Bay St. George, as well as in the Bay of Islands, there are two castes of Indian, known as Mi'kmaq and Montagnais. They have joined together and form a population of 80 to 90 individuals. The former are originally from Cape Breton, and the latter from Labrador.

They live chiefly from hunting and fishing. They sell their furs and their fish to the English living in St. George's, who give them in exchange necessities at a very high price, and treat them quite badly—they scarcely allow them to fish for salmon.

These savages are all Catholic. They are very devoted to the French, and some of them are the offspring of Basque sailors who fish in the area. One of our former sailors, named Benoit, married 30 years ago a savage woman with whom he has nine children. This man is a very good pilot of the southern part of the coast. He lives at the harbour of St. George's, on the side opposite the English.

It would be very desirable for the government to pay some attention to these individuals, who might be extremely useful to French fishermen, if they were employed as guardians of the harbours, rather than the English, who sooner or later will be a hindrance to the government with their claims.

Every year they should be sent a priest taken on as almoner by the commodore of the station, to enlighten them about the Catholic religion which they fervently profess; this would be one more way to put them on our side. One Sunday I listened to their prayers; they sang a high mass from a book written by them, the characters of which I include here, which the missionaries must have learned to be able to teach them the Catholic religion. They had raised a small altar decorated with a figure of Christ and various holy images, next to which on the right there was the portrait of His Majesty the King of France, and, on the left, a picture showing His Royal Highness the Duc de Berry. I added to their prayers the *Domine salvum*, the tune to which they picked up perfectly. I repeat, these Indians appear to be very attached to the French, and if we were ever to form settlements in Newfoundland, they could be even more useful, since a great number would come over from Cape Breton, with which they are frequently in contact.

There is a third caste of savage in the interior of the island, known as Red Savages, who do not communicate with the inhabitants of the country or the Indians. They kill all those that they come across, and are believed to be cannibals. The English have tried in vain to civilize them. They are few in number, and for several years they have not been seen, which leads one to believe that the intense cold that has been experienced in Newfoundland may have destroyed them.

Products

This island produces various kinds of fir trees, but of inferior quality to those of northern Europe. Some very fine ones are found in the Bay of Islands and at the head of Bay St. George. The masts that are made from spruce are very good for two or three years, after which they dry out and become brittle.

Pin cherry, balsam fir,[174] birch, sweet cherry, hazelnuts, and strawberry plants are all very common on the west coast, where there are also a few apple trees. Angelica, maidenhair ferns, sarsparilla, raspberries, gooseberries, and currants are found in all parts of the island.

In Bay St. George, 7 miles [c. 11.2 km] from the harbour, going up the coast from the south, there is a limestone and plaster mine.

In the second river, 2 miles [c. 3.2 km] upstream from the coast, there is a spring with very salt water.

In another river, 2 miles [c. 3.2 km] from the former and 10 miles [c. 16 km] from the shore, there is quite a large coal mine.

I took samples of these three products, which I will deposit at Brest.

There is a considerable quantity of wild animals: black and polar bears, various kinds of wolf, many stags known as *caribou*, foxes, marten, beaver, otters, and seals.

There is a great abundance of seabirds, but as for land birds, they are not very numerous. There are eagles, two kinds of partridge, two kinds of thrush and other small birds, wild geese known as Canada geese, and curlews, which are migratory birds.

It appears that the island does not have any poisonous plants, animals, or reptiles; however, there are enormous numbers of mosquitoes and field mice (wild rats).

The English who inhabit the French part of the west of Newfoundland are very successful in planting hard and soft wheat, oats, barley, buckwheat, potatoes, and all kinds of vegetables, but since they are very lazy, they barely grow enough grain for their cattle.

---

174   The text published in the *Annales maritimes et coloniales* has "bananier" (banana tree), an obvious error in transcription. The original document in the Archives nationales, Paris, MAR CC5 610/602 (cote groupée) has "baumier" (balsam fir). (Translator's note.)

Agriculture

The soil is generally good, especially all of the land around Bay St. George, which, due to its position, its climate (which is not as cold as in other parts of the island), and all the resources it contains, is capable of becoming the finest settlement that we have.

A report on the season's activities by Captain Gautier, captain of the naval schooner La Gentille,[175] *based in St-Pierre, to the commandant of the islands of St-Pierre and Miquelon in 1846.*

Report addressed to the commandant of the islands of St-Pierre and Miquelon on the fisheries on the west coast of Newfoundland allocated to those islands, by Mr. Gautier, captain of the state's schooner the *Gentille*.

Commandant,

On entering the Gulf of St. Lawrence, the first fishing places that one comes across are the northwest cove of Cape Ray and the two rivers at Codroy. These three areas have never been occupied, even though they are capable of sustaining permanent settlements. The rivers in particular would offer considerable resources for salmon fishing. Then there are Codroy Island, Bay St. George, Red Island, and Port-au-Port. Of all these fishing places, only two are in gainful use, Red Island and Codroy Island, and even these are occupied by a company from mainland France. The other harbours at the disposal of St-Pierre and Miquelon are to all intents and purposes abandoned by these fishermen. The only areas used by them are the small banks in Bay St.

---

175   Archives des Colonies, Série C11C. Microfilm 505, Library and Archives Canada. The title page also has the following note, in a different hand: "Since it appeared likely to be of interest to H. E. the Minister, this report was sent to the Department by the Commandant of St. Pierre and Miquelon." (Translator's note.)

George, where in the past few years they have been coming to carry on their trade with bultows.

Before entering on a study of this bay, the most important of the areas mentioned above, offering the most attractions to foreigners, let us cast a swift eye over the other dependencies of these islands.

Codroy

The passage between the mainland and the island forms a kind of harbour where small vessels with a draft of 8 or 10 feet can anchor. The southern passage is the only one used, though the north one could also provide a way through for the schooners that frequent these parts. This is the main reason why I decided to undertake the topography of this island, which has I believe never before been mapped except on a very small scale. This is an excellent fishing area and it is difficult to explain why it has been abandoned by the schooners from St-Pierre and Miquelon, an abandonment that would, without the foresight of the administration of these islands, already have turned Codroy Island into a little English colony, such as for example berth no. 3 in the table.[176] But the temporary concession to a company from France prevents any foreigners from settling there. It is true that there are irregularities in the way in which this company operates, the greatest of which is that it is not possible to apply to it the regulations in effect for our other Newfoundland fisheries. For example, on Codroy Island there are about 140 men with not a single master; they are all independent, and they have contracts with their supplier, represented by a clerk, who has to take their product on the spot and in exchange to provide them with what they need. Since it is in the interest of the supplier to provide as many goods as possible,

---

176   Gautier is referring to the table drawn up in France every year showing the allocation of fishing berths in all harbours frequented by the French in Newfoundland. (Translator's note.)

spirits are naturally among the items traded. And how can we prevent this abuse? By ensuring, when the trading vessels arrive from St-Pierre, that their manifest corresponds to their cargo, which must not exceed a certain figure in alcohol. To do that would require as many naval schooners as there are places to oversee, since Codroy is not the only locality in this position. Moreover, let me hasten to add that during the time that I spent in the Gulf, I never saw any fights due to drunkenness break out among the fishermen.

But if there is some irregularity in the manner in which the harbours allocated to St-Pierre and Miquelon are operated, does this not carry within itself a corrective that should temper its effect? For with a population of foreigners such as exists today in the areas close to Codroy, would it not be extremely difficult, if not impossible, to prevent the fraudulent sale of fish, if schooners, as in the past, acted on their own behalf? The companies operating at those points, apart from the fact that they acquire more fish than they would like from the men they supply, also have to control those same men who, almost always at war with their suppliers, would not fail to denounce them at the slightest appearance of illicit trafficing.

One might think that the figure of 140 men that I referred to above as inhabiting Codroy Island during the fishing season is exaggerated, since the table of allocation of harbours in Newfoundland shows only two berths, nos. 1 and 2, for this fishing spot, berths capable of providing for 22 boats, that is, 66 fishermen, for by "boats" in Newfoundland they mean a boat crewed by three men. But the census that I carried out at Codroy this year gave me 53 boats crewed by two men, i.e., 106, not counting the shoremen attached to the room to dry the fish.

The beaches on the island are of little extent, but could be enlarged by the use of flakes[177] like those found in large numbers on the east coast of Newfoundland, and even be more useful for drying fish than the rocky headlands on the island where the cod quite frequently burns.

---

177   Flakes are wooden drying platforms like those made in France, in Retz, Marseilles, and La Rochelle. (Author's note.)

Red Island

Red Island, operated by the same company as Codroy Island, unfortunately has no harbour, and anchorage there is not practical with offshore winds. However, it seems to offer great advantages for the fishery, since, this year, drying areas have been set up at the top of the island, where the fish is carried up by means of winches to a height of more than 60 metres. In the past it was dried on a rocky headland stretching to the northeast, but it often ran the risk of being carried away by the sea, which, in strong winds from the northwest, sometimes makes this beach completely disappear. In addition, this place is profitable only for a large establishment which has transportation for large volumes, for the product would risk spending the winter there if they waited for the late season to take it away. As I have already mentioned, there is no safe anchorage there, so we do not have to fear the presence of foreign populations. A few families from Cape Breton have nevertheless settled on the mainland, 2 miles [c. 3.2 km] from the island, where they devote themselves entirely to raising cattle and to cultivating the land.

Port-au-Port

The harbour of Port-au-Port, located 7 leagues [c. 38.5 km] to the northeast of Red Island, is nowadays frequented only by a few ships from St-Malo who come in the spring to carry on their early fishery, while waiting for the arrival of the caplin, at which time they sail off to the harbours which are their main destination. Several ships from the islands of Jersey and Guernsey, like ours, begin their fishery at Port-au-Port, and the good relations that they have mean that our fishermen from France find on the coast of Labrador[178] an equally warm welcome.

For some while, schooners from the islands of St-Pierre and Miquelon

---

178 The French treaty shore never extended to Labrador, but a number of French ships fished there quite regularly. (Translator's note.)

have abandoned this area of Newfoundland. In the past they nearly all carried out their early fishery there, and later went to the Magdalen Islands. But today the greater part of them make for the banks that are close to St-Pierre, and from there make their way to the Grand Banks.

Port-au-Port nevertheless has one establishment like those on Red Island, but it is far from having as fruitful a fishery, which is hardly surprising, since the cod disappear from these parts with the caplin. So this year the fishermen went to set up in the Bay of Islands, at Little Port, as soon as the ships occupying that harbour had left, that is, around the end of June, when the latter, with their product, make for the east coast of Newfoundland.

In the spring, herring is plentiful in Port-au-Port, as in Bay St. George, but it does not appear to offer the same attraction to foreigners, who have not yet set up any establishment.

In all the fishing areas that I have just discussed, the seine, which is so common on the east coast, is not used at all. On Red Island, as at Port-au-Port, the fishery is carried on with warys, or small flat-bottomed boats crewed by two men who nearly always make their way by rowing, because of the violent gusts of wind which are common in these parts. In Codroy the fishermen use small boats, built on the spot by the English, that handle well under sail. On all of this coast the fishery is carried on with a hand line.

St. George's (see sketch at the end of this report)

In 1817,[179] when we returned to take possession of the harbours that were granted to us by treaties, we found a few families established in several of them. Bay St. George had five who had been living there for a long while from father to son. Among them was even a former French sailor by the name of Benoist who, married to an Indian woman, had a progeny of

---

179 During the Napoleonic period the French Newfoundland fishery was suspended, and it was a couple of years after Napoleon's defeat at Waterloo in 1815 that this fishery fully resumed. (Translator's note.)

more than 60 people. The other inhabitants were the Denys, the Perrys, the Stuarts, and the Messerveys, whose offspring form the nucleus of the population of this bay. The main industry of these families was the salmon fishery, which was particularly abundant at that time, since there were only a few salmon fishing stations occupied, along a coast where rivers and streams meander everywhere.

If one is to rely on the proclamation of Sir Charles Hamilton,[180] governor of Newfoundland in 1822, it would appear that prior to that date no serious claims had been made to the English government to turn us away from our fisheries. It should be noted that if this proclamation did not bear fruit, the fault perhaps lies with us, for at that time the English prosecuted only the salmon fishery, and did no harm to our subjects, for whom catching this fish had been of little profit,[181] and who devoted themselves exclusively to the cod fishery. This gave rise to a regrettable tolerance on the part of the commodores of the naval station who, receiving no complaints about the invasion of foreigners, allowed in some places a whole population to form, a population which today considers it a right to carry on the fishery, concurrently with us, along the entire west coast.

I said regrettable tolerance, for it appears that none of the commodores of the station before M. Fabvre, except perhaps for M. Bazoche, now rear admiral, made it known to these foreigners that it was purely out of the goodness of our hearts that they were allowed to carry on their trade freely on a coast which, during the fishing season, was ours; on other occasions we would allow this as a reward for services rendered, as is proved by a certificate conveyed to M. Bazoche by an Englishman in Bay St. George, a certificate which still exists today.

And we should not disguise the fact that for a very long time there was either no warship present in Bay St. George, or it was heavily

---

180   The Hamilton proclamation of 12 August 1822 reminded Newfoundlanders that, according to the peace treaties signed between Britain and France, the French Newfoundland fishery was to be on the same footing as it had been prior to 1792, and ordered both fishermen and officials to ensure that the French were not hindered in the prosecution of their fishery. See https://thediscoverblog.com/tag/premiere-series/ for the text of this proclamation. (Translator's note.)

181   A ship fitted out for this fishery in Le Havre (France) had completely failed in this fishery in St. George's. (Author's note.)

neglected. Port Saunders was the anchorage where the ships of the station were based, that is to say 6 leagues [c. 33 km] from the spot with which we are concerned today. This distance is explained by the fact that for a long time the home country had little or no relations with Bay St. George, where only a few traders from St-Pierre came every year and frequently even left behind French sailors who contributed in no small measure to the increase of the population of this part of the coast. The man named Duquesnel, for example, during the close to 12 years that he monopolized the bay, one might say, left 40 deserters, and since, in exchange for his goods, he received foreign products, one might assume that he was far from wishing for frequent visits by the station. This Duquesnel was succeeded by a more enterprising company operating on a larger scale, but their business was soon subject to inspection by the captain of the *Dassas* and the schooners under his orders, and the administration of St-Pierre did the rest. Today there is no trace of fishing rooms or beaches belonging to French subjects. The entire shoreline, both of the point and the cove, is lined with foreign houses or stores. Moreover, it is easy to gain an idea of the growth of the population at this point by comparing the map drawn by Mr. Le Saunier de S. in 1830 with the sketch[182] that I have the honour of attaching to this report. I am considering here just the part of the bay known as the village, noting that the hamlets established on the rivers along this coast have also increased considerably.

Here I shall attempt to explain why there is a continual influx of foreign inhabitants in this area, while at the same time our fishermen practically abandon the place. (I say practically, since the results obtained by a few schooners from St-Pierre and Miquelon in 1845 would seem to require this qualification.)[183]

I am coming to the main point: apart from the seamen in the fishery who,

---
182 September 1846. (Author's note.)
183 Fishing with bultows was attempted, quite successfully, on the small banks in the bay, especially in the late season. The schooner *La Virginie* from Miquelon took 10,000 cod there, of the same size as those on the Grand Bank (1846). (Author's note.)

some to escape the continual recruitment,[184] and others out of desire for a change, annually abandon their flag to remain in St. George's, there are also the continual migrations of people from Cape Breton and New Brunswick who flock to Newfoundland to settle, some in the area around Cape Ray but many on the rivers at Codroy and in Bay St. George's. Presently in this bay there are 35 of these families making up no less than 200 people. They are known as Jacotars,[185] and my efforts to discover the origin of this name were fruitless. In abandoning their home country, these newcomers simply intended to escape the taxes that the government would impose on them as on all of its subjects. At the same time, they wanted to carry on the eel fishery, which is the main source of food for a great number of them.[186] These Acadians, of French origin but practically abandoned to their own devices, respecting no law or religion since the English took power, form a completely separate population, a population that is weakened and bastardized, living from day to day, distinguishing themselves from their English neighbours only by their inertia and laziness. Nevertheless, they cultivate the land enough to harvest sufficient potatoes to last, with their supply of salted eels, until the arrival of the herring which, at the onset of spring, comes into this bay to make up the main harvest of the other inhabitants, a harvest which has replaced the salmon fishery and which, today, is the most productive, the most reliable, and the least costly of fisheries. Salmon seem to have become very rare, and the cod fishery is hardly carried on at all by the English of St. George's. One observation worthy of note: several families in the south and southwest of Newfoundland are also in the habit of coming to settle around St. George's. One of them, of whom I asked the reason for this change, answered that here, at least, we have no collector, whereas everywhere else there is the tax to pay to our government.

---

184 The French government paid outfitters a bonus for each fisherman employed in the Newfoundland fishery. A condition of this bonus was that, following the completion of the fishery, fishermen had to be available for service in the French navy if circumstances required it. This is why fishermen who jumped ship to stay in Newfoundland were known as deserters. (Translator's note.)

185 See Chapter 5, note 85, for a possible explanation of the origin of this term. Gautier's understanding of the term is a little different. He applies it to deserters from the French fishing fleet and incomers of French origin from Acadia. However, he also notes the mixed French/Mi'kmaq origin of the Benoist family noted earlier. (Translator's note,)

186 This fish is so abundant in the area known as Flat Bay that it is no exaggeration to say that the bottom is paved with them. (Author's note.)

It is during the months of April and May that all of them, men, women, and children, devote themselves to bringing in the herring. A few Acadians, some of the least lazy, are employed by the English as labourers. At that season, which is really harvest time, this spot offers the most lively sight in all of Newfoundland. Hundreds of boats are ceaselessly busy taking this fish from nets that are teeming with them, to the point where they often sink under the weight. The anchorage is invaded by boats coming from all parts of the coast, from Nova Scotia, New Brunswick, the Magdalen Islands, and Lower Canada. This fish, once it has been prepared and salted, is put into quarter barrels and mostly exported to the St. Lawrence. At present on the English markets it sells for 14 to 15 francs a barrel. This is also the price that merchants pay for it locally, but in goods. The inhabitant of St. George's has nothing to lay out to obtain a few hundred quarter barrels of herring, except for the cost of the salt and the initial cost of the nets. He makes the barrels himself out of local wood, and his involvement in the cod fishery in summer is little to none.[187]

So the presence of large numbers of foreigners in St. George's is the result of:

1. The abundance of herring, which for the past dozen years has acquired an intrinsic value on the shores of Upper and Lower Canada,
2. The complete and total freedom that they enjoy, with no controls and with no payment of dues or taxes.

But let us consider whether this foreign population is the reason for the place being abandoned by our subjects. I do not believe this to be the case, for it should be remembered that since herring from the coast of Newfoundland is prohibited in France, in order to promote that industry

---

[187] As a general rule they use 100 kilograms of salt to prepare a barrel of herring. This is where they have their greatest expense, since in Newfoundland they need only a few kilograms to salt 50 kilograms of cod, but the former is much more quickly and reliably caught than the latter. However, there are still a few ships that fish for cod in Ship Cove on the north shore of the bay, though in very small quantities. (Author's note.)

along our coasts, the English subjects are not in competition with our nationals. Furthermore, it is quite likely that, if cod were as plentiful in this bay, and easily fished with lines or with seines as in certain harbours along the east coast, France would not have ceded it to the islands of St-Pierre and Miquelon. It is precisely because France found no benefit in this fishery that it handed it over to those islands. The depth of the bay and the almost complete disappearance of cod after the caplin have been there are, I believe, the two main reasons why our fishermen have decided not to set up there, therefore leaving the way open to foreigners. If it is not overstating the case, I believe I can say that St. George's is lost to us, and what would have been easy to do in the past has now become practically impossible. Indeed, we could, before the start of the herring fishery, have encouraged the prosecution of the salmon fishery in all parts of the bay capable of accommodating a salmon-fishing station. We could have set up an industry in competition, and if the English government found this unacceptable (which it certainly would), we could have objected that our settlements were no more contrary to the treaties than theirs, and insisted that their withdrawal be a condition of ours. But today they have too firmly taken root for this strategy to be practicable, and, in any case, the herring fishery alone would be sufficient to keep them there.

Despite this invasion of foreigners and the little inclination that our subjects appear to have for our fisheries in this area, I believe that it is prudent not to abandon our rights in St. George's, particularly since the most recent measures taken by the British government with regard to herring and caplin exports to St-Pierre; if this were to be cut off from us, we could then, for lack of anything better, fall back on this bay to supply our ships from France fishing on the Banks. Unless, however, we were assured that the islands of St-Pierre and Miquelon would be supplied by English coastal boats from the South Coast of Newfoundland, as they always have been up to the end of 184[5?].

Let me recapitulate: St. George's now appears to be struck from the map of our fisheries. The government in St. John's has established a spiritual ministry; a Protestant minister adds the task of schoolteacher to his other duties. A church and an educational establishment have been built for him for this purpose. The main authority in Newfoundland has perhaps not yet dared to send a magistrate there, although one would be just as useful as the other, for, since this place is much sought after by English captains intent on committing barratry, disputes—often very serious ones—arise almost daily, and since might is right, fights and violent altercations are a common result.

This, Commandant, is the outcome of my observations during my station on the west coast of Newfoundland. I hope that you will appreciate the devotion that I feel for the good of the service and the national interest.

Please accept, Commandant, the assurance of the deep respect of your most humble and devoted servant.

Gautier
Captain of the schooner *La Gentille*
Codroy 1 October 1846

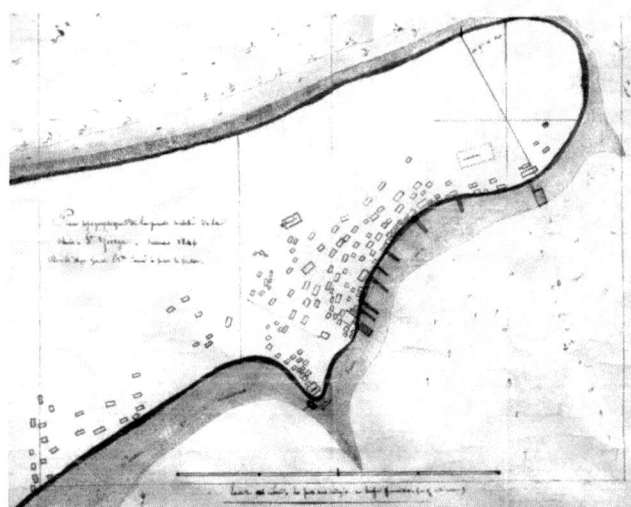

Handwritten inscription: "Topographical map of the inhabited part of Bay St. George, September 1846, by Mr. Ange Gautier, Captain of the schooner *La Gentille*."

A report on the season's activities by Captain Mer, commodore of the French naval station in Newfoundland in 1868, to the minister for the navy.

Report to the Admiral Commander in Chief of the Naval Division for the West Indies, the Gulf of Mexico, and North America on the Expedition to Newfoundland in the Year 1868.[188]

20 September 1868

Admiral,

During the period of command that I have just completed on the coast of Newfoundland for the protection and the surveillance of our fishery, I have had the honour of acquainting you in my different reports with the movements of the *Pomone* and those of other vessels of the Subdivision.[189] The table attached[190] summarizes the movements carried out by each ship, both for the inspection of the harbours and for carrying mail.

The result is that every harbour on both coasts was visited several times, eight bags of mail from Europe were distributed, and letters for

---

188 Archives nationales, Paris, MAR BB4 886 (1868).
189 As the title of the report indicates, the French naval ships sent to Newfoundland every year for the duration of the fishing season were a subdivision of the West Indies, Mexico, and North America Division. (Translator's note.)
190 The table Mer is referring to was not included in the report consulted in the Archives nationals, Paris.

France were sent five times via Sydney[191] or St. John's.

Nevertheless you will observe, Admiral, that due to the late arrival from France of the aviso[192] *Curieux*, as a result of the change of captain for the *Belette*, and then to the recall to France of the *Levrette*, the means at my disposal were to all intents and purposes limited to the *Pomone* and the *Curieux*. However, I believe that no task was put in abeyance and there was no lack of surveillance or protection anywhere.

It would however be desirable next year for the surveillance of the west coast between Férolle and Flowers Cove to start earlier than this year. This is the only area where disputes arose between our fishermen and the locals; it is also the only point which requires practically constant surveillance throughout the fishing season.

Observations on the Composition of the Subdivision

The presence in St-Pierre of two schooners for the local service of the colony had for many years naturally resulted in these two small vessels being assigned to the surveillance of the fishery during the four months that this industry is carried on. Then force of habit caused this utilization to become fixed, and when it was necessary to replace the *Fauvette* and the *Gentille* because of their antiquated condition, two new schooners were sent out from France to replace the old ones.

Experience has proved both to me and to my predecessors that these vessels are quite unsuited to providing good service and that two small steamships like the second-class gun boats outfitted for the Russian war[193] would meet all the conditions one could wish.

The duties of these schooners consist mostly in visiting the harbours

---

191 As Mer explains later, French naval ships regularly went to Sydney, Nova Scotia, to replenish their supply of coal. (Translator's note.)
192 An aviso was originally a small ship used for carrying dispatches, but was later used to describe medium-sized warships used in the colonial service.
193 Mer is referring to the Crimean war (1853–56) between the Russian Empire and the Turkish, French, and British coalition. Seven French gunboats of this type were deployed during those operations. For details, see the website by Alain Clouet at http://dossiersmarine.free.fr/fs_ca_G2.html. (Translator's note.)

or rather the creeks where our fishermen set up operations, and they are often held there for very long periods by the difficulty of getting out once they have gone in.

In fact, our fishermen are in the habit of setting up their operations not in good harbours with easy access, but in those where they are as close as possible to the fishing grounds; so they often prefer dreadful, rocky creeks where they moor four together for the whole season, and yet these are the harbours or so-called harbours that the schooners often have to inspect; hence it is not uncommon to find them held there for weeks at a time by headwinds, unable to carry out their surveillance of the local Englishmen who, well aware of the situation, are able without fear to use seines and other forbidden gear.

With two motor gunboats, this disadvantage would disappear. Surveillance would be constant and effective. It could begin much earlier and all harbours would be inspected much more often than is possible with the schooners.

Lastly, at the end of the fishing season, these two small gunboats, instead of being laid up in the barachois like the schooners, could be used to establish easy and regular communications between St-Pierre and Miquelon, which, despite their proximity, have no communications during practically all of the winter season.

The use of two motor gunboats would naturally require the setting up of a coal storage depot on the west coast, but that is a very easy thing to do; coal is not expensive at Sydney, and the *Eurydice* on making its way to Croque could drop off about 60 tons at Port Saunders, where there is a location that is most suitable for such a depot. This coal would be sufficient for the gunboat on the west coast, and the other one, responsible for the east coast, could obtain its supplies at Croque.

This combination would in addition would allow us to dispense with the aviso that we have to take from the West Indies division.

Finally, with just the two gunboats in question, it would be very easy to maintain a regular mail service; they would alternate going to Sydney and St. John's to pick up mail, and on every trip they would fill up with coal.

I believe that this would greatly facilitate everything, and save one vessel whose presence on the West Indies station could be indispensable.

As for the usefulness of the schooners in the surveillance of the fishery, I find it to be practically non-existent, and yet once the fishing season is over, they are laid up, and their crews are used simply to patrol the streets of St-Pierre.

A proposal similar to the one that I have just outlined has already been made by M. de Jonquières, when he was in command of the subdivision, and M. Lapelin was following a similar line of thinking in requesting two gunboats and two schooners.

I believe that the schooners would be superfluous if there were two gunboats, which would reduce to three the number of vessels comprising the Newfoundland subdivision.

The Grand Bank, Banquereau, and St-Pierre Bank Fishery

According to information that I have obtained, it appears that the fishery this year is poorer than last year's, which itself was worse than the preceding years.

This fishery, which is the largest in terms of the number of ships outfitted by us, occupies a very large number of ships and men; on my arrival in St-Pierre in early June, the roads provided a magnificent sight, holding more than 200 vessels, all outfitted for the Grand Banks and for the southern banks.

The colony of St-Pierre also fits out quite a large number of schooners, which usually fish on the St-Pierre Bank or on Banquereau Bank.

Discipline among the Crews of the Bankers

Discipline among the crews of the bankers leaves something to be desired. The profession of fisherman on the Grand Banks is so harsh and so dangerous that when the ships put in at St-Pierre to take on bait, the crews unfortunately indulge in excessive consumption of alcohol, which frequently results in disorder and acts of insubordination. I received quite a large number of complaints from captains of these ships; I imposed a certain number of disciplinary punishments, and I called two Maritime Commercial Councils to judge two quite serious cases. In one of them, the first mate of one of the ships had sworn at and struck his captain, while the other was a case of a sailor who had refused to board one of the fishing shallops on the Grand Banks, despite the example bravely set by the men in charge of the boats. I would have had a large number of other cases to attend to if I had been able to stay in St-Pierre, but the non-arrival of the *Curieux* forced me to leave for the coast, leaving the complaints in the hands of the Commissioner of Maritime Registration.

The experience of this year proves to me that it is indispensable for the commodore of the station to prolong his stay in St-Pierre until the middle of June, when all the bankers leave, in order to put down and punish acts of indiscipline that are committed among the many crews that are present in the roads at that time.

This duty is in fact much more important than the surveillance of a few ships spread out in the harbours along the coast, where in any case they are protected by the other ships of the subdivision.

I should point out that in the absence of a warship in the roads at St-Pierre, the responsibility for dealing with acts of indiscipline and imposing penalties belongs to the Commissioner of Maritime Registration (in this case an assistant commissioner, I believe) who at that time of year is so busy with the presence of 200 or 300 ships that the majority of the time it is impossible for him to deal with the complaints that are made to him; at least this is what several captains have told me.

In order to eradicate an unfortunate situation so detrimental to discipline, it would be essential at that time of year to always have a warship in the roads; it would be sufficient for this purpose to have the schooner assigned to local service, the *Mouche*, brought out of the barachois; it is under the command of a lieutenant. Then, according to Section 6 of the Disciplinary and Penal Order for the Merchant Navy, the right to impose discipline would belong to this officer, as soon as his ship is in the roads rather than in the harbour.

Gulf Fishery

The captains all agree that the Gulf fishery would have been good if the ships had been able to reach their fishing grounds as early as last year. But the exceptional length of the crossing from France, and the persistance of ice in the Gulf, which prevented them from reaching their harbours until the first two weeks of June, caused them to lose more than a month of good fishing.

The results are not those of a good year; nevertheless, the vessels on the west coast are practically all less unfortunate than those on the east coast.

Accidents

Two most unfortunate accidents occurred among the ships on this coast. The *Nautonnier* of the Guibert company making for the harbour of Little Port was lost at sea and its captain drowned. The *Courrier de Terre-Neuve* of the same company was lost in the Strait of Belle Isle on the coast of Labrador while tacking in thick fog.

I was able to report these unfavourable conditions myself, since I was passing through the Strait of Belle Isle on board the *Pomone* on the very night that the shipwreck occurred.

In this latter accident the ship was lost, but there was no loss of life.

The most exaggerated rumours were circulating about the circumstances of this shipwreck. It was claimed that the English locals had taken the vessel by boarding it, and had pillaged and sacked it. The captain, blinded by his misfortune, had even made a complaint along these lines to Captain Parish, in command of the *Sphinx* of the English navy, which was in Port Saunders when the French captain arrived there.

Captain Parish went to the scene of the shipwreck and carried out a thorough investigation, which I sent to you in its entirety, Admiral, from which it appeared that, far from indulging in scenes of savage piracy (those are the terms used in the complaint) the locals immediately went to the assistance of this wrecked ship, put out anchors and floated it; they did all that they could to save it, and they would probably have succeeded if they had been directing operations on their own. Finally, after the mooring lines broke, and the the ship was definitively lost, they helped in carrying the goods to land and later repatriated the crew to Port au Choix.

It is nevertheless clear that after the ship had been abandoned, many lines were taken by the locals, but it is also clear that the French captain had promised wages to these Englishmen, who are very poor and had worked for him for a full day. The English are not in the habit of working for nothing, and since the captain was not in a position to pay them, they thought that they were entitled to pay themselves by taking the rope that was on the beach and was not guarded by anyone.

In addition to the loss of these two ships, unfortunately we also have to report several men missing.

When the *Douze Juillet* put into Bay St. George, it found itself without a sailor, who became lost in the woods and all efforts at finding him were fruitless.[194]

---

[194] Sometimes men would deliberately leave a French fishing ship with the intention of staying in Newfoundland to begin a new life, and hiding in the woods until their ship had left port was one way of accomplishing this. (Translator's note.)

The *Mogador* of Little Port lost a boat crewed by three men.

The *Normandie* also lost a man and a fishing shallop abeam Barbace Cove.

East Coast Fishery

The ships on the east coast were less fortunate than those in the Gulf, and from Cape Onion to La Scie, practically all of them will have no more than a third of their normal catch.

There are however three exceptions. The *Jeune Polixène* of l'Anse du Dégrat had a fine fishery. The *Jeune Henriette* at Three Mountains and the *Jean Bart* at Boutitou state that they are quite satisfied. And the ships sent by the Guibert company to the Grand Banks have succeeded quite well, improving the overall total.

Accidents

The *Élisabeth* at Quirpon lost a boat with three men.

The *Eugène* of St. Anthony also lost a boat and the three men who crewed it. And the *Calculo*[195] lost an apprentice while setting a seine.

Salmon Fishery

Of the three salmon-fishing stations granted this year, only one, in Hare Bay, has given satisfactory results.

The one at Castors River was not even used, as the manager for the Larsonnent Company did not even cover his expenses last year.

All along the coasts of Newfoundland and Labrador, as well as Cape Breton and Prince Edward Island, the past few years have seen a considerable reduction in the salmon fishery, which should be no surprise given the enormous destruction of this fish that is being carried out.

---

195   This is the spelling given by Mer. *Calculot* is the term used in St-Pierre for the Atlantic puffin. (Translator's note.)

In the past, salmon was fished only at the mouths of watercourses where their instinct led them to go upstream to spawn in waters that are colder than the sea, and those that escaped would reproduce in considerable numbers.

Today salmon are tracked not only at the mouths of streams, which are practically all blocked by nets, but it can also be said that the entire circumference of Newfoundland and all of the coast of Labrador is set with salmon nets, a kind of fixed net set at every cape and at the points outside every bay, so that the destruction is enormous and the renewal is not sufficient to fill the gap.

The decrease in salmon is perhaps even greater on the English shore than on the parts that are reserved for us, for the nets there are much more numerous on account of the greater concentration of inhabitants.

Herring Fishery

In spite of the favourable provisions for the entry into France of herring fished on the coast of Newfoundland, our captains do not appear to be disposed to undertake this fishery on a large scale. Upon their arrival on the coast, they fish herring as bait to catch cod, but very few of them have any desire to take a chance on them; all seem afraid that this fishery would involve a loss of time, and hence compromise their main operation, the cod fishery.

The ships that put into Bay St. George this year in June nevertheless fished a few hundred barrels of herring, but they could have taken several thousand if they had wanted to, such was the abundance of this fishery. The local inhabitants took more than 30,000 barrels in a period of two weeks.

I strongly encouraged the captains not to neglect this alternative opportunity in years when the cod is not present, and especially to ensure that they have the certificates required for the duty-free importation of this fish. But, once again, few of them seem disposed to undertake this kind of fishery. The manager of one of the chief companies with whom I was discussing the advantages that our captains might derive from it said to me: "What products come from herring? None, or very few."

Discipline among Crews on Both Coasts

During my tours of the two coasts I had to impose only one disciplinary punishment, and the captains of the other ships of the Subdivision also had to impose only a few insignificant punishments. Everywhere I found the punishment logs blank, and I was able to confirm the excellent morale among these crews.

It was not without admiration that I saw these good people identifying themselves with their outfitters and taking the keenest interest in the success of the operation, being on the lookout for news about whether other ships were doing better than they were, wherever they were always taking the side of the outfitter. One hears again and again people repeating that it would be most unfortunate if their outfitter lost money, since he provides a living for so many people in our country. I state again that these men are not paid mercenaries; they are good sailors contributing conscientiously and with all their might to the success of the operation.

Bait Fishery[196]

Sometimes there is not enough bait in the Gulf along the coast reserved for us, while it is most abundant on the coast of Labrador, and our fishermen are in the habit of going there to obtain some, either by buying it from the

---

[196] The supply of bait was a source of friction between Newfoundland and France, culminating in the Bait Act of 1887 prohibiting Newfoundland residents from selling bait to the French. The measure did not prove to be very effective, as the French found other ways of procuring supplies, including catching it themselves. However, for the French to catch it outside the limits of the French Shore (in Labrador, for example) was a violation of the treaties. (Translator's note.)

English residents or by fishing it themselves when the opportunity arises.

A few years ago, some difficulties arose regarding this trade in bait, and the English schooner tasked with overseeing this coast even arrested some of our boats; since then, the government of St. John's has recognized that trade in bait is allowed on the coast of Labrador and that the French could freely go there to purchase it. It appears that this year our fishermen by agreement with a few English along this coast went there not to purchase bait, but to fish for it with their shallops, and that, when a complaint was made to the commodore of the English station, the inhabitants in question are reported to have replied that they were free to hire the French to work for them if they so wished. The English commodore told me that he had informed them that they were correct, but I know that fresh complaints were made by the majority of the inhabitants, probably those who previously sold bait to our fishermen.

Since this is a service offered to our subjects, I told the English commodore that it was up to him to do as he saw fit, but still insisting that the bait trade should not suffer any interference if our fishermen needed it.

Labrador Fishery

Several schooners from St-Pierre were surprised fishing illegally on the coast of Labrador; the English ships of the station treated them with great kindness and the commodore refused to give me their names. In such cases the English make an important distinction between the ships from France and those outfitted in St-Pierre; the latter, the English commodore told me, are on our side: they are from Newfoundland.

Local Fishery on the Islands of St-Pierre and Miquelon

The local fishery in St-Pierre has been poor this year, while the one at Miquelon has been very plentiful, a particularly fortunate turn of events, since for two or three years fish have been scarce at Miquelon and the population of that island was in dire straits.

English Fishery

The fishery appears to have been quite good on the south coast of Newfoundland, and on the east coast as far as St. John's, but beyond, going north, it has been as bad as on the coast reserved for us.

On the coast of Labrador, south of the Strait of Belle Isle and in the Strait, it has been very poor. In the north, however, it has been very productive, with the cod becoming more plentiful moving further north.

The schooners which went furthest north quickly filled their hold and exhausted their supply of salt; they could easily have made two trips in the season if they had wanted to.

English Schooners Fishing in Northern Labrador

For a few years this fishery has been giving such good results that the number of schooners going there every year has been growing constantly, and I have been assured that this year there were more than 500 or 600.

So our captains have nothing to fear from the presence of English captains in our harbours; they sometimes put in there to rest on their way to Labrador, but they have no interest in staying to fish, since they are sure of having a much more plentiful and easier fishery by going to Labrador than they would by fishing clandestinely in our harbours.

State of the Rooms on Both Coasts

All of the rooms occupied by our fishermen are generally in good condition and well maintained; the same is true of the small number that are not occupied but are guarded.

As for all of the others, they are falling in ruins everywhere; a large number have completely disappeared over the past several years, leaving no trace behind, and the remainder will not be long in following suit.

I understand the regrets of the captains who are *Prud'hommes*[197] of certain harbours, such as Quirpon among others, and the complaints that they make every year about the extent of the devastation suffered in the winter. While unfortunate, it is inevitable, and it would be puerile to believe that, given the Newfoundland climate and the actions of men, such unguarded and unmaintained rooms can stand up for very long.

The only effective way to preserve them would be to give a salary to the former guardians, who, since they receive nothing as long as the rooms remain unoccupied, have no interest in its preservation and are perhaps the first to help themselves to wood for heating during the winter.

These former guardians are practically all reduced to extreme poverty, and if our outfitters wish to keep their stages and outbuildings, I see no other effective way of ensuring their preservation than paying a salary to some of these unfortunate people, who would then become responsible for them.

Rooms of the Migratory Fishermen in the Gulf

The rooms of the migratory fishermen in the Gulf always leave a great deal to be desired; however, the number of cabins is increasing, and the number of sailcloth-covered shelters decreasing. The men do not complain; these are men who are so used to poverty and so hardened to fatigue that as long as their food is assured, the rest counts for little.

---

197   The *Prud'homme* of a harbour frequented by the French was a fishing captain elected by the others and responsible for settling disputes. (Translator's note.)

Theft of Salt in Quirpon

Last winter there was a theft of a considerable quantity of salt in one of the unguarded rooms at Quirpon. It was impossible to discover who was responsible; the inhabitants claim that the theft was committed by sealers who put in at Quirpon in large numbers in the spring. These crews are, it is true, made up of buccaneers capable of anything, but it is possible that the inhabitants also took part and put the responsibility on the backs of the sealers; however, in the absence of any evidence or any indication whatsoever, it was impossible to undertake any regular proceedings against the guilty parties.

I pointed out to the Prud'homme in Quirpon how necessary it is not to leave any salt or other material at the disposal of these poor people who are starving, and that even in France, if one left salt for an entire winter with nobody to guard it, it would inevitably be taken away.

Nevertheless, I informed Sir Musgrave,[198] governor of Newfoundland, of this fresh offence, and he responded that if I could provide him with any indications of the identity of those responsible for the theft, he would hand them over to justice.

Cabins for the Sick

In all of the sedentary stations there is a cabin, or at least a place set aside, where the sick can be placed. Fortunately, the climate of Newfoundland is sufficiently healthy for them to be used only rarely.

Provisions

Provisions are generally of good quality; the bread in particular is excellent. Each station has an oven, and the men nearly always have fresh bread.

---

198   Sir Anthony Musgrave (1828–88), governor of Newfoundland 1864–68. (Translator's note.)

Cider, which is the usual drink, is poor, but the men do not complain; some outfitters give their men wine twice a week.

Contraventions of Regulations

First, I will note an error in the distribution tables, where a room is shown for Ingornachoix Bay at Port Saunders; no fishing room exists at Port Saunders. The ship *Hyacinthe Marie*, to which it was allocated, has not put up any building there of any kind. That ship anchored there on 5 June, then went to set up at St. John Island at the room known as Mazagran.

It was doubtless the understanding that the *René* and the *Hyacinthe Marie* would be in the same bay that led the administration to allow these two ships to be grouped together for health care purposes, so that the *René*, which is on its own in Ingornachoix Bay, finds itself without a doctor.[199]

Unoccupied Room

On 30 August the *Lévrier* of the Fontan company, which had been allocated room no. 1 in the harbour of St. John Island, had not yet taken possession of its room. On that date this ship was at New Férolle and was preparing to go to Fisch Island to load cod.

In response to the observation made to the manager of the Fontan company by the captain of the *Belette* that the *Lévrier* had not yet taken regular possession of its room, the response received was that it would soon be doing so. But, given the fact that the season is well advanced, that ship will not be able to meet the conditions of the order to carry out an effective fishery there, since according to the provisions of the order of 19 October 1851, made to implement the act on bounties of 22 July of the same year, occupation cannot be for less than 30 days.

---

199   Mer is referring to the practice of sometimes allowing ships that are to be fishing out of the same harbour to be exempted from the regulation requiring a doctor on board each one. (Translator's note.)

I note that the *Lévrier* is one of the two ships for which Mr. Fontan was sentenced last year to a fine of 3,000 francs for failure to occupy his room. In addition, because the agents of that company persist in conducting themselves outside that regulation, I believe that is appropriate to apply to that outfitter Section 13 of the order, since the *Lévrier* has no more filled the conditions set down by the order than it did last year.

I am ordering the captain of the *Curieux*, when he goes to St. John,[200] to have the Prud'homme prepare a record of this breach of regulations and to pass it on his return to the Commissioner of Maritime Registration in the port from which he left.

Observation on the Substitution of the Anchor Point Room for the Tonnelle Cove Room

Room no. 5 at Tonnelle Cove, St. John Island, which for several years people had been eagerly requesting to have listed, has never been occupied, and in the partial draw held this year the Fontan company was given the room at Anchor Point instead of the Tonnelle Cove room, which it has completely abandoned.

But if this room at Anchor Point is substituted for the Tonnelle Cove room, it becomes sedentary, like the latter, and hence must be occupied on a permanent basis. Yet the Fontan company has not begun building any structure there this year.

The captain of the *Levrette* noted that at that room there was only a simple cabin and an oven built several years ago by a M. Richard. This officer rightly points out that the privilege granted to the Fontan company entails certain obligations and that the agents of that company are very quick to disregard them while at the same time proving very protective of their rights.

---

200   Mer is referring here to St. John Island, on the northwest coast of Newfoundland, not the capital, St. John's. (Translator's note.)

Damage at the Savage Island Room

Yet another complaint has been made about the agents of this company.

Captain Houet of the Guibert company complains that last year a cabin and two salt houses on Savage Island were removed by Captain Laignet, manager of the Fontan company, and is claiming their restitution.

Captain Laignet understood that he could occupy that room last year in the absence of the *Douze Juillet*, which had returned to France for repairs.

He admits having destroyed one of the stages and a cabin, but claims in his defence that since he understood he could permanently occupy that room, he thought he was entitled to demolish one of the stages that was falling into ruin, and a cabin located in the middle of the beach, to improve the rest and to make it serviceable, which he claims to have done.

Such an excuse cannot be accepted; you do not improve a fishing room by demolishing a stage and a cabin, and I believe that Captain Huet's claim is well founded; this captain declares that, far from having found the room improved, he saw that nothing was serviceable, that there was no salt house, and that he would have faced great difficulty if he had caught any cod as soon as he arrived.

East Coast

Captain Lamy of the *Eugénie*, anchored in the harbour of St. Anthony, made a complaint to me about his predecessor regarding various damages carried out at that room at the time when the latter is believed to have left it last year; I do not have the necessary information to assess the value of this claim; in any case the damages were very slight.

Infractions in the Use of Fishing Gear

I have received no complaints about the simultaneous use of seines and bultows, or about the use of any unauthorized gear. I believe that in this respect the regulations have been observed everywhere.

The suppression of the hiring of surgeons on board ships sent to the fishery was once again requested at the last meeting of outfitters.

I cannot reject such a request too strongly, and without attempting to judge the reasons why some outfitters wish to free themselves from this requirement, I believe that we have gone much too far in the liberty that they have been allowed in this respect; I consider that the tolerance of the administration has been much too great.

At first they were allowed to take health officers in place of medical doctors, then medical students, then people who are nothing more than cod splitters.

The ships that were all together in a single harbour were permitted to have a single doctor; there are even harbours such as Little Port, where there are four ships and no doctor.

For medical purposes, even ships fishing in different harbours have been grouped together, and some ships were allowed to leave with no surgeon on account of the difficulty in finding one, or so it was claimed.

There is nothing surprising about such difficulty given the life to which these poor young men are subjected. It has become quite evident to me that, with the exception of two or three surgeons at the most, all the others split cod. When this is pointed out to them, they reply that this is true but they do so voluntarily; however, I am convinced that if they did not do it, they would no longer be employed.

So the result is that the great majority of these practitioners are incapable of giving proper care to the sick and even most of the time of recognizing an illness.

I shall cite just two examples:

A sailor having had a fractured arm for a month was declared able to carry out his duties, and if the chief surgeon of the *Curieux* had not identified this fracture and applied a device, this poor man would have been crippled while being regarded as an idler.

In another harbour an entire crew was poisoned by the use of containers having lead in their tinning, without the illness being recognized. On a great many occasions, the surgeon of the *Pomone* intervened to care for sick men and indicate the treatment that should be followed.

I believe therefore that in the interests of the health of our many crews, the administration should show itself to be very strict in the taking on board of surgeons.

Grouping several ships together in the same harbour, as in the case of Little Port, should never be allowed.

Ships fishing in different harbours should never be grouped together, as in the case of the *René* fishing at Keppel and the *Hyacinthe Marie*, or the *Jeune Henriette* fishing in Three Mountains, which is grouped with the ships in St. Anthony as far as the surgeon is concerned.

This grouping involving different harbours is as if one expected doctors in St-Malo to treat the inhabitants of Granville.

Finally, it should never be permitted for a ship to leave without a surgeon when it will be occupying a harbour on its own.

The outfitters claim that it is very difficult, if not impossible, to find surgeons for their ships. One could respond by saying that if they were to be properly remunerated, and if these practitioners were not asked to carry out work as repellant as cod splitting, they would find as many as they might wish for.

English Residents on the Coasts

We know that the English population settled on the part of the coast of Newfoundland reserved for us would not exist if our outfitters had not had the lack of foresight about 40 years ago of setting up English guardians on their stages; once they had married and had a large number of children, they formed the basis of this population. Today the evil cannot be undone; centres of 10 or 12 families have formed, making up small villages, and it would be completely impossible to drive these unfortunate people away from the ground that they cleared and where they have built houses. In some places this population is showing a tendency to increase; in others, it is static, and almost everywhere it lives in the most abject poverty. The soil of Newfoundland is too barren to provide an adequate subsistence through agriculture; it is fishing that provides their living. The only families that have a reasonable life are those of the guardians, in the harbours where we have settlements, and where our outfitters pay them for their care with provisions. Other families, without this advantage, live from day to day in a most precarious situation; since the fishery failed for them this year, several of them are in danger of starving during the coming winter.

I have looked closely at this population, which practically everywhere I have found to be honest and industrious, well aware of our rights and obedient to the slightest command. And I received almost no complaints about these local inhabitants.

Our captains and crews are generally on very good terms with these people and they render services to one another. However, difficulties sometimes arise. For example, while inspecting one fishing harbour, on one of our unoccupied stages I found young Englishmen busy splitting and preparing cod. When I commented on this, the Prud'homme replied: "Oh! They are not doing any harm; they are children." So it is our captains who nearly always are the first to give permission for contraventions that little by little grow into abuse and dispossession, and then, when the problem becomes too big, they have recourse to the ships of the station to put a stop to them. It would, however, be much better to prevent these abuses rather than having to punish them.

The English in the area around Anchor Point and in Flowers Cove are the only ones about whom we received well-founded complaints this year. It appears that not only did they use seines to fish before the arrival of our ships, but they also wanted to carry on using them after their arrival.

Captain Galopet states that he was greatly hindered by them and that they refused to stop using their seines, saying that they would obey only the officers of the Imperial navy and not merchant captains. It is true that they were quite submissive as soon as the *Belette* and the *Curieux* showed up in that area; nevertheless, it is a locality that requires special surveillance, and it may be necessary to confiscate a few nets next year if, despite their promise, they continue to try to use them.

An officer from the English corvette *Sphinx* visited Flowers Cove when Captain Galopet was having difficulties with the locals and there was a rumour that he had given them permission to use seines as the French do. Captain Parish, to whom I have since spoken, told me that this rumour was entirely groundless and that his duty officer had given no such authorization.

Relations with the English Station and the Authorities in St. John's

This year the English station was under the orders of Captain Parish, in command of the *Sphinx*. This senior officer had come to St-Pierre with the intention of seeing me a few days prior to the arrival of the *Pomone*, but I had the pleasure of meeting him on three different occasions in St. John's or Croque harbour.

We had the best and most cordial relations, and I became certain that in all of the difficulties that might arise between fishermen of the two nations, he would always act with the most conciliatory intentions and in a manner likely to facilitate an amicable solution.

I also had extremely good relations with the authorities in St. John's, principally with the bishop, who is perhaps the most important person in the colony; he came on board the *Pomone* to return my visit, and on his departure I gave him a nine-gun salute.

On my arrival in St. John's, Sir Musgrave, governor of the colony, was in England. I had cordial visits to his replacement as well as with different authorities in the colony.

In Croque I had the opportunity to see the schooner of the colonial service with Mr. Marsh on board, the superintendent of fisheries in Newfoundland and Labrador. This Mr. Marsh is independent of the English station, answering only to the colonial authorities. A few years ago, he raised some difficulties regarding bait that our fishermen were going to buy in Labrador. This same Mr. Marsh had at that time shown great strictness with respect to our fishermen, and even carried out arbitrary acts regarding them. This was at the time of irritating discussions in the St. John's assembly on the proposed Convention between France and England.[201] I was expecting to find in this Mr. Marsh a most recalcitrant Englishman; I saw with pleasure that he was a very peaceful man who assured me of his good and conciliatory intentions with respect to our fishermen.

Reduction in Fish on the Coast of Newfoundland

The captains are unanimous in reporting the gradual reduction of fish on the coast of Newfoundland, and as this reduction coincides with an increase in the number of ships fishing on the Banks, they are inclined to reach the conclusion that the gear used to catch cod on the Banks, that

---

201   In 1857 authorities in Paris and London negotiated an Anglo-French Convention on the fishery, which was not to be put into effect unless ratified by Newfoundland. Newfoundland angrily rejected it, and there was considerable ill-feeling on all sides. (Translator's note.)

is, bultows or trawls, is the cause of the reduction of fish on the coast. They state with some reason that the Banks are criss-crossed by such a prodigious quantity of baited lines that the cod stay there, since they find abundant food there, and no longer come in to the coast. They also assert that spawny fish are taken mostly by the Banks fishermen and that that too is one of the main causes in the reduction in the numbers of fish.

It is difficult to reach a definitive opinion on such a question. We cannot consider modifying in any way the manner in which bankers fish; the only method that they use is the bultow. Moreover, I believe that we do not sufficiently understand the habits of cod, the direction of their migrations and the areas where they prefer to lay their eggs. Whatever the case may be, the extraordinary abundance of fish on the north coast of Labrador proves that if they come from the south, lines set on the Banks do not prevent them from passing through.

I think that the cod have simply become less numerous in certain areas because very large quantities have been caught several years in a row, and that for the stock to attain higher numbers a certain amount of time is required, just as with the reproduction of game in the countryside.

Fishing Gear

On the west coast they have successfully continued to use trawls, which are in favour with the captains, who believe that this device gives very good results. On the east coast, on the other hand, they are used only after 15 August. Opinions are very divided. It is true that on the east coast the fishing grounds are less favourable for the use of trawls than on the west coast.

I therefore believe that no modification in the regulation of fishing gear is needed, and that if any change were to be introduced, it should be aimed at greater freedom, that is, at allowing everyone freedom to choose the most appropriate means to obtain fish.

Reduction in the Number of Ships Fitted Out

An examination of the table showing the allocation of harbours over previous years shows that there is a progressive trend to a reduction in the number of ships we send to the fishery. This year, the total number of ships registered is only 65 for both coasts, and it is to be feared that this number will fall again next year.

The main outfitters have concentrated their ships in certain harbours such as Fichot, Cape Rouge, and La Scie, etc., and it is disappointing to see over half of the harbours on the east coast completely unoccupied. For example, Bay du Nord, Griquet, White Cape, Les Bréhats, St. Lunaire, La Crémaillère, Goose Cove, etc., do not have a single ship, and the rapid destruction of the fishing rooms in all of those harbours will make it impossible or at least very expensive to take possession of them again.

Faced with such a situation, I feel that one way likely to put a stop to this difficulty would be to make an appeal, and to use bounties to encourage small operations by allowing those who apply even outside the annual drawing by lot to come and settle their ships in the unoccupied harbours. In fact, the only way to prevent the English from gradually invading our fishing rooms would be to always have at least one ship in every harbour on the coast.

This is a simple question that I am putting, with no intention of settling it, since the adoption of this measure would entail modifications to the order of 2 March 1852.

Table of Allocation of Harbours

The tables of allocation of fishing rooms for 1868 did not reach me until early August. As a result, there was nearly a conflict between the fishermen. Since the captain of the *Levrette* had not received this document, and unaware therefore that Anchor Point had been granted as a replacement for Tonnelle Cove, he had given permission for two schooners from St-Pierre to stay there. Once the captain of the new *St-Pierre* had shown his form authorizing possession, the matter was settled, but, I repeat, it would be highly desirable for this document, dated 15 June, to reach the ships of the subdivision sooner.

Assistance to Fishing Ships

As is done every year, the blacksmiths and mechanics of the ships of the subdivision repaired a great number of items and objects used by the merchant ships; in particular, a large number of furnaces were tinned.

I went to Cape Rouge with the *Pomone* with the aim of giving all possible assistance in careening a ship that was leaking heavily. The point where the water was coming in was discovered, making this operation superfluous.

Our assistance even extended to foreigners: an English schooner on its way back from Labrador with its mast cracked at the level of the deck asked us to render assistance; its mast was strongly fished[202] and the vessel was able to continue on its way.

I took on board the *Pomone* two merchant sailors suffering from very serious complaints. One of these was completely cured and sent back to his work as seine master; as the other needed a dangerous surgical operation he was left at the St-Pierre hospital.

Health of the Crews

The climate of Newfoundland is very healthy and requires no special measures to maintain good health; normal precautions against cold and

---

202 To *fish* a broken mast is to carry out a repair at sea by applying a piece of timber as a splint and lashing the joint in place. (Translator's note.)

dampness are sufficient. However, numerous cases of lead poisoning, that is, dry colic, were noted this year among the fishing crews and in particular among those from the port of Binic.

These accidents call for very serious attention to the way in which utensils used for the cooking of food are tinned.

However, the chief surgeon of the *Pomone* considers that it is not simply the tinning of these utensils with pewter adulterated with a mixture of lead which may have caused the accidents noted. He believes that there may be another contributory cause.

The fishermen consume cider as a drink, and on board several ships, tin containers are used to take the cider from the barrels at mealtimes. Surplus cider remains in these containers in contact with the metal for a long time.

On board other vessels they use for the same purpose common earthenware containers with a lead-based glaze.

This simple contact is all that is needed for the cider to become a drink that is dangerous to health, and we cannot be too careful in making our captains aware of the serious problems that can result both for their crews and for them.

I have been told that cases of paralysis were quite frequent among Newfoundland fishermen; it may be that no other cause of this illness needs to be sought than lead poisoning, since paralysis is one of the most common outcomes of this complaint.[203]

---

203   In 1835 outfitters of merchant ships were advised of the dangers of using lead containers for serving wine on board their ships.
"It appears that some of our merchant ships have continued to use containers made of lead for serving wine to crews. Three men of the same ship were recently treated in one of the hospitals in our colonies for lead colic, which cannot be attributed to anything but the containers made of this metal used on board for serving wine. Lead colic is a painful and persistent illness which often gives rise to very serious sicknesses.
"We believe it is useful to notify outfitters and captains of merchant ships of this fact and to urge them to abandon the use of lead containers for the distribution of wine, which, through its action on this metal, may bring about terrible colic and paralysis of the limbs, in short, full-scale poisoning."
Annales maritimes et coloniales 1835, v. 58, Partie non officielle, 824. (Translator's note and translation.)

Spruce Beer

The crews of the ships of the subdivision were regularly supplied with spruce beer, whose beneficial and antiscorbutic properties have been known for a long time.

This is a drink made with molasses and young shoots of spruce; one soon becomes used to it, despite its resiny flavour, and on board the *Pomone* we learned how to make it sufficiently well to make it such a pleasant drink that it was freely available, and the men consumed great quantities of it.

Live Cattle

The live cattle picked up in Sydney by the *Pomone*, the *Eurydice*, and the *Curieux* were a most valuable resource for the crews and for different tables. Once these cattle were put to pasture, they grew fatter and allowed us to have at least one meal of fresh meat every week throughout the whole season.

Newfoundland Clothing

The Newfoundland clothing—boots, oilskins, sou'westers—delivered to the *Pomone* were of quite good quality and were of very great service to the crew.

These items came from the port of Cherbourg. I set aside a special place for these effects, mostly for the boots, which were hung on the wall in the tween deck and accessible to the men. I believe that this is an essential condition for the preservation of this footwear, which deteriorates very quickly when it is stored in an enclosed space.

These boots are certainly not a luxury or fashionable item on board; in expeditions such as those to Newfoundland, one has to adapt to circumstances in everything that may be useful for the health of the men.

Almoners

The outfitters from the bay of Saint-Brieuc used to be in the habit of sending two almoners to Newfoundland every year for the religious needs of the fishermen. These two almoners carried out tours, one going to the north and the other to the south, in whalers set aside for this dangerous service.

Only one priest came to Cape Rouge this year, who despite all his eagerness and goodwill was able to make only one tour of the coast; this clergyman nevertheless visited all of the harbours from Cape Onion to La Scie.

The absence of an almoner on board the *Pomone* appeared to upset greatly the inhabitants of some harbours where we anchored. They normally count on the passing of this almoner for baptisms, marriages, and other requirements of the Catholic faith.

Justice

A woman from Conche came to make a complaint to me against an inhabitant of that place who had fired a rifle shot at her husband; I told her that it was impossible for me to involve myself with that matter, and that if it had been a case of a conflict with our fishermen, I could have intervened, but that I could not intervene in private disputes between English inhabitants, and that she should make a complaint to the authorities in St. John's. I have since learned that when Captain Parish was passing through Conche, having quite extensive judicial powers, he carried out an investigation into this matter.

Hydrography

As Commodore Lapelin finished the soundings along the coast that he had begun earlier, I extended the sounding lines offshore to a distance of 30 miles [c. 54 km]. The results obtained demonstrate to me that these soundings can be of no great utility for fishing vessels heading for land, since those ships are not in the habit of sounding at depths as great as those we found.

In addition, I sounded all of the bays where the *Pomone* anchored to check the accuracy of the charts and to attempt to find any few rocks that might have been overlooked in the earlier operation.

Lieutenant Rallier of the *Pomone* drew with great precision the views of the entries to the principal harbours on the east coast.

I have been assured that, in addition to two rocks located in the Bay of Islands near Pearl and Tweed Islands, the position of which was recognized and determined by the *Armorique* last year, there is also a third. The high wind that remained constant during my stay in Governor's Bay did not allow me to send anyone in search of this hazard.

The currents in the Strait of Belle Isle and on the east coast of Newfoundland were observed with care. In normal circumstances, on the west coast the current runs to the north at a speed of about one mile [c. 1.6 km] an hour. It becomes stronger as one moves further north. The one in the Strait of Belle Isle generally runs toward the north following the direction of the Strait at a speed of between 1 and 1.5 miles per hour, and even 2 miles [up to 3.2 km] an hour. At Cape Norman the direction tends toward the northeast until it meets the polar current, which causes it to turn to the southeast. On the east coast the current generally is to the southeast, with a speed of from 0.5 to 1.5 [c. 0.8 to 2.4 km]. I have found it to be close to 2 miles [c. 3.2 km] an hour one mile [c. 1.6 km] from the coast from Cape Bonavista to Cape Race.

Unfortunately, the force and the direction of these currents are not constant and they are greatly influenced by the wind.

An English steamship is at the moment taking soundings around the Funk Islands and Fogo Island. These are very bad areas where fresh dangers are discovered every day.

Device for Food on Boats Sent out on Duty

On an expedition such as the one to Newfoundland where it is continually necessary to send boats far from the ship to inspect fishing ships, we derived great benefit from a very simple device, a model of which the first mate of the *Pomone* had seen at an exhibition and which we constructed on board. It is made up of a simple wooden box lined with wool and horsehair, leaving a space where one puts a cylindrical boiler made from a beef can. In this boiler one puts boiling water with meat and soup seasonings; it is then covered with a wool and horsehair cushion, and the box is closed with a padlock to prevent the men from inspecting it too often; three or four hours later the soup is ready, the meat is well cooked and the dish has lost only a few degrees of heat. This is a very simple device that is easy to make anywhere; all that is necessary is to cover the boiler where the food is to be cooked with a sufficiently thick layer of material that does not conduct heat, such as wool, horsehair, sawdust, etc. We often used this device and we derived great benefit from it on every occasion when we had to send boats far from the ship. Instead of a simple ration of cheese, the men had a soup that was as good and as hot as that served on board.

*Provisions Delivered to the Guardian
of the Subdivision's Establishment*

As in previous years, I left Patrick,[204] the guardian of the stores of the subdivision, the same quantity of provisions that we have been giving him for many years for the supervision and care that he takes of our settlements.

---

204 This was Patrick Kearney of Kearney's Cove, Croque. (Translator's note.)

Petition of Boat Masters Carrying on the Local Fishery at the Islands of St-Pierre and Miquelon

At a meeting of fishermen to which the Admiral paid me the honour of requesting me to attend, the masters of boats carrying on the local fishery around St-Pierre sent him a petition bearing more than 400 signatures.

The object of this petition was to obtain the total prohibition of trawls or bultows throughout the fishing season in the area where their industry is conducted and to institute active surveillance to suppress the abuses that they report.

The petitioners represent more than 400 boats crewed by approximately 1,000 men, mostly from the areas of Granville and St. Malo. They come to Newfoundland in April and leave at the end of September; one-tenth of them only remains in St-Pierre, where their families are settled and continue the fishery in the fall.

They are all very courageous and honest sailors, most worthy of attention.

Their petition is very well composed and its main goal is to obtain an effective surveillance of the implementation of local fisheries regulations so as to prevent the financial hardship caused to them by the lack of enforcement of an order from the governor of the islands of St-Pierre; according to this order, the use of trawls or bultows is forbidden within a radius of 9 miles [16.2 km] around the island.

To reach this goal, they propose making contributions to set up a sworn guard selected by them who would be responsible for this surveillance.

The boats used by the fishermen are *warys*,[205] none of which is capable of setting lines at the distance required by the local order; most of them limit themselves to fishing by hand line a short distance from

---

205 "Wary" is a French term that was commonly used in St-Pierre to describe a small fishing boat, a forerunner of the dory. The name may be derived from the English "wherry." (Translator's note.)

land, but unfortunately there are offenders who set bultows, and it is to bring such abuses to an end that they request more effective surveillance.

They are all in agreement in stating that in a fishing spot where there is a bultow set with numerous baited hooks, the cod stay there and do not come closer to shore; they say they have often learned to their cost that in the middle of a plentiful harvest of fish, the setting out of a few bultows in the area is all that is needed to bring the fishery to a complete halt.

They also point out that among the signatories to the petition are a large number of those who have used bultows but who would be quite prepared to give them up if there were an effective measure forbidding them to everyone.

The request of these fishermen seems to me to be very fair and well founded, and the force of the reasons cited in their petition is so real that this question had already been brought to the attention of the governor of St-Pierre. It was the basis for the order of 21 August 1860 governing the use of bultows and setting at 15 miles [c. 27 km] the distance from the shore at which it would be permitted for them to be used from 1 April to 31 August every year.

This order was naturally made in the interest of the local fishery; however, the last element, with the aim of permitting schooners returning from the Banks to use their fishing boats to fish with bultows from 1 September, does not seem to me to be fully justified. It is certain that if schooners are returning from the Banks before 1 September, it is because they have had a plentiful fishery there, and it would not be fair to give them an advantage at the expense of the local fishery.

I consider therefore that there are grounds for extending the prohibition of bultows within the set limits to the entire duration of the fishing season.

In short, the order exists in part only, and what the fishermen are requesting is its enforcement.

I find therefore that the request of the fishermen is very fair, and the grounds for it are strengthened by the fact that those who had committed violations are in agreement with the others, and that all are prepared to contribute to put in place at their expense a sworn guard appointed by them and charged with carrying out effective surveillance to prevent violations.

However, such a measure cannot be implemented except as a consequence of fresh provisions decided upon by the governor of the islands of St-Pierre to put into practice the arrangements requested by the petitioners.

These same fishermen informed the Admiral of the presence of American schooners this year setting enormous bultows between Langlade and Le Colombier,[206] and who, under the pretext of catching halibut, fish indiscriminately for that fish and for cod; these foreigners are therefore in contravention of the order of 20 April 1860. They are causing great harm to the industry of our fishermen.

These fishermen assure us that last year only three American schooners came, that this year there are seven, and that they are very afraid that next year this number will increase yet again.

Finally, these fishermen request more effective protection against the English ships which at caplin time come in large numbers to fish at Langlade and Miquelon at the same time as they do.

In order to provide bait for the many ships that wait for that bait to sail to the Banks, we allow the English at that period to come and fish at Langlade and at Miquelon alongside our fishermen. But it seems that, as they are present in great numbers, they abuse their numerical superiority by hindering the industry of our nationals with huge nets.

These are questions relating to local policing that concern principally the authorities of the colony, but it would be nevertheless useful to bring to the attention of the governor of St-Pierre to them.

---

206 Le Colombier (= dovecote) is a rock located just off the northern tip of the island of St-Pierre and facing the island of Langlade. (Translator's note.)

In concluding this report, I believe it is my duty, Admiral, to inform you how delighted I have been with all of the senior officers of the *Pomone* as well as all the other officers under my orders.

The captains of the *Eurydice* and the *Belette*, the *Levrette*, and the *Curieux* demonstrated great zeal, intelligence, and activity in the many missions I entrusted to them and I could not be more satisfied with their services.

The crew of the *Pomone*, made up of very young men, also developed very well during this expedition; they are now fully aware of the duties that they are called upon to carry out. I would be most satisfied if Your Excellency were to decide to retain the same officers and crew for the next expedition.

Coastal Pilot

Mr. Ledret, a former captain from St-Pierre, taken on board the *Pomone* as coastal pilot, was also extremely useful to me on going into and leaving all the harbours. The thorough knowledge that he has of all the coasts of Newfoundland makes his assistance invaluable to the commodore of the subdivision. Moreover, he is an excellent sailor, very eager in carrying out his duties, and I can only reiterate the well-founded praises that Captain de Lapelin has already bestowed on him.

With the greatest respect, Admiral, I remain your most obedient servant.

Captain in command of the frigate *Pomone* and the naval subdivision of Newfoundland.

Signed: Mer.
On board the *Pomone*, 20 September 1868.

ACKNOWLEDGEMENTS

I would like to express my deep appreciation for the assistance provided by my wife Frances in the translation of the material in this book, as well as to Dr. Claire Wilkshire for providing invaluable assistance in polishing the manuscript. The staff of the Centre for Newfoundland Studies at Memorial University's Queen Elizabeth II Library have been unfailingly helpful in assisting my research. Thanks are also due to Dr. Michael Collins, who provided helpful advice on Newfoundland plants, to the late Dr. Gordon Bennett, who assisted with advice on mosquitoes, and to Stephanie Porter of Boulder Books for her sterling work in editing this volume.

ABOUT THE AUTHOR

Michael Wilkshire moved to Newfoundland from his native England in 1966 to teach French at Memorial University in St. John's. He earned an MA from Carleton University and a doctorate from the Université de Dijon, France, and continued to teach at Memorial until his retirement. He has written extensively and published on the French presence in Newfoundland, with a particular emphasis on 19th-century writings of French visitors to the province and the iconography of the French Shore, as in *A Gentleman in the Outports: Gobineau and Newfoundland* (Ottawa: Carleton University Press, 1993), Wilkshire's edition of Gobineau's works inspired by his diplomatic mission to Newfoundland in 1859. *A Mixed Marriage* is Wilkshire's latest contribution to the field.